Flesh Wounds

Flesh Wounds

The Culture of Cosmetic Surgery

Virginia L. Blum

UNIVERSITY OF CALIFORNIA PRESS

Berkeley   Los Angeles   London

University of California Press
Berkeley and Los Angeles, California

University of California Press, Ltd.
London, England

First paperback printing 2005

Library of Congress Cataloging-in-Publication Data

Blum, Virginia L., 1956–.
  Flesh wounds: the culture of cosmetic surgery / Virginia
  L. Blum.
    p.   cm.
  Includes bibliographical references and index.
  ISBN 978-0-520-24473-3 (pbk. : alk. paper)
    1. Surgery, Plastic—Social aspects.   2. Surgery,
  Plastic—Psychological aspects.   I. Title.
RD119 .B58   2003
617.9'5—dc21
                                    2002154915

Manufactured in the United States of America

13   12   11   10   09
10   9   8   7   6   5   4   3   2

The paper used in this publication is both acid-free and
totally chlorine-free (TCF). It meets the minimum
requirements of ANSI/NISO Z39.48–1992 (R 1997)
(Permanence of Paper).

To my father, David Blum
and to my mother, Fern Walder

CONTENTS

ACKNOWLEDGMENTS

Many people have contributed to this project, from reading chapters to helping me think through a range of ideas and possibilities, from providing close editorial scrutiny to sharing enlightening telephone conversations. For their encouragement, good humor, and editorial advice I would like to express my gratitude to my writing group, Susan Bordo, Dana Nelson, Suzanne Pucci, Sue Roberts, and Ellen Rosenman. They were my first guides on this project, and their criticisms, both compassionate and critical, were indispensable. I thank Claire Kahane for an early and crucial response to the project as well as Steve Pile and Dan Smith, who both raised important questions. To Jim Kincaid, who read the whole manuscript in less than two weeks, complete with abundant notes and encouragement, I cannot thank you enough for what I can only describe as heroic feats of friendship.

Thanks to those people who sent me materials and made recommendations along the way: Mardel Blum, Sandy Blum, Bonnie Burman, Janet Eldred, Susan Kessler, Heidi Nast, and Michael Uebel.

Thanks to my two brilliant workaholic graduate students who assisted me with the research, Ann Beebe and Ann Ciasullo. Thanks also to Meredith Jones for her painstaking transcriptions.

I thank the Institutional Review Board of the University of Kentucky for advising me through this project and finding ways of accommodating someone with so little experience in the realm of human subject research. I especially thank Graham Rowles for his time and effort in teaching me how to conduct interviews.

Thanks also to the University of Kentucky for generously supporting this project with a research grant and research assistant stipends.

I want also to offer particular thanks to the numerous surgeons and cosmetic-surgery patients who contributed so generously to this project. While their names remain anonymous for the reader, I am deeply grateful for their sincere commitment to expanding the range of commentary on this complicated cultural phenomenon. Special thanks go to those surgeons who allowed me to observe their surgeries. I thank as well their staffs who gave me so much information about the nature of the procedures, not to mention good-naturedly tolerating my intrusion into their work space. I thank the patients for their willingness to speak with me so openly.

Thanks go to my project editor, Cindy Fulton, for all of her efforts toward making this a better book. Without the expertise of my copyeditor, Robin Whitaker, this book would be considerably less readable, so I cannot thank her enough. And thanks so much to Sierra Filucci, assistant to the editor, for all her time, attention, and concern. Finally, I thank Naomi Schneider, my wonderful editor at the University of California Press, for her extraordinary patience in seeing this project through.

ONE

The Patient's Body

THE BEGINNING

My first nose job was performed by an otolaryngologist (otherwise known as an ear, nose, and throat doctor) who, in concert with my mother, encouraged me to have surgery. Without consulting me, my mother made an appointment and then convinced me to go with her—just to see what he had to say. He had operated on the nose of a neighbor, and my mother liked her result.

Having a parent criticize a physical feature is a complicated emotional experience that induces both anger and guilt. You feel as though you have let the parent down. Why didn't you come out right? At the same time, the pervasive mythology of parent-child relations tells you that parents think their children are perfect, no matter what. From my mother's perspective, however, criticism of my nose didn't seem harmful because it wasn't permanent. Such problems could be resolved—fixed. Ballerina Allegra Kent writes about the nose job similarly imposed upon her by a mother invested in "conventional beauty" (79). "Allegra [said her mother], if you had a little more chin and a little less nose, you would be so much prettier" (78). And then: "Aren't you interested in a face that would be closer to perfect proportions? Then you would be beautiful" (78).

When a friend had her nose fixed at age seventeen, that settled it. She and I never spoke about her surgery, but somehow the mothers got together and conferred. Even though I couldn't see the difference myself following my friend's surgery, my mother was more than enthusiastic. I suppose her postsurgical nose was slightly smaller. In those days, the only kinds of noses that made me think of surgery were very large noses. Slightly large (like my friend's) or wide noses (like mine) or noses with bumps all seemed fine to my adolescent perception of faces.

Young children and adolescents receive their body images wholly from the outside. The adolescent girl, especially, enters the world tentatively and waits for it to say yes or no to her face and body. Now that my face had emerged from its childish amorphousness, it was finished enough to predict its disadvantages. Negotiating adolescence can feel like traveling in a herd of sorts, always under fire or under threat of some dangerous predator; you hope that you will escape notice. Then one day you are singled out—shot down in the field—just when you imagined yourself safely swallowed in anonymity.

My experience of learning there was something wrong with my nose is inscribed in my mind (and on my body) as a story of imperfection that "required" correction. The story goes this way: Your body is recalcitrant. It came out wrong. If you don't intervene on some level, you are compounding the original failure. A plastic surgeon I interviewed corrected my terminology: "It's not an intervention. I hate that word. Let's call it what it is. It's surgery." But psychically, it feels like an intervention in the body's wayward path. This holds true for both image-changing surgeries like rhinoplasty and rejuvenation surgeries like a face-lift. Your body is heading in a certain direction that threatens to make "you" worthless unless you rise up in resistance—unless you intervene. With surgery. It is important to remember that if you don't intervene *now* while there's still time, you will lose. Something. Everything. Love. Money. Achievement. This is what we learn even from the body-image scholars who write about how much easier it is to thrive in the world if one is good-looking. I worry about these supposedly objective studies, because I think they have the unfortunate effect of making us all more anxious than we already are. You! Yes, *you there*, because you are plain, you will be sentenced to ten years in prison instead of three. And *you*—don't even think about applying for that job until you have those jowls and double chin sucked smooth. We require streamlined faces to match our precision office spaces. Body-image studies become yet more fodder for plastic surgeons, who explain to me that men "need" to have their eyelids tucked in order to be considered young and energetic in business.

The story of my household is like that of many Jewish American families whose assimilation is symbolized through physical appearance. Features, body styles—these have meaning. They tell stories all by themselves. Certain kinds of noses speak Jewishness. I have heard too many people say that he or she "looks" Jewish on the basis of the size of a nose. Jews assimilating into a largely gentile culture thus strip from our features the traces of our ethnicity. We have other aesthetically assimilating rituals. We straighten curly hair, dye dark hair light. We get very thin to disguise what we often imagine are Jewish-coded thighs and hips. What we choose to treat are precisely the features that are culturally selected as our distinguishing physical traits. My nose was not what my family would call "typically Jewish." It was wide. It was turned-up but "too wide," as my mother declared. Every picture of me would become an aesthetic catechism. "Do you know why this is a flattering picture? It's taken from the side so your nose looks good." There was that picture of me from my tenth-grade play. I was looking up at another actor, pointing my perfect gentile profile at them, concealing the disappointing full-face version. That picture became a kind of emblem—how good-looking I could be if only I held myself in profile. Dr. Eileen Bradbury says of people self-conscious about their noses: "If you are concerned about your nose from the side view, then you will do everything you can to prevent other people from seeing it from the side. You develop a whole pattern of very anxious behavior that is intended to camouflage and conceal that part from the world" (*Plastic Fantastic,* "Horn of Plenty"). But, unlike the cultural fantasy of typical plastic surgery candidates, who walk around in a huddle of physical shame until one illuminating and determined moment they decide to take their bodies into their own hands and offer them up to some whiz of a plastic surgeon, I remained unselfconscious about a feature I considered perfectly acceptable. It was only after I became surgical that my features were reorganized into categories of pass and fail—a trail of sites viewed through surgical eyes. I had expected to reach my twenties with my body parts intact. This was not to be.

When surgery enters your experience, the mirror becomes a kind of blueprint on which you project and plan the future of your body. This happened with my nose. At first, I looked at my nose and it looked fine. I couldn't really see the problem my mother had identified. It looked like "me." There is a difference between looking in the mirror and imagining what you will look like as a grown-up and picturing a surgical transformation. In contrast to the protracted process of development and aging, surgery feels like a kind of magic.

"What we do," said a surgeon, "is a very powerful magic." Most surgeons tell me about the technical aspects and the logical desire to improve your appearance along with the high satisfaction rate if the patients have reasonable expectations. This is so different from the emotional reality of a practice that feels, as this one surgeon admitted, magical. You go to sleep one way and wake up another. It is the stuff of fairy tales. How different, ultimately, is cosmetic surgery from the story of, say, Sleeping Beauty, who goes to sleep a young, isolated maiden and wakes up to love and perfect happiness forever after? This is what you want at the end of the surgeon's wand. They will never admit as much to me—that it's what we all want. None of us is rational when it comes to surgery, no matter what we say to them, no matter what rational claims surgeons assert. It won't change your life, most of them tell me. But of course it will, one way or another. And indeed, at the same time as the surgeons offer me their professional "truth," in confidence they claim, Oh yes, this will change people's lives. "Once they look better, everything will change."

One young woman who had her nose fixed describes it thus: "I always looked in the mirror and thought, I want that bump out. I've thought, Oh, I feel hideously ugly. But I've always thought, it's like you have a car that has a dent in it—if you got it fixed it would be quite a nice car. So I thought, apply the same thing to your face" (*Plastic Fantastic*, "Horn of Plenty"). Notice how her nose is both her and not-her, something that makes her feel "hideously ugly" at the same time that it's as materially distinct as a car. This is what happens to your body when you start changing it surgically. The "you" who feels ugly is linked to the defective piece but is also imaginatively separable. Partly, this double effect of your body that is both "you" and replaceable feels like a split right down the center of your identity. I am my body and yet I own my body.

THE SURGEON

"A bad outcome of a rhinoplasty can be devastating for a young girl," observed the surgeon I was interviewing. "It can ruin her appearance." We echoed each other's moans over the plethora of otolaryngologists barging into a field best left to board-certified plastic surgeons. I confessed that I was one of those teen-aged victims of an inept ENT. He paused, then responded cautiously, cordially: "Your nose isn't so bad." I wanted him to protest with surprise, "But your nose looks great," even though I know it is merely a rescued nose—a good enough nose reconfigured into reasonable shape after the original, botched job.

From the moment I entered his office, the surgeon had me. I instantly transferred my need for approval from my mother to him. This relationship forged with the plastic surgeon is a perfect example of what psychoanalysts mean by the process of transference, whereby unconscious attachments to early figures are transferred onto contemporary people in one's life. The parentified plastic surgeon is nowhere more apparent than when parents take children to the surgeon. When the parent is the one who determines the need for surgery, the surgeon inevitably becomes a parent surrogate. This role is freighted with responsibility. In part, what I wanted from this surgeon was for him to become the good parent who would tell the bad parent she was wrong, her daughter was beautiful. Go home. Let her get on with her life.

He looked at me and smiled ingratiatingly. He was an ugly man with a large sagging face; his eyes seemed almost attached above an enormous nose. Thatches of gray and dark hair erupted unevenly from his head. This is how I remember him at least. I remember him as a monster, as the slayer of my nose, the creator of a surgical subject.

I've asked surgeons what they do about the mother problem—the mother who drags a demurring daughter into the surgeon's office. "I talk to the daughter alone," one surgeon replied. "I ask the mother to leave us alone until I've had a chance to talk to the daughter about what *she* wants." Some surgeons go on to say they won't operate if the daughter says she doesn't want the surgery. But, in general, the surgeons have surprised me. They've said the daughter wants the surgery, that's why she's there. Even though her mother made the appointment, told her to get ready for the appointment, drove her to the appointment, and explained at length to the surgeon what she wanted for her daughter's nose while the daughter sat in an abstracted silence as if not there or as if just accompanying her body part, her infamous nose. They've told me that you need to get her alone so she tells you what *she* wants for her own nose. They don't consider that she might want nothing. Better still, what if the surgeon were to say, Your nose is really fine; it suits your face. None of the surgeons told me this story. I was hoping for just one. But this isn't what surgeons do. They see the defect from the other side of the room. The defect (or deformity, as they term it) hails them, flags them down, implores their assistance. They see, in other words, the need for surgery. They don't recognize the daughter's need to be sent home, surgery-free. In part, this has to do with their construction of a particular kind of reality populated with bodies requiring correction.

*A surgeon tells me: "When I walk into a room, anywhere, I can't help
thinking about what I could do to make improvements in the faces around
me." I shudder as he looks me over and smiles coolly.*

Certainly, a surgeon who preyed on maternal fantasies and the insecurities of young girls wasn't about to let me go, not once he had me in
his orbit. I made it clear how little I wanted this surgery. He said that he
would never operate against my wishes, but I should be aware that this
rhinoplasty would make me beautiful. "Now," he began impressively,
"you are better looking than eight out of ten girls." He hesitated slightly
before elaborating more profoundly: "With this surgery, you will be
a ten." My mother almost exploded with vicarious narcissism. Never
mind that she knew as well as I that I had plenty of other flaws in my face;
did doctors lie? The doctor must see beauty in her daughter that had
eluded her own eyes. This was exactly how he seduced me into surgery—through being the better parent, the one who would compensate
for all the cruel deficiencies in the real parents. In this sense, the deficiency cured by the plastic surgeon takes place in the transference itself—the implicit promise he makes to be the parent who will call you
beautiful. The surgical transformation is only a literalization, then, of
what happens psychically in the moment when he makes, or you imagine he makes, this promise.

He showed us a picture of his most famous patient, an early 1970s
model. "She came in with the same problem," he explained. "Her tip was
bulbous." He showed us a picture of the pre-op woman, whose nasal tip
was wide, although not as wide as mine, nor was the bridge as wide. He
was telling me I had the same nose, and I found myself seeing her nose
as though it were like mine, even though at another level I recognized
the enormous difference between them.

This moment when your perspective intersects with or is overtaken
by the surgeon's is crucial to the process of transformation itself. He
functions as the aesthetic expert, the one who plumbs the deepest secrets of faces and their potential beauty. If he tells you thus and thus will

make you better looking, it is difficult to resist your conviction of his privileged knowledge. If you are the child of critical parents, you are especially at risk—both because the transference will be more entire, and because one's need is more abject. Years later, when the second surgeon operated on my nose, he casually mentioned that he was going to put a cartilage implant in my nose to offset the problem of my weak chin.[1] For twenty-seven years, I had never once seen my chin as too small, but for several years following this off-the-cuff observation I considered a chin implant. This effect that a plastic surgeon can have on one's body image is extreme in my case, but I would argue that for everyone who undergoes plastic surgery there is a degree of dependence on the surgeon's perspective.

Not only did I confuse my own nose with the famous model's, I confused my whole face. Showing me her picture was a brilliant stroke. It created what I would call a metonymic chain of desire in which the nose became representative of the whole face—that would be mine (the ten, me as a ten) with surgery. I wanted her pre-op face as much as I wanted her post-op nose. The change he made to her nose became irrelevant in the overarching fantasy of having the face of a supermodel. Showing before and after pictures is misleading to patients, because we tend to focus on the whole image instead of the isolated alteration. Many plastic surgeons discourage showing before and after photographs, both because they stoke the expectations of prospective patients and because they violate the privacy of former patients. Each surgery is different. People have different tissues, bone structures, healing mechanisms. Avaricious surgeons out to increase their patient load will show pictures because they have such a seductive effect. In the case of the famous model, it was nearly impossible for me to separate the nose from the rest of the face that was being served up to me as a forecast of my future status as a "ten."

The originally slightly rounded tip of the model's nose was exchanged for a precision tip. There were indentations in it that I coveted because at the time they signified refinement; only subsequently did I perceive them as a grotesque imitation of the "upper-crust" nose. No nose ever came from nature with those chinks in it. With elaborate pride, he showed us a magazine article detailing the model's features, among which her nose was described as almost too chiseled, as though some surgeon had become overeager. I later learned that this model's nose job was considered a notorious disaster among plastic surgeons.

I was only eighteen, so it is no surprise that I was thoroughly taken in by this unctuous and unscrupulous man, who preyed on the insecurities of young women on the verge of college, in the throes of the all-absorbing question of how we would be received. Would we find dates? How would we rate? Ten. He promised. Like the model. Look at her. There you will be. It's so graceful, really, like a card trick.

Why did my mother take me to the plastic surgeon—especially when I didn't want plastic surgery? She wasn't atypical. Many of my friends were taken by their mothers for cosmetic surgery to their noses. Some of them said no, while others agreed. One friend describes the tactful way her parents put it. They told her that she had a large nose they would pay to have fixed—if she wanted it. But it was up to her. When your parents identify a flaw in you, your response depends on your overall relationship. Two friends say they were unequivocal about the nose job pressed upon them by mothers with whom they were in endless conflict. The "no" to the nose job was like any other "no" flung into the mother's detested face. Children more anxious to please parents will in turn be more willing to correct the perceived flaw.

Meanwhile, my mother considered it parentally irresponsible not to do what she could to make me more "marketable." These decisions are motivated by both broadly social and narrowly narcissistic impulses, which are in the end interlinked. The daughter successful in the marriage market, the ambitious son—these are familial achievements that raise parental value in their own eyes and in the eyes of the world. The failed child is a sign of parental neglect of some kind. They are clucked over by the parents' circle. Just as it may swell the mother's own self-esteem to send into the world a beautiful daughter, she will also be taken to task for her daughter's failure to thrive in the world according to socially conditioned guidelines.

For my mother, good looks meant marrying well. Marrying well, by the way, meant marrying a successful Jewish man; yet it was just these Jewish men who, supposedly, were most desirous of the too-small, imitation-WASP nose. In other words, our bodies weren't being honed and refashioned for a gentile market of prospective husbands. It was our own cultural and ethnic "brothers" for whom we were being redesigned in the conventional WASP image. It was as though circulating among us was a tacit agreement that Jewish men prefer gentile looks superimposed on originally Jewish bodies.

The Asian American community has been experiencing a similar cultural schism. Mothers take their sixteen-year-old daughters for double-lid surgery; they present it to them with love, kisses, and their blessings as a high school graduation present. Surgery on the epicanthal fold gives the effect of the Caucasian double lid so prized among the Asian community as the preeminent sign of beautiful eyes. One Asian American woman explains the system: "'Our mothers want us to be beautiful because being beautiful is one requirement for getting married. Big eyes are supposed to make you beautiful'" (Accinelli E4). Yet surgery to the eyelids of Asian daughters is intended to appeal to the aesthetic taste of young Asian men, who presumably share the very racial traits they want changed. These surgeries we perform to transform ethnically and racially different bodies into "mainstream" bodies are not in the service of thorough integration into WASP/Western culture, because the aesthetic changes are for the pleasure of our own kind. Rather, such surgeries are the badges of parental success in the "new land." A nose, a double lid—these dominant culture codes of beauty are etched into our bodies in token of our parents' simultaneous submission to the dominant culture and accomplishment *within* it. The entrance fee is the daughter's rehabilitated body.

SURGERY

It wasn't until the morning of the surgery that the surgeon admitted he might have to break the bone after all. I hesitated. Then I murmured, "Only if you have to," as though I hadn't known from the moment he brought up the possibility that it was inevitable. The bridge would be broken. He'd known all along, and only now, as the pre-op sedatives were beginning to take effect at 6:30 in the morning—after waiting in anticipation for three months, fantasying the beautiful future of my face, after going to bed early and having no food or water in my stomach since the previous evening—only now did he divulge the whole truth about the surgery. They need to reel us in slowly.

I came in and out of consciousness during the surgery, which was performed under a local anesthetic. Not long after I awoke in my hospital bed, feeling a kind of weight and intensity in the middle of my face, I was handed a mirror. My nose was in a cast and heavily bandaged, but what struck me immediately was that the bottom of my nose was now flat where once it had been rounded. Even then, recognizing on some level that too much was missing, I was in that postsurgery haze of pure expectation—when the result could be anything. After surgery, you lie in bed waiting for your day. Instead of obscuring your face, the bandages seem more like a blank field of possibility—of the beauty promised, of the happy ending to the surgical story.

This relationship between the male surgeon and the female patient is so powerful that more than twenty years later, as an interviewer, I found that surgeons continued to have the same effect on me. Regardless of the professional career, the expertise, the presumed "grown-up" resistance to their blandishments and insinuations, no matter how big the desk between us or how sophisticated my insights—no matter how enlightened I am as to the way they harness cultural power over women's bodies in the service of their practice—these surgeons continued to be able to tell me who I am, to construct an identity for me that emerges in relation to an aesthetic standard they come to represent as the ultimate body crit-

ics (and perfecters). In their hands lies the route to the promised world
of tens. Many of us can say no to the surgeon (most people never consider surgery), but it's more difficult to rise entirely above a culture
where ten is something worth being.

During my interviews with plastic surgeons I found that, despite my
role as interviewer, at times they assessed me as potential surgical material. Having spent a great deal of time in their offices, I am now hyper-
conscious of a general institutionalized distribution of power that has
very little to do with the aesthetic particulars of each woman's face and
body. Unless they asked, I rarely informed the surgeons that I have had
surgery. For one thing, I hardly wanted them to comment on the outcome or recommend further surgery. I wanted them to interact and respond outside a surgeon-patient dynamic, which would have been all too
available for them once they could position me as "patient." For the
most part, the surgeons did not talk to me as though I was a prospective
patient. They respected the interviewing boundary; my body remained
beyond the scope of the interview—at least as a subject of discussion.
Nevertheless, there were those who could not help but overstep, who
seemed compelled to see me as a patient despite the institutional imperatives against doing so (the original exchange of letters, the process of
signing consent forms, turning on a tape recorder). It was at these moments that I gained (harrowingly) much deeper insight into how men's
and women's bodies perform in relation to preassigned roles of those
who get to look, operate, impress upon, and make versus those who are
looked at, assessed, receptive, and changed. It was as though the still-
powerful cultural, allegorical roles of masculinity and femininity were
ever straining against the fragile boundaries of the professional situation. The remainder of this chapter will concentrate on just this tension
between my positions as interviewer and patient and how the interview
process itself made me realize how perilously close I always am to laps-
ing back into the patient position. The demands of my damaged and
vulnerable body continue to defy the rigors of half a lifetime of cultural
inquiry and feminist protest.

DAMAGE

Viewing themselves as "healers" of cosmetic defects and emotional desperation, plastic surgeons need not interrogate their own psychological necessity for intervening in the appearance of healthy bodies. We could argue that cosmetic surgery is markedly different from the life-saving efforts of, say, the general surgeon, because in cosmetic surgery we find harm being done to a healthy body, cuts being made, blood flowing for no known medical reason. This is why plastic surgeons tend to justify their practice through the claim of psychological necessity. Psychological damage takes over for physical impairment. Healthy bodies begin to appear "diseased." In countries with national health programs, this argument is taken quite literally. In Great Britain, for example, a woman can still receive a state-funded breast augmentation if a qualified psychologist deems it necessary to her emotional well-being. The sociologist Kathy Davis documents at length the criteria established in the Netherlands (also under national health insurance) to evaluate the "necessity" for the cosmetic operation:

> For example, a breast lift was indicated if the "nipples were level with the recipient's elbows." A "difference of four clothing sizes between top and bottom" was sufficient indication that a breast augmentation or liposuction was in order. A sagging abdomen which "made her look pregnant" was enough reason to perform a tummy tuck. For a face lift, the patient had "to look ten years older than his or her chronological age." (35)

While this program of government-subsidized cosmetic surgeries impressively levels the playing field between those who can pay out of pocket and those who cannot, such an approach to determining a patently aesthetic "necessity" colludes with the idea that people might need to put themselves at surgical risk in order to heal their self-esteem. Plastic surgeons operate under the pretext that the damage has already been done in the form of the cosmetic defect, hence they are simply correcting a problem that originated elsewhere. They can overlook the damage inflicted by them under their supervision in their operating room. They can project onto the other, the patient, the psychological damage as well.

It is possible that plastic surgeons are acting out in a socially sanctioned way their aggression on bodies that have been shaped by forces other than their scalpel. Such "forces" are either natural (what the patients were born with) or surgical (the results of other surgeons' work) or traumatic (car accidents, etc.); whatever might be the cause of the body's appearance, it induces in the surgeon a form of rivalry. This would explain the extraordinary level of in-fighting and competition among the surgeons, which include their readiness to "correct" the mistakes of other surgeons. Indeed, open any plastic surgery journal or women's magazine and you will find plastic surgeons bemoaning the failures of other surgeons as they extol their own corrective techniques. While it is certainly admirable that medical professionals are as attentive to psychological forms of impairment and dysfunction as they are to physiological forms, I suggest that we also consider what kind of gratification might be in it for plastic surgeons. How might their sincere regard for patients join with and disguise this double action of damaging and repairing?

Moreover, whose aesthetic prevails? Whose body, ultimately, is it? When friends ask my advice, I tell them to go to the surgeon whose surgical results look like what you want on your own face or body. Many surgeons criticize their colleagues who reproduce a particular look on every face and body touched by their scalpel. They talk at length about tailoring the change to the individual. But then I look at their own work, and all their patients as well look like members of a not-so-extended family. There's a surgeon whose face-lifts I would recognize anywhere. His procedure is always the same: yank up that brow, stretch back those nasolabial folds, insert a silastic implant into the chin. His patients look uncannily alike in their "after" photographs, staring brightly into the camera, chins stiffly prominent, every element on their faces that could crease or fold now permanently affixed as though by a rubber band.

PATHOLOGICAL CONCERN

"Do you think you're attractive?" one surgeon asked me.

"I'm okay," I replied. Of course, this is the stock response—one always replies "okay" to such a question—or "reasonably" or something neutral. One must be prudently modest. Think of all those models and actresses who "confess" to their aching insecurities. "I've always hated my mouth," Michelle Pfeiffer admits. Are we supposed to accept at face value that she dislikes her most celebrated feature? That she really believes she looks like a duck?

At the same time one must not cross the line into flagrant self-doubt, because then you will be pathologized as "disordered" by those who specialize in body-image disturbance; you will be said to suffer from a psychological affliction, body dysmorphic disorder, an extreme dissatisfaction with one's appearance, that they will promptly and efficiently try to "cure."[2] Surgeons are trained to be wary of such individuals. But throughout the literature on body dysmorphic disorder, one is aware of an extraordinary insensitivity to the fact that some people are considered more attractive than others and that some people are considered unattractive by a significant number of people with whom they interact. How do body-image theorists reconcile their pathologization of beauty-obsessed people with their own work suggesting that the good-looking profit in all respects.[3]

The cognitive behaviorist Katherine Phillips claims to have proved that body dysmorphic disorder (BDD) is biological in origin. Not only does she advocate treating it with a combination of antidepressants; she is also optimistic that brain scans will eventually locate the very scene of pathology. She concedes that BDD can seem related to "normal appearance concerns." But, in order to qualify as having BDD, you need to spend more than an hour a day engaged in BDD-related behaviors. Phillips considers (briefly) the cultural origins of preoccupation with appearance. She argues that while body dysmorphia may be exacerbated by the excessiveness of beauty culture, it is by no means caused by it. Her proof is that if the appearance-centeredness of the culture were to blame, more women would suffer than men and, in fact, it's the reverse. Yet, we could speculate that since men are not supposed to care as much about their appearance, it would only stand to reason that more men than women would be diagnosed as disordered for caring so much.[4] "Normal" for Phillips seems to mean those of us who respond to magazine articles on "perfect thighs in this lifetime" and the possibility of going "'from so-so to supersexy'" (182). To respond to a cultural preoccupation with appearance is, of course, normal. But you can care too much. Then you have a disorder. Plastic surgeons follow a logic similar to that of Katherine Phillips. Normal, apparently, is to want your ethnic nose fixed.

I wound up with one of those noses surgeons display as the "before" picture for a botched surgery. My turned-up nose became Roman. It twisted to one side. It hooked. The tip was flattened out from the removal of too much cartilage. Allegra Kent describes her own disastrous result: "My new face was grotesque. It was shockingly distorted. It was not me. The doctor had done a bad job, and I recuperated slowly. My mother's obsession with externals and what could be done about them had been played out on me" (80). Both our mothers assumed that surgery was a kind of miracle, that there was no dreadful aesthetic risk involved, that these (urgent) beautification rituals inevitably made one more beautiful. Afterward, my mother and I complained, but the surgeon dismissed us as having absurd expectations. There was only so much he could do—"the bones have to go somewhere," as he put it to my mother in response to her wondering how my nose had gone from turned up to turned down. Many years later, as I was going under anesthesia for my second rhinoplastic surgery, I heard the operating surgeon say to his nurse: "Look what some joker did to this poor girl's nose." Nevertheless, the first surgeon considered his work successful—or at least he claimed as much in the face of our dissatisfaction. While I may have been condemned as a perfectionist by surgeon number one (expectations out of line with predictable outcome), surgeon number two identified me as a legitimate case for correction.

ROLE REVERSALS

"Do you think you're attractive?"

What does it mean for a plastic surgeon to turn to a woman he doesn't know (and who's not there for surgery!) and ask her if she thinks she's attractive? Does he imagine he has the right by virtue of what he does—territorial rights, to be exact, over all women's bodies? He also knows (who knows better?) that it is the essential question for women. To be attractive for women means they get what they want. But what is it that women truly want—beauty or its putative social rewards? After undergoing extensive plastic surgery to make her ugly body beautiful, Fay Weldon's protagonist Ruth in *The Life and Loves of a She-Devil* is still dissatisfied because she remains too tall. "'You must be satisfied now,' Dr. Black [one of her surgeons] was saying to this blond, simpering doll on stilts, 'if grown men are fighting over you. . . . You are beautiful, you are popular, you can go to a party and cause infinite trouble: you are the showgirl type. The balding businessman's dream'" (261). Not quite perfect enough, Ruth demands further (life-threatening) surgery. Dr. Black doesn't understand, because Ruth already has everything he imagines women could want—mainly, to be desired by most men. This, he takes for granted, is why women want to be beautiful. Certainly, Ruth wants to appeal to men (particularly her philandering ex-husband), but it is ultimately her ideal image of her body that she pursues. In other words, what women may want in the end is just beauty itself. While the number of potential partners may increase, this is perhaps not the goal but rather the proof of beauty, the approving stares and the expensive gifts and the proposals simply registered on the checklist of beauty's accomplishments. Just as the measure of a religion's truth is often made according to the numbers of its adherents, a beautiful woman achieves value through discipleship.

This is what Freud has to say on the subject of what he calls the secondary narcissism of the beautiful woman: "Strictly speaking, it is only themselves that such women love with an intensity comparable to that of the man's love for them. Nor does their need lie in the direction of loving, but of being loved. . . . Such women have the greatest fascination for men, not only for aesthetic reasons, since as a rule they are the most beautiful, but also because of a combination of psychological factors" ("On Narcissism" 89). The love object, then, is neither the partner nor the self (in any permanent sense) but instead the body and only when it's beautiful. Freud seems to have captured a cultural turning point when just being beautiful took over as the object of desire. We generally assume that women want beauty as a means to certain ends, the various benefits that become more available to beautiful women: more financially successful partners and the material pleasures they bring. But it is possible that the accomplishment of the lifestyle serves merely as an index of her value on the open market of desirability. What appear to be the cultural rewards, in other words, are just the evidence of—the thing she has, the only thing she wants—her beauty. It is not surprising that beauty has come to this pass.

In *Beauty Secrets*, Wendy Chapkis describes the received relationship between beauty and its benefits:

> Real life and real appearance are not enough when the goal is to live in a travel poster with a beautiful person at your side and in your flesh. If only we were more stylish, if only we had more money, if only we had accomplished something more remarkable, if only we were really beautiful, then life could begin.
>
> But as it is, we know we are too flawed to deserve it—yet. Meanwhile we wait, buying the props if we can afford them, trying to turn ourselves into closer approximations of the beautiful. We wait, aware that beautiful people are not old. (140)

What is most telling about Chapkis's wish-list is how the chain of "if onlys" culminates in beauty itself. The travel poster is the ubiquitous cultural metonymy for "the place" of success, which entails becoming beautiful in a beautiful place. When success looks like a place and place is just an appearance—the place where you are perfectly beautiful—then most of us can simply try to be "closer approximations of the beautiful," never truly "inside" the pictured paradise.

"One day," Fay Weldon writes, "we vaguely know, a knight in shining armor will gallop by, and see through to the beauty of the soul, and gather the damsel up and set a crown on her head, and she will be queen" (*She-Devil* 63). But in the end Weldon's *She-Devil* heroine, Ruth, doesn't even really want the knight—she just wants to be the queen of beauty; the knight, her ex-husband, in all his defeated confusion, merely guarantees her sovereignty. It's not that the man in the heterosexual woman's fantasy of beauty is incidental; no, he is central. He is part of the package.

What am I saying, exactly? That beauty is its own end? It seems almost too astonishing; at the same time it is such an obvious consequence of a culture that bombards women on all sides with beauty regimes, beauty solutions, beautiful images—the exigency, in other words, of beauty. It was inevitable that the thing women needed in order to be "successful" as women has ascended to the thing itself. If you tell us enough times and you show us enough appealing examples, then we will begin to believe utterly in beauty as its own reward.

As we are increasingly influenced by the ubiquity of beautiful female bodies on television, in movies, on the cover of virtually every magazine in the supermarket, it is no wonder that the identification with the image of beauty itself is so compelling. The art historian Francette Pacteau discusses the connection between men's near fetishistic representations of beautiful women and women's fascination with these images. She advances the perplexing possibility that "man-made images of female beauty are, at least in part, a product of the man's attempt to meet the desire of the woman—to accede to being *her* desire, by presenting her with an ideal image of herself" (190). Contrary to the commonly received notion that it is men who dictate the demand for and the terms of this female beauty, Pacteau intriguingly suggests that to some extent men are giving women what men think women want—representations of female beauty. These images serve women's demand for identification with beautiful images.

Art historian Lynda Nead emphasizes the emergence of the female nude as the favorite subject of nineteenth-century painting, which suggests not only the new centrality of the female body as the object of the gaze but also the circulation and availability of images of the female body. Thus, what I point to as the overinvestment in beauty as its own goal is the historically specific result of both identifying women with (beautiful) visual images and raising women to identify with the image of their own beauty.

"Do you think you're attractive?"

What am I supposed to do with the "think" in that sentence? What if he had asked me, "Are you attractive?" A yes or no question that people feel as though they can't answer about themselves. To ask us if we "think" we are attractive implies the power of the mind over the body. If you feel beautiful, then you are. But the plastic surgeon's very role in life is to overturn dramatically this already quite impoverished cultural fiction.

A beautiful woman in my family loves to assert that beauty doesn't make you happy—"Just look at Elizabeth Taylor," she will urge. As though Taylor's beauty interfered with her pursuit of happiness. So invested is my relative in this myth that she kept secret from me her own rhinoplastic surgery—even when I was about to have surgery myself (that first surgery). It was her cousin who accidentally spilled the beans, because he didn't know the degree to which women guard their beauty secrets. When I confronted her with her cousin's story, she conceded that, yes, she'd had a revision, but only a very little one, only a slight refinement of the tip. It is impossible ever to tap into the whole truth of these family fictions, but what I learned from her was that narcissism is shameful, and what could be more narcissistic than having cosmetic surgery?

"Do you think you're attractive?"

To be asked by a plastic surgeon whether you think you are attractive is a reversal of the real question hanging between the surgeon and the patient—Does *he* think you're attractive? When he asked me, "Do you think you're attractive?" what naturally sprang to mind was his opinion, not mine. Whatever I thought, he was going to tell me the truth; moreover, his question brought to light what I work hard at forgetting when I am in the company of these surgeons—the degree to which they are immediately, reflexively almost, pronouncing aesthetic judgment on me as I walk through the door. When he asked me, "Do you think you're attractive?" I felt as though I were being quizzed by a teacher who knew in advance the correct answer.

"Have you had your nose done?" he pursued.

I think back to that first surgeon pinching the tip of my nose between his thumb and forefinger. "I was checking the cartilage, in case she was Hispanic," he explained to us. "Hispanic noses don't have the right consistency for reshaping."[5] My mother was instantly impressed with his cross-cultural expertise in the distribution and pliability of nasal cartilage. Afterward she kept referring to that moment when she had witnessed his expertise in practice, when he had pinched my nose. These surgeons trade on the cultural conviction of their ability to analyze the body's surfaces like a form of corporeal exegesis. It takes so little. A soothsayer of the body, reading my parts, my ethnicity—as though it weren't obvious. My last name is Blum. Not exactly Hispanic-sounding.

"Have you had your nose done?" He smiled. It wasn't a casual question. He may as well have been pinching my nose between his thumb and forefinger.

"Yes," I told him. He wanted to know who had (re)operated on me.

"Um, yes, I know him," he commented. He asked me to turn off the tape recorder. It was my turn to be scrutinized—as though the lamp had suddenly swung across the desk from his face to mine. He chain-smoked in my face in his small office.

My anxiety—that any moment any one of them could turn on me, tumble me off my high horse and into the muck of defective female plastic flesh—was lived out with this particular surgeon. My reaction was an extreme version of the pervasive and understood relationship between heterosexual men and women in Western culture. We are always dependent on their restraint, their charity, their ability to refrain from taking advantage of the power reposed in them. This surgeon simply acted upon the power any one of them had.

Just the same, where this power is located is not altogether clear. The power he assumed in that massive reversal was a power I attributed to him as male, as plastic surgeon, to evaluate me aesthetically. He could not have the power unless I turned it over. But I was helpless to withhold it. In other words, while his power cannot happen without my complicity, my complicity is an inevitable corollary and consequence of his cultural power. There is no choice involved in this relationship. If his effect happens only through my response, I can at the same time argue that my response wells up uncontrollably to the positional power he commands over my body. Recall that I could have turned the tables once again. I could have made his face and body an object of my gaze—I could have asked him if he had had surgery. Why didn't I ask him about his eyes, for example, because certainly they appeared operated on? But I instinctively withdrew, and it is this "instinctive" withdrawal that is ultimately structural. This institutional power is inextricably tethered to the degree to which women are the perfect subjects of and for cosmetic surgery.[6]

I will illustrate my point through my various encounters with plastic surgeons. Early on, I was alerted to my vulnerability when a Kentucky plastic surgeon, discussing the kinds of cosmetic procedures he would and would not perform, remarked that he would do only "really bad noses," for example, "real honkers," as he put it. Then, in an offhand manner, he added: "I wouldn't do your nose, for instance." Now, I didn't take this as a compliment; rather, he was using my nose as an example of features that weren't sufficiently displeasing for him to bother reshaping them. As he emphasized, in light of his practice, which was predominantly reconstructive rather than cosmetic, the cosmetic procedures had to be such that he "could make a significant difference." Whether his comment was indifferent or aesthetically evaluative was irrelevant to my stunned recognition that he was looking at me in that way—that he could not help but appraise me, moreover that anyone who walked into that office was subject to his professional look. This particular circumstance applies to men and women alike. Given the surgeon's customary experience of the doctor/patient relationship taking place within his office, it was no wonder that he would see me in light of my context—that very office.

They see us all with an aesthetic gaze that is additionally a transformative gaze—what they can do for the defective face and body. Many surgeons acknowledged that often they found themselves looking at people with an eye to what aesthetic revisions they might want to make. "When I went to church more frequently," a surgeon said, "I used to while away the time looking at people and wondering what I would do if they consulted me. And that's a lot of fun." By way of showing me an example of too-heavy eyelids, one surgeon handed me a picture of his nineteen-year-old daughter. "She'll probably need something done in another ten years," he pointed out. What might this be like for the daughter of a plastic surgeon? I felt bad for her. I had noticed her photograph early on in the interview—it was a large photograph and prominently displayed. I had mistaken the gesture of the enormous photograph for a father's pride; rather, she was there as a strategy for personalizing defects. See (I could imagine him explaining genially to a patient), my own daughter suffers from this defect; in another few years, she will need the very surgery you require today. He allowed that I had eyelids. But later in the interview, as he commented on some pictures of face-lifts and noted how impossible it is to correct the nasolabial folds, he pleasantly added, "You have them already, and you're a young person."

AESTHETIC JUDGMENT

I was already wearing a mask when I entered the operating room. This was the first time I was meeting the surgeon in person, so he had no idea what I looked like. This mask covered my face from the top of my nose to my chin. Nevertheless, as he inserted a cadaver-harvested septum into the patient's nose, he asked me if I'd had my nose done—a nose he had not yet glimpsed. I was a Jewish woman raised in Southern California, writing a book on plastic surgery; I suppose it was a likely assumption. He, too, wanted to know the name of the surgeon. It was a casual question. Just as casually, after describing the transformations he was making in this woman's facial contours via the addition of a number of silastic implants, he asked me what my jawline was like, if I had a strong chin.

I was sent off to a private room to view a videotape of the surgeon describing his silastic implantation technique. He looked different to me in the tape—older, with a narrower face. Had something been done in between the filming and now? Was he surgically altered, or was I just projecting onto his face his own aesthetic fantasy? Was I seeing him as his own work-in-progress simply because I was caught inside his world at that moment—a world in which all faces are simply variations on a particular surgical theme? After surgery, he came into the room and showed me slides of his work—a series of implant miracles where flat, narrow, chinless faces suddenly bulged with the eminences of jawlines and cheekbones—tiny little features like rosebud mouths and narrow-set eyes now caught amid the mountainous terrain of their plastic bone structure.[7] Out of the blue, he announced: "You have great eyes, full lips, good jawline and chin, a cute nose, but you need cheek implants to widen your face."

I laughed. I wasn't offended. I half expected him to say something of the kind. It was endearing in a way, thoroughly ingenuous. This is what he does—he adds bits to people's faces to make them more nearly match the current fashion in bone structure. My face is too narrow. I need cheek implants. In order to do what he does for a living, he cannot help but view the world around him as divided into those who do and don't need augmentation of their bone structure. It wasn't in the least aggressive. I had the feeling, in fact, that he would give me the surgery for a reduced rate, as a courtesy. He wants to make people happy.

I realized that I had to phrase my refusal cautiously—this is his life's work, after all. I told him I wasn't comfortable with the thought of foreign substances in my face. He looked bewildered, slightly wounded. "What do you mean?" "It's just me," I mumbled apologetically.

Most of his slides were impressive. I remarked on the extreme changes for the better in his patients' appearance. I hesitated, however, over one set of before and after shots. The young woman started out fine, but I didn't much care for her after photo. I was trying to figure out what had gone wrong. I wondered if perhaps she had gained weight, because her cheeks seemed too round. The surgeon interjected: "This woman has a facial shape just like yours. See the difference I made with the cheek implants." I stared. She had chipmunk cheeks. This is what he wanted for me. I explained to him that I didn't care for the changes. He was immediately uneasy. "Well, that's okay," he said. "You probably like it because it's like your own face and so that's what you're accustomed to looking at." It was unlikely, I observed, that I would use my own face as any kind of standard. "I'm confident about the work I did on her," he assured me. "It's all right that you don't like it, because I don't have any doubts about it."

Suddenly, I understood that he was anything but confident—that the point of showing me all of these slides was to win my approval. I was his perfect audience, both because I know a great deal about surgery (enough, in other words, to validate my judgment) and because I am not a surgeon myself. There is a danger in revealing one's work to another surgeon because of the element of rivalry that inevitably surges through the relationship between two "master artists," especially, perhaps, two male artists. I am a woman, and I am not a surgeon. Yet, because I have interviewed other surgeons, reviewed a great deal of the literature, in other words, momentarily borrowed their prestige, my approval goes a long way toward shoring up the surgeon's self-esteem.

As Susan Bordo puts it in "Reading the Male Body," what feminists commonly dismiss as the male objectification of women (in pornography) may not be desubjectifying at all. Quite the contrary, for the fantasy to thrive, the woman *must* be a subject who accepts the male body and its performances on any terms:

> The attempt is to depict a circumscribed female *subjectivity* that will validate the male body and male desire in ways that "real" women do not. The category of "objectification" came naturally to feminism because of the continual cultural fetishization of women's bodies and body parts. But here it is perhaps the case that our analysis suffered from mind/body dualism. For the fact that women's bodies are fetishized does not entail that what is going on in their minds is therefore unimplicated or unimportant. Rather, an essential ingredient in porn . . . is the depiction of a subjectivity (or personality) that willingly contracts its possibilities and pleasures to one—the acceptance and gratification of the male." (276)

Bordo's analysis of a male construction of female subjectivity coincides with what I experienced at the hands of the surgeons. It is not that they are just objectifying my body (and those of their patients) as so much meat for their transformational miracles. There also needs to be an appreciative subject of the surgery who can afterward look in the mirror and recognize the surgeon's skill. While surgeons may be objectifying the body, they depend on the living subject who can evaluate outcome, insist upon a revision, go to another surgeon (where both patient and surgeon will pool their scorn for the "lesser" surgeon), then praise the "greater" surgeon to all her friends and family as a miracle worker.

THE SURGICAL TOUCH

I try to walk in prepared; if they're published authors, I take out a photocopy of at least one article they have written in order to illustrate my

interest in them. Since most of the surgeons I have interviewed specialize in cosmetic (rather than reconstructive) procedures, imagine what it
must feel like to have a woman come in who is paying attention to *them*.
He who spends his days nursing the narcissistic grievances of dozens
of women suddenly takes center stage. "There are a lot of women," one
surgeon confides, "who have too much money and too little sense. In
fact, I would say that the more they have of money, the less they have of
sense." He wonders how he is supposed to render beautiful a woman of
two hundred pounds—what does she want from him, after all? More
than one surgeon has expressed the frustration of occupying the position of handmaid to rich, idle, overweight women who imagine that a
little liposuction will restore their youthful contours. Yet why shouldn't
these women be hopeful, given the proliferation of tabloid stories on
astonishing body transformations?

So, imagine me there, sitting in the place of the patient even as I offer the services of a therapist. It's a complicated shift of the conventional
daily situation obtaining in their offices. The relationship between us is
so precarious, always on the verge of tipping over into the other arena,
that it implies throughout the very thing it is not. I am not the patient.
He is not in charge. He has something to give me that is so very different from what he gives his patients. Instead of the surgeon listening to my
woes, I listen to his. To his patients he offers up (to a greater or lesser degree) the fantasy that they can become more beautiful. Some of them
think they will come out looking like a favorite actress. Some of them
are instructed to lie back and look in a mirror. "This is the best I can do
for you," the surgeon tells them regarding the face-lift surgery. They
look up into the mirror to see their skin falling back into their ears—
their facial contours reemerge from the flesh that has converged in the
middle of their face and sloped from the jawline.

Regarding younger face-lift interventions, a surgeon tells me, "I
don't want to do a surgery that the patient won't notice. There has to be
a noticeable difference in order to make it worthwhile." It's still not clear
to me how this decision is reached. "You, for example," he continues. "If

we were to do a face-lift on you, the result would be so minimal, you would hardly notice. Let me show you." He rises with a mirror in hand and approaches me. I have suddenly become a patient; before I even knew what was happening or could adequately prepare myself for the descent of those surgical hands, he has me. I ask him to stop as he begins to put his hands on my face. "I don't think I want to do this," a weak protest thrown up against his expeditiousness.

"Why not?" he is surprised. "Don't be silly. See here," he very gently lifts my cheeks and jawline.

"Here, look." I see myself in the mirror with my cheeks lifted—younger-looking no doubt. But the invitation to look registers as ironically hollow in the context of my feeling stripped of the ability to decide; my looking now feels as though it can only be passive and grateful. How does the woman view her future face-lift in the mirror? Consider that she is at once subject and object? I say, "It looks good." What else could I say? Worse yet, it *did* look better—to me, at least. I have many friends who all ardently insist that the "natural" contours of aging always look better to them than the surgical intervention. But not to me. (Indeed, certain actresses not yet "outed" for their surgeries are always claimed to be more beautiful than the surgery junkies.) What was lower was made higher. Isn't that what we're supposed to want—what we *do* want? What I "want" for my appearance is inscribed in the culture that shows me, everywhere I turn, what is supposed to be my ideal image—from the fifteen-year-old faces advertising makeup marketed to forty-year-olds (we're told that very young models are used because their skin tone is more regular!) to drastically underweight twenty-year-olds with enormous hardened silicone breast implants distending the fragile chest walls, puckering out from the sides of their sleeveless tops, stretching the buttons apart, like the taut skin beneath, barely able to contain the threatened excess. Far below the huge breasts linger the eighteen-inch waist, the thirty-inch hips—a comic strip heroine made flesh.

I was startled by the surgeon's hands as they swept up the contours of my cheek and jaw—ever so slightly, but permanently nonetheless:

the glimpse of an imaginary future, seeing my face as though through cheesecloth draped over the camera lens, like the expanse of a morning beach flattened back into smoothness by the tide after being rumpled and pitted by visitors the day before . . . everyday we can start fresh. I glanced in the mirror tentatively, then turned away abruptly and pushed his hands from my face.

"Yes, that looks good."

"You see that?" he asked me. He glowed. "Well, then, you would be a candidate for a face-lift. If you can see it, it means you would be pleased with the result." This was the point he was trying to make to me—that the surgeon is dependent on what the patient "sees," what the patient thinks is worth the surgical price in all senses of the term. He said: "What I would do now is send you in to my nurse to discuss price and set up a date for the operation." (Like a date for the prom.) This surgeon was no monster. When he put his hands on me, he was not trying to harm me. Indeed, he was trying to illustrate for me that I would not see any difference, that I didn't have enough sag for it to be worth my while to have surgery. He was slightly surprised that I could recognize the change.

He was a nice man. He was a caring father. He talked about his daughter and her career expectations. Nevertheless, he would not have touched a male interviewer—I have no doubt about it. This does not lead me, however, to an uncomplicated revelation of the imperturbable sexism underlying all interactions between men and women in our society.

Instead, I have a heightened understanding of just how difficult it is even to evaluate let alone change a system sustained on so many different levels within the culture as well as through and within our bodies. Dismantling this system might entail a dismemberment of what we take to be the body itself. The impulse that made him rise and touch me, the retreat and submission on my own part, and then the furtive look into the mirror—even against my will, wherever that "will" might be located, which certainly wasn't in my body, not that day, not in that surgeon's office, not in relation to the mirror he held up to challenge all my superior academic distance—all of these events are part of a more wide-scale social drama of how masculinity and femininity circulate through our bodies like something that feels as basic as a life force.

Let's isolate the multiple physical and psychical events that occurred within the space of sixty seconds. We were in our places on either side of the desk, and this arrangement had a visibly disorienting effect on the surgeon (as it frequently does), because I was in the patient's chair yet the one interviewing him. You would think it would fortify the surgeon's sense of his own place, his position in the world, his doctor's position. Yet it seems to do the reverse. It is as though his position mocks him. His inability to truly occupy the place where he believes he belongs and the place he has earned through many years of medical school, through a thriving surgical practice, involves a disjunction between the arrangement of our bodies and the distribution of power, confronting him per-haps with the ultimate uncertainty of all such social spaces and the roles associated with them. Yet my aging female body beckons the roles to re-vert to the normative—for me to become the patient and him the doc-tor. There is a radical break, then, between my role as interviewing sub-ject and my body that is a perfect object for his inspection. It is my body that obligingly (despite myself) drifts back into its familiar patient-role, where it supinely invites the surgical touch.

What is it about the relationship between the plastic surgeon and the female body that allows for such instant intimacy? Beyond the simple fe-maleness of my body, on what other basis did he know me? I could have been his wife, or daughter. I could have been his patient.

Lynda Nead discusses the dilemma of being simultaneously subject and object for *oneself*. As she puts it, "Woman [plays] out the roles of both viewed object and viewing subject, forming and judging her image against cultural ideals and exercising a fearsome self-regulation" (10). It is just this predicament of being the object of one's own remorseless gaze that acts out most transparently in the plastic surgeon's office. In a way, he feels like an extension of me—what, after all, is the difference between his hands reshaping my face in the mirror and my own doing so? Moreover, once I'm in pursuit of his skill, once I'm in the chair asking him to look at me (in the patient position), the surgery has as good as taken place. The leap from speculation to scalpel is so narrow once the surgeon considers the possibilities that hover before me like another planet drawing me into its orbit, holding out its promise of difference and specialness—a new life, a new you. In the case of the anorexic, Nead continues, "Woman acts both as judge and executioner." To execute means both "to kill" and "to make happen." So which is it? "Life Is What You Make It" is the newest advertising slogan of the American Society of Plastic Surgeons. What they don't tell you, though, is that first you need to unmake the former life.

While we all might agree that even today, despite our array of achievements, women are always being judged on our appearance, there is much less agreement when it comes to the surgical changes themselves. The otherwise seamless cultural fantasy of the "beautiful" woman is thrown into question by the enormous diversity of practiced aesthetics. Frequently, the patient and the surgeon disagree over the result. I am not talking about poor surgery here; rather, I'm talking about the confrontation of two different aesthetic paradigms, the surgeon's and the patient's, that become evident only in the aftermath of surgery. One woman complained bitterly to me about her surgeon. He wouldn't pull her face tight enough because he wanted her to look natural, while she wanted to look, as she told me, "plastic." They also disagreed on the most suitable shape for her nose. This dispute over the body (who knows best what it should look like) is a place where the apparent universality of aesthetic judgment can be undermined and revealed most clearly for the social and political act it always is.

As we can see, there is nothing inherently malevolent in the surgeon viewing the patient's body as raw material on which he can improve, because she came in looking for just this kind of judgment; moreover, she had already judged herself a fitting subject for the plastic surgeon's arts. Accustomed as they are to this particular relationship between them and the women who visit their offices, it was inevitable that I was cast as more of the same. Moreover, it doesn't really matter ultimately if it's men or women occupying the surgeon position, because it's an assumed instrumentality that acts out gendered characteristics and gendered relations but is no longer gender specific.[8]

Having these surgeons discuss my nose reminded me that it doesn't really belong to me. There are numerous accounts of how long it takes after surgery for the patient to integrate thoroughly the changed body part into the body image.[9] A surgeon explained the following: "A woman who has breast implants or who has her nose changed incorporates that into her body image within forty-eight hours. It's dramatic. Because I always ask them, 'Does it feel like a part of you?' and for the first couple of days, they feel like it's going to fall off, but then within forty-eight hours, or three days, it's a part of them. When you do breast reconstruction, you can't make that up. Really, if my kids were to look at the picture, the best they would say is, 'Yuck.' Yet this too gets incorporated in the body image almost instantly." On the basis of questionnaires and interviews, the researchers smugly present body integration statistics on face-lift versus nose job versus breast implant. Missing from these studies is any recognition of a culture in which women never really own any of our body parts, let alone those parts manufactured for us at the hands of the plastic surgeon. The implanted breast might feel as though it belongs to the woman but only insofar as breasts ever belong to women and are not culturally coded for visual pleasure, as a signifier of femininity. Consider as well the culturally normative "part-object" status of women's bottoms and legs.[10] According to psychologist Joyce Nash's account, the swiftness of such bodily incorporations is vastly overrated. "Jackie reported that for nearly a year after her breast lift and augmentations she would awaken from a dream in which her breasts had shriveled up and become distorted and ugly. Following breast surgery, it is common for patients to dream that their nipples fall off or to experience their breasts as 'pasted on,' not their own, or foreign" (119). Breasts, which are an integral part of the public spectacle of femininity, are in many ways foreign to or separable from the bodies that possess them — even naturally. The experience of gaining the breasts that symbolize the to-be-looked-at-ness of femininity (as Laura Mulvey has put it) could imitate (and even exaggerate) the cultural drama taking place around "real" breasts. It's not just obvious secondary sex characteristics like breasts, however. Once you look in the mirror and think, Hmm, maybe I should have my nose done, or maybe I would look better with a chin implant, then what you possess "naturally" feels no more natural than a superadded or altered bit. Thus, it means nothing really to say that we incorporate changes almost instantaneously, when we consider that the incorporations of transitory parts are necessarily (structurally) transitory.[11]

There is a borrowed quality to women's bodies. For the surgeons to ask me about the changes to my face (as though all of our features are potentially artificial—as though they looked at me in search of artifice) is to underscore not only that the cosmetic change is never "owned" by the cosmetic subject, but also that everything I have is only provisionally mine. This gaze of theirs that is registered in a particular way by my own surgically altered body at the same time sweeps the world with its inquiry: Did she do it? Or he? While this surgical gaze may be originally based on how men look at women—may, in other words, owe its cultural power to the inequality of gender roles—it is itself taking over as the predominant cultural look. The surgical gaze is shared by many people in this culture as we microscopically assess the faces and bodies of our favorite celebrities, as we dutifully peer into the mirror everyday to check our wrinkle quotient, challenged by Melanie Griffith from her surgically and digitally altered Revlon face: "Don't deny your age. Defy it." We take for granted that we can in diverse ways transform the body—either by way of exercise or makeup or hair color . . .

or surgery; the body that is seen as transformable is the body at the other end of the surgical gaze. More and more it seems that what was once the relationship between the male gaze and the female body/canvas is now experienced in the relationship between technology in general and any body at all.[12]

TWO

Untouchable Bodies

"I had huge zits . . . I had a huge cold sore on my lip . . .
stretch marks all over my butt . . . birthmarks, bruises. You
name it. It's airbrushed."

MTV show host (and Playboy playmate)
Jenny McCarthy, revealing the secrets of
her best-selling poster, Glamour *magazine*

A young woman took a summer job as a receptionist in a local plastic surgeon's office. Always troubled by the fullness of her lower face, she read about a procedure for removing the pockets of fat (buccal fat pads) from either side of the mouth. Eager for this slimming effect from what was described in the literature as an extremely simple operation, she asked her summer employer to perform the surgery.

She woke up from surgery without cheeks. In place of what were once sumptuous curves now extended a flat plain that had been liposuctioned clean. Meanwhile, the fat on the sides of her mouth remained untouched. The surgeon somehow had misunderstood her request, determined what he believed needed "correction," and ruined this young woman's appearance. In contrast to the narrowed upper face, the lower face seemed even broader than before.

She has sought the help of another plastic surgeon, who is trying to compensate by injecting fat into her cheeks. From what many other surgeons tell me as well as what we have learned from the long-term studies on fat injections, however, this approach will not work; the fat will continue to resorb or be uneven. Eventually, thousands of dollars later, she will probably find another surgeon, who will offer yet another makeshift "cure." Perhaps she will try cheek implants, although there is a relatively high rate of complications associated with this surgery. They may or may not work for her. She is only twenty years old, so she probably has years of surgery ahead of her. The surgical damage to her face can be corrected only through more surgery. Nevertheless, if the surgery had worked and made her more beautiful, she very well might have gone on to consider further surgeries. It would feel too good to resist. Either way . . .

I met a woman whose nose had been operated on when she was twenty-five by an osteopath in Los Angeles. He had left a sizable dent in her nose, which he attempted to repair by direct injection of liquid silicone. More than twenty years later, her nose became inflamed, and hard red spots progressed across her face. She was producing what are called granulomas, which are an allergic response to a foreign body. The problem with liquid silicone—as we now all know since the press has presented various exposés about it and the FDA has banned it—is that once it begins to travel through your body, it is almost impossible to control. You can try to excise it at visible sites, but this is a haphazard process with limited success. What was most concerning was the question of whether or not she was going to lose her nose altogether as the granulomas spread and the tissue slowly died. A plastic surgeon famous for repairing noses ruined by other surgeons chose to remove the silicone from visible sites—her nose, between her nose and upper lip, on her chin, along her forehead, wherever these masses of silicone snaked under the skin. She was beautiful before these nodules overcame her face, and she remains resiliently attractive through all the damage. In the last few years, she has developed rheumatoid arthritis so severe that she has needed hip replacement surgery. The causal relation is unclear—whether the silicone has compromised her immune system, or a weak immune system precipitated an allergic reaction.[1]

If the nasal tissue dies, she will need a new nose built from a flap of skin brought down from her forehead. This is an old technique for restoring lost noses—performed at least as early as 600 B.C. in India (Margrave 12). She chastises herself for her youthful vanity, as though this were the root cause of her current suffering.

We all feel this way when things go wrong. But even worse than the endless regret over bad decisions or our own uncontainable urge to intervene in the bodies we were born with is the obsessive thought that somewhere there is a surgeon who will finally, once and for all, give us what we want.

You go to wash your hands in a public restroom. What happens when you catch sight of your own reflection? Or in the rearview mirror of your car? Applying lipstick or flicking a limp eyelash—do you linger there? Have you glimpsed something new that bothers you, or is it the same old problem returning to haunt your image?

Does the mirror own you? Is it the place where you are in danger of falling apart? Is it the only place where you can be put back together?

Have you ever shredded your face into pieces?

Do you measure the length of your chin or the distance between your eyes, or do you worry about how your eyes slant down at the corners instead of up, not to mention the increasing laxness of your jawline that every year slips farther into your neck? Do you see these things not as a whole but in parts, fixate on them for the hour or the day—sometimes a week at a time? And then every face you meet, or view on television, or in a magazine becomes a site of comparison—a place where the defective events on your own face either happen or don't.

If you map your face by breaking it down into its component parts, then you are the perfect candidate for plastic surgery.[2] You see your face the way the surgeons see it. They will feel as though you share a common goal.

When I interview plastic surgeons, they discuss the face and body in aesthetic microunits. They elaborate on the nasal angle and the relationship between the bottom and the top lip. They divide the face into thirds and measure the relative proportions. If the bottom third is too short, they believe they should add a chin implant or move the lower jaw forward. They pore over the face as though it were an astral map of the aesthetic universe. When they put knife to skin, it is as though they are merely tracing the lines already etched in imagination—following the arcs and angles of beauty that are dormant in the subject, until one day awakened and lifted to the surface by the plastic surgeon. He can see deep inside you, this "holy crusader against ugliness"; he knows where your beauty hides (Goldwyn, *Operative Note* 95).

Many surgeons tell me they won't operate on patients with diffuse expectations of just "looking better." "What is it exactly that you don't like about your appearance?" they pursue. The patient hesitates—it's her nose, really, she just doesn't much care for it. "What is it about your nose? Is it too long? Too wide? The bump on it?" They demand exactitude from the prospective patient, because, without this, they know that patient is unlikely to be satisfied with the surgical result.[3]

It is true, if you grind down the face and body into subsections of beauty, each surgical intervention will feel as though it's improving upon this localized defect. The nose will be narrower. The cheekbones will be broader. Those fat deposits around your hips will vanish. Whether or not you "look better" is another question. Consider the sweeping trend of the nose job that overtook Jewish and other ethnic communities in the 1960s and continues to have a certain amount of popularity. The nose job of the teenaged middle-class Jewish girl became a rite of passage. What was wanted, however, was an extreme version of the "Irish" nose, apparently the archetypal gentile nose in the

Jewish imagination. Nostrils too flaring, tips too uptilted and too narrow. For the most part this nose created on the surgeon's table had no relationship whatsoever to the rest of her features (or any human nose that I know of). It didn't matter. The nose itself was the mark of a coveted cultural assimilation. This nose that stands for the rest of gentile culture, now somehow internalized in the Jewish girl through being planted in the middle of her face, is an example of how most cosmetic surgery works. The physical transformation emblematizes a cultural ideal.

There are psychologists who specialize in "body image"; a term originally coined by the psychoanalyst Paul Schilder in 1935 to describe the mental representation of our bodies, body image involves a psychological picture, not an objective one, which is why someone with an eating disorder can see fat in the mirror despite weighing less than a supermodel.[4] Current experts in this area recommend adjustments to body image through a combination of psychotherapy and pharmaceuticals.[5] In marked contrast to Schilder, whose use of the term "body image" was meant to challenge any distinction between an objective body and a subjectively experienced body, contemporary body-image specialists routinely assert (indeed, depend on) this very distinction. Here's an example from the literature: "Individuals who are homely or who have a facial deformity are more likely to be socially withdrawn and inhibited" (Pruzinksy and Cash 345). While such a statement seems straightforward enough, consider that body-image specialists think the person suffers from a disorder only when the specialists themselves recognize a significant difference between the ostensibly objective body and the person's internal representation of that body. Pruzinsky and Edgerton write: "Body parts are the inkblots onto which some people project their discontent. This may account, in part, for the recent increase in the numbers of patients requesting cosmetic plastic surgery who have previously undergone cosmetic surgery procedures on other parts of their bodies" (231). What if we were to broaden this account to suggest that body parts are inkblots onto which *everyone* projects his or her discontent; or rather, what if we were to argue that body parts become inkblots only when cultural circumstances deeply link these parts to identity? More-over, in a culture where fashions in beauty change rapidly and various degrees of ethnicity and mainstream WASP go in and out of the covers of fashion magazines and films, it's nearly impossible to hold on to a no-tion of an objectively beautiful body.

Not that there ever was an objectively beautiful body. The difference between our culture and traditional societies of the past is that their ideal images were longer lasting, giving the effect of a notion of beauty liter-ally carved in stone.[6] Increasingly subject to the vicissitudes of taste and fashion over the past few centuries, beauty is now as disposable and short-lived as our electronic gadgetry, more impermanent than even the flesh it graces—an airbrushed smile in a woman's magazine, which soon becomes paper garbage; a glowing and toned thigh illuminated in am-ber brilliance on the film screen, which briefly holds the most intangi-ble projections of light. Marshall McLuhan emphasized the profound cultural effects of the media we use: "The heavy and unwieldy media, such as stone, are time binders. Used for writing, they . . . serve to unify the ages; whereas paper is a hot medium that serves to unify spaces hor-izontally, both in political and entertainment empires" (23). "Sculp-ture," he writes, "tends towards the timeless" (188). These media are embodied; McLuhan calls them "extensions" of our bodies that not only project our bodies into the world but also inform the very means of inscribing our body image on our mental screen. The material of this screen likewise shares the weight of whatever substance into which we extend ourselves. Now paper is as outmoded as stone, and our extensions are digital as we pursue hypertextual trails through computerized spaces, where identity is exuberantly virtual and bodies linger dully behind. No wonder these bodies would rise to the occasion urged upon them by their extension into virtual worlds.

BODY LANDSCAPES

There is a famous plastic surgeon who specializes in correcting body skin laxity. After he performs what is called a lower trunk lift on a woman's body, her bikini-line scar perfectly traces the line of a bathing suit bottom—concealed by underwear or a bathing suit, no one would ever know. In front of a sexual partner, however, there would be no denying this Frankenstein-like sign of surgery. She is left with a hip-to-hip wraparound scar that suggests she has been cut in half and sewn back together.

Notwithstanding the unmistakable scar on the woman's naked body, this surgeon is also very interested in her appearance without clothing—in rejuvenating the pubic line, pulling up the sagging groin skin, transforming, so he claims, the pubic region of, typically, a forty-five-year-old woman into that of a nineteen-year-old. At a plastic surgery convention, he showed before and after pictures of his surgical correction of one woman's pubic area, isolated from the rest of the body. The audience was properly enthusiastic over the result. He then went on to report that this particular pubic area belonged to a ninety-four-year-old body. The other surgeons were both amazed and amused. "What does the rest of her look like?" queried one surgeon, presumably joking. "Oh, the rest of her looks ninety-four, but this bit looks nineteen." While there was a certain amount of self-parody in the surgeon's cavalier presentation, the isolated rejuvenation of a ninety-four-year-old woman's pubic region is not unlike juxtaposing a young-looking body with its telltale scars. She displays the gestalt of her youthful and desirable body to the eyes of a partner, who is (unconsciously perhaps) forced to choose between two very different aesthetic goals. Which is "uglier" in our inventory of the beautiful—scars or sagging thighs, buttocks, and abdomen?

One surgeon expressed utter revulsion at the thought of a woman with such dramatic scars on her body. "Who would get near her!" he expostulated. This surgeon tends to talk women out of the surgery. At the same time, notice the way he pictures his patients as women he either would or would not have sex with. Another surgeon who frequently performs the procedure insisted that the women were thrilled with the results. When I pursued the question of their partners' responses, he was dismissive: "The scars fade. It's not as bad as you think." These women were purely patients to him, not imaginable as partners. There were others around when he said this (nurses, technicians); they shot me significant glances. Another surgeon expressed this about the situation: "You need to compare the benefits and the drawbacks of any surgery. If you dislike big scars more than your sagging skin, then that surgery isn't for you." So, ultimately, it seems to come down to one's aesthetic—scars or sag—as simple as that. What you can live with versus what you can't. But these seemingly personal "tastes" are not so individualized as they might at first appear. Our preferences are very much informed by our respective backgrounds, personal experiences, subcultures, professional lives, and so forth.

We each have what I will call a body landscape. John and Marcia Goin refer to a "history of the body," which influences a whole lifetime of aesthetic choices (*Changing the Body* 66). I choose "body landscape" to place more emphasis on the body's surface, on the experience of the body's topography as the (always transforming) location of where inner experiences of "self" intersect with the outer body image. What feels like taste (scars or sag) or choice (surgery or not) is simply the effects of this body landscape. By "body landscape" I mean the individual's sense of where one's body begins and ends, the hierarchy of the body parts, which parts one esteems or values or invests with more thought than others, the degree to which this body is perceived as transformable or having been transformed. There are buried stories in the body, waiting like prehistory to be "discovered"—a scar on my knee that I don't think of for twenty years and then one day I realize that I don't even remember how it happened. Most important for the purposes of this book, one's body landscape determines one's own threshold for and reaction to different kinds of transformations (puberty, disfiguring injury, piercing one's ears, aging, cosmetic surgery, . . .). Consider the instance of an academic woman who believes that the loss of half her leg to cancer is nowhere near as disfiguring as the loss of a breast. I felt shocked to think that something so *public* as the loss of part of a leg, which involves a significant decrease in mobility, could be considered easier to live with than a mastectomy.[7] Clearly, she and I have entirely different body landscapes around not only leg versus breast but public body versus private—in other words the social body versus the body I see in the shower, share with my partner.

Through the perspective of a body landscape, we can raise certain questions that neither psychological nor sociological accounts of the human subject can illuminate. Why, for example, do some people wince at the thought of pierced ears while others think little of being anesthetized for a five-hour face-lift? Just as we recall through all of our senses any place where we have lived or visited (the dampness of a seaside cliff, a forest hike through the dense whir of black flies, the scent of industrial waste suffusing a certain highway), our bodies are held together with the residues of everything they have been, should have been, were not, could be, are not. Take the body of a woman who wanted to be pregnant but never was. In part, her body landscape will consist in being a place from which no babies were born. Compare her with the women undergoing lower trunk lift surgery, most of whom have experienced several pregnancies. Their sagging breasts and loose abdominal skin forever mark their bodies as having given birth. Yet, when they decide to have surgery to "correct" the results of childbirth, how will that alter the story their body tells? It is not just a question of the physical results— scars tracing the elimination of redundant skin and fat; it is how the woman herself both sees and imagines her body as the culmination of a series of transformative processes. Furthermore, what might it mean to her to have surgically removed from her body the evidences of her maternal past? Her body landscape would at once disguise and preserve the cumulative events of her bodily history. The scars will evoke simultaneously all three events in that history.

The bodies of women in a postsurgical culture are all compromised regardless of whether we choose or refuse surgical interventions. When intervention in one's appearance emerges on the cultural scene as a possibility for many instead of just the rich and celebrated, when it becomes a middle-class practice (and statistics indicate that it has), then we are inevitably in a relationship to surgery regardless of whether we actually become surgical.[8] We cannot be indifferent to the surgery that is everywhere around us, advertising on late-night television, beckoning us from the back pages of women's magazines, from right there in the middle of the newspaper we open during breakfast. These advertisements no longer even disturb the cream in our morning coffee, so familiar have they become, like anything else in a consumer society. We are hailed by cosmetic surgery as a practice to which we must respond (in one way or another). There is no longer an "outside" of this story.

When I mention my project to people (both men and women), they instantly personalize: "Oh, I would never do that" or "I've thought about it but I don't know if I could go through with it." Even a surgeon I interviewed responded in this fashion. Thus, when I posed to him the general question of whether surgeons typically have work done, he said, yes they do, but that he hadn't. As though recognizing the implications for his practice, he promptly added, "But I would if I needed it." Another surgeon said he would if he could find someone as good as himself!

I am reminded of the discourse on virginity. Once you take the step into surgery—once you open yourself up to the scalpel, to a bloody and material intervention in the formerly pristine sheath of your skin—you are a cosmetic-surgery patient from that point on, with more surgeries always on your horizon of expectations. It's taking that first step, a feared precipice, and then it's over—was it really so bad? There are surgery virgins. "I don't know if I could ever go so far as to have *surgery*," they say. Then comes the all-important transition, relinquishing the body to the surgeon's mastery—the fall. Many women talk about whether or not someone has "held out" or, in whispered circles, whether she's "done it." One patient told me that she thinks willingness to have cosmetic surgery is related to one's sexuality. "I am a very sexual person," she said. "I am comfortable with my body." Insofar as conventional heterosexual male and female sexualities are experienced psychically and represented cul-turewide as the relationship between the one who penetrates and the one penetrated, surgical interventions can function as very eroticized ver-sions of the sexual act. A surgeon noted the erotics of postsurgical con-versations among women: "They always want to know, 'Who *did* you?' It's not, 'Who was your surgeon?' Instead, they talk about surgeons 'do-ing' them."

My project is heavily informed by interviews of plastic surgeons as well as patients of plastic surgery.[9] I am a literary critic, not a social sci-entist, and thus my decision to do what is called qualitative interviewing was a highly unusual one, to say the least. Some might say, given my dis-ciplinary background and biases, I really had no business getting into this side of things. The members of the Institutional Review Board of my university, from whom I had to receive approval to conduct human-subject research, were especially concerned about what kind of addi-tional psychic injury I might inflict on these patients who had already suffered, as one IRB member put it, from "damage" to their body im-ages. What I learned from them is just how divided our culture remains between people for whom surgery seems normal and those who con-tinue to pathologize it as an extreme solution.

Wanting to avoid a patient population with excessive grievances, I decided to find patients through surgeon referrals.[10] Although it may seem that surgeons would pass on only their happiest patients, as it turns out, patients who contacted me through the surgeons varied from pleased to critical. I also used word of mouth to locate friends of friends.

I located the surgeons mainly through the aid of Barbara Callas and Leida Snow, past and current media directors of the American Society for Aesthetic Plastic Surgery. Because I was after a sense of the general cultural discourse of surgery, I traveled to multiple locations in the United States in order to register regional differences, which are significant in terms of the kinds of surgeries being requested, the patient population, and, most important, the aesthetic parameters. To this end, I also interviewed surgeons in England, where they are in the midst of the kind of media blitz on cosmetic surgery that began in the United States over ten years ago.[11] In the end, I interviewed thirty-nine surgeons; most of these interviews were face-to-face. I interviewed eleven patients; five were telephone interviews and six were face-to-face. I also interviewed a number of friends who were glad to share their experiences. The people I interviewed ranged in income from the very wealthy to those who were going to be paying the surgery off on a credit card for quite some time. Two of the patients were Latina, and the rest were white, mainly gentile. I interviewed only two men. I observed seven surgeries, including two rhinoplasties, one breast augmentation, and four face-lifts.

In some ways it was easier to interview the surgeons than the patients, because the surgeons were less likely to draw me into their surgical stories. After one woman asked me what I thought of her nose, I amended my consent form to include the following: "I also understand that the principal investigator cannot make any comments on my appearance." Such experiences also motivated me to stick to telephone interviews with the patients. But this isn't a study in the sociological sense of the term, and I am not using my interview subjects to make truth claims.

So why did I do it? I'm a literary critic and a critical theorist, meaning, first, that I work with texts, not people, and, second, that I tend to be wary of overconfidence in empirical evidence. But given that I am exploring a cultural trend involving real people, I was after what I can describe only as an ethical engagement with that trend's practice. My particular use of these interview materials, moreover, is what distinguishes me from a social scientist.

Many of the surgeons expressed confusion over my intentions. Why was I interviewing them? What did I want to know? It was difficult to explain, because what I really wanted was to hear how they talk about it. I wanted to know how they characterize their cultural role as plastic surgeons and to hear them describe what they do, how they feel about it, how they perceive patients. From the patients, I wanted to hear the ways in which they explain their reasons for having surgery, how they assess their bodies—what terms they use to describe a perceived flaw and their dissatisfaction with it—and how they describe the surgery and its aftermath. As should become clear during the course of this book, in many ways I treat the interview materials in much the same way as I "read" literary and filmic texts. In that sense, they are just more cultural texts, with the central difference between them and other cultural texts being that the interview subjects speak from the location of material, embodied experience.

My own body has been at risk since I began this project. When I called to arrange an interview with one well-known surgeon, he bluntly asked my age.

"Forty."

"Oh, well, yes, of course, you are right on the line of thinking about face-lifts."

Of course, he's right. The world of rejuvenating surgery beckons me as an option—all along, offering this conviction that I don't have to age if I don't want to, if I'm prepared to intervene, if I can afford to, if I can tolerate the surgical route.

Here's where I feel the relationship between my theories and my personal practices rapidly deteriorate into pure desire for the product (rejuvenation) that several plastic surgeons I've interviewed have held out to me as simply reasonable personal maintenance. During a follow-up interview over the telephone, a surgeon urged me to go read his recent article, where I would see the spectacular results of his latest face-lifts. Truly, the results were spectacular. It is so hard to resist.

And why would I want to?

The answer to "why resist?" no longer works as a feminist conundrum—even for feminists, who relentlessly quarrel among ourselves over our social obligation to perform our politics. Plastic surgery has unfortunately become another arena for feminist infighting as we accuse each other of submitting to the culture of appearances or providing the wrong role models, making each other feel bad/guilty.[12] The debate is predictable, yet also necessary even in its predictability, because we do need to at least account for our practices, if only in the name of leaning toward an understanding of what drives our social experiences.[13]

But there are larger cultural forces at work. It seems that men are the most current body-culture victims. The spate of men's lifestyle magazines (*Men's Health*, for example) underscores an identifiable shift in the gender ratio of body-consciousness.[14] We could argue that men are falling prey to the same image-centered social forces that have for so long oppressed women. This is certainly likely. Men are having more and more surgery, including the notorious penile augmentation, as though to confirm that male desirability is equally vulnerable to idealized cultural images.

How identity became susceptible to two-dimensional images, however, is the story that most interests me. Here it's useful to invoke what Fredric Jameson has called a "periodizing hypothesis" in order to articulate the relationship between the desire of individuals and their cultural circumstances and pressures. By "periodizing hypothesis," Jameson means a history comprising a chain of events that can be read not with chronological ease and exactitude but rather with the sense that one can recognize what he calls a "cultural dominant: a conception which allows for the presence and coexistence of a range of very different, yet subordinate, features" (4). Thus, while I acknowledge the interplay of multiple cultural positions, identities, experiences, and practices, I also generalize about a dominant contemporary image of the mutability of the subject—and the extent to which such mutability is *culturally desirable*.

My particular periodizing hypothesis could simply be called a culture of postnarcissism, after Christopher Lasch's more predictive than descriptive 1979 *Culture of Narcissism*. Nevertheless, although my book will dwell at length on the way narcissistic patterns have literally reshaped us (mind and body), I will instead name this pattern of which I speak "the culture of cosmetic surgery." To underscore "surgery" instead of simply "narcissism" places emphasis on the ways in which we experience the body as shaped by multiple external forces (environmental pollutants including cigarette smoke, ultraviolet rays, exercise regimes, even the food and vitamin supplements through which we imagine we introduce life- and health-changing elements from the outside in).[15] As for the social experience of one's identity, surgery is presented as a necessary corollary to the oddly relentless coercions of a youth-and-beauty-centered culture, despite the actual statistical aging of the United States. That we're desperate to be seen as fit and energetic and young and attractive makes sense when we are told on so many tacit and overt levels that we will find neither work nor sexual partners without these attributes; moreover, we are fated to lose both if we don't retain at least the superficial vestiges of the original assets. As a result of such extreme cultural imperatives, we cannot help but locate who we are on the surface of our bodies. The "culture of cosmetic surgery," paradoxically enough, is a postbody culture inasmuch as the material body seems to lose all its pathetic vulnerability in the face of a host of medical/technological advances meant to keep you perfect from the beginning to the end, indefinitely. In this sense, the body itself is both more and less important.

In coming to terms with this culture of cosmetic surgery, it is important to resist the easy (and understandable) urge to condemn such widespread social submission to a "plastic" body image. The proliferation of what feel like the supervening images of youth and beauty certainly seems suspect when their outcome is the (inevitable) imposition of a number of unattainable paradigms on individual consumers. The negative effect on a culture full of individuals who, stricken with panic, check our faces for the slightest hint of aging or rush to liposuction out the half-inch increase of the thigh's circumference is obvious, and this book takes account of the pressure on the individual to live up to the social image. At the same time, however, we need to ask if the rush to surgery (5.7 million cosmetic surgical and nonsurgical procedures in 2000, up from 2.8 million in 1998) [16] isn't about more than the external pressure of social images overwhelming "natural" human beings, who would otherwise live happily with their cellulite, wrinkles, and oversized noses. We need to reconsider the simple and recurrent binary between human beings and our social imperatives. The subjects who "submit" to images are the selfsame subjects who create them; so, while we might feel (literally) impaled on the perfectible body of postmodern culture, each one of us is linked to this body by cords of affiliation stronger than the one-way visual impingements of a television screen.

Rachel Bowlby has captured expertly the built-in impasses of the notion of agency in a consumer society. On the one hand, as she notes, we are active consumers of just about everything, to the extent that even health care is represented as being controlled by the power of consumers to comparison shop. On the other hand, consumers are depicted as helplessly capitulating to desires thrust on them from the outside but experienced as though spontaneous and authentic.

> The two types of consumer are complementary insofar as they turn upon a fixed opposition between control and its absence, between behaviour that is knowing and conscious of its aims and behaviour that is imposed on a mind incapable of, or uninterested in, resistance. A perfect accord, which is also a ready-made, and a custom-built, tension, exists between the passive and the active, the victim and the agent, the impressionable and the rational, the feminine and the masculine, the infantile and the adult, the impulsive and the restrained. (Bowlby 99)

These opposed social deployments of the idea and practice of consumption suggest why feminist responses to plastic surgery range from freedom of choice to utter subjection to the regime of beauty culture. Even the term "buy" contains the paradoxical combination of agency (one chooses to buy something) and victimization (one "buys into" as a form of submission). A surgeon invoked a shopping analogy to explain why he considers men to be better patients than women:[17] "A woman will spend all day shopping, trying on everything in the store, and then never being completely satisfied with what she gets. A man walks into the store, chooses something and takes it, puts it in his closet, and never worries about it again." Men are decisive consumers; women, erratic—infantile perhaps. The very reason we want surgery arises from our innate ambivalence, right? We can't ever be satisfied with what we have.

When we get into the habit of buying/buying into bodies, however, then the stakes seem especially high. Once bodies are on the line, well, things have gone too far. But, as Bowlby suggests, things were already pretty far gone by the time we turned the corner into an advertising culture of consumption that used the insights of psychology to regulate appetites and buying habits on a mass scale.

Just as consumers are both active and passive, beauty culture can be simultaneously coercive and liberating—another paradox. Regarding an emergent early-twentieth-century beauty culture, historian Lois Banner describes how it allowed older (postforty) women to value their sexuality and appearance: "Here what seems significant is that the elderly were no longer viewed as old, that women of whatever age were permitted and even encouraged to act as they liked and to look as young as they wanted" (223). Such a radical change in the way postforty women appeared to themselves and to the culture derived partly from feminism and partly from the incursions of commercial beauty culture that offered means for maintaining a more youthful appearance.[18] But there lay the source of what was, from its beginning, the double bind of beauty culture—if it pressed apart the gates, it nevertheless left intact (even exacerbated) a joint goal: youth, beauty identified with youth. No longer taken for granted that they would respectably disappear from the beauty scene, women would have to toil away at their complexions and bodies for another couple of decades. Such double binds ensuing from what Banner calls the "democratization of beauty" seem to plague us.[19]

This double bind is part and parcel of plastic surgery culture, which oddly invokes the rhetoric of democracy. Anyone can be beautiful. Anyone can afford the surgeries—you can find a cheaper surgeon or take a loan or even finance the surgery by arrangement through the surgeon's office. Apparently, the poorest and plainest of us can have breast implants and achieve perfect body contour. Can this be bad for us? Or, to put it from a slightly different perspective, can it be any worse than being stunned senseless by the impossible glow of "beautiful people" from our film and television screens, from our billboards, from magazine layouts? To borrow Rachel Bowlby's point about consumer culture—beauty can have *you*, or you can have *beauty*. It can oppress you as a social law, or you can hop in your car (or on a bus) and get some for yourself. Meanwhile, the surgeons, those empowered purveyors of the mystical quality of beauty itself, are there for us the moment we hold out our credit cards. What they do for a living shakes up not only the social order but also the very conventions of identity itself, as I will argue.

Once beauty becomes available to everyone, from all classes, races, and ethnicities, then it is exploded as a site of privilege—right?[20] Open any magazine lauding the wonders of cosmetic surgery, and you will find some reference or other to just how leveling it is for us that the miracles of cosmetic surgery are no longer hoarded by the rich and famous. We are so lucky that it is now available to a wide range of socioeconomic consumers. Is democratizing surgery a cultural boon? Or does this mean instead that now everyone must be beautiful according to a certain streamlined logic? Will everyone begin to feel as though she or he needs to take advantage of the surgery that once was available only in the remote domain of the privileged classes?

Most important, for the purposes of what will be my central argument about the deep relationship between celebrity culture and cosmetic surgery, the people who have benefited most (notoriously) from cosmetic surgery have been celebrities in general and actors in particular. Long before its currency among the general public, cosmetic surgery was associated with the Hollywood machinery of forging particular looks and impressions. Yet, finally, in a consumer culture, as Bowlby maintains, "everyone is . . . in relation to everyone else, a consumer, taking in as well as giving off impressions; 'paying' or withholding his or her attention and interest" (95). And thus cosmetic surgery, originally the special preserve of those whose appearance had exceptional value, has become equally (in more than one sense) available and important to the average consumer concerned with making an impression.[21]

IMPERFECTLY PERFECT

We are told that we know no limits in our pursuit of this perfect body; this is the concern voiced by those who worry that cultural toys like endoscopic lasers and other miracle-making tools of science will stave off for us the necessary encounter with the reality of the flesh—and ultimately its mortality.[22] We driven souls who turn to the gym to lose weight and flab and to the surgeon to hone what the gym can't adjust are told that we need to understand that the body itself is the limit-term we are trying to subjugate with our armamentarium of devices and our utter conviction that if you have the money and find the right surgeon, you can overcome even the hint of ugliness. Why, the stakes are raised on the category of ugliness itself, which can now be as minimal as the slight bump of a mole or eyes that aren't absolutely symmetrical. In contrast to this account of runaway grandiose narcissism, however, I suggest that it is the reverse. It's not that we are giddily disregarding the very real pull of mortality and the flesh. We aren't trying to transcend the limits of our bodies so much as we strive to create something from nothing.

The body is nothing until it's jolted into being by the image of something it could become—a movie star, a supermodel, a beautiful body. It's a body you have only when it's *the* body. Perhaps we want to possess the body we don't have to begin with. Working out, having surgery, just dieting—these are acts that give the body cultural reality. It's not only the puritanical, subjugated body that submits to cultural regimes of the beautiful.[23] Rather, we invent regimes as routes toward inventing this body. In other words, it's not a question of distinguishing between disciplined bodies that strive for perfection as they deny the limits of the flesh and presumably liberated bodies that engage the fact of their corporeality. This is a pretend conflict in the service of sustaining a conviction of a "real" old body struggling beneath the ceaseless assaults of dangerous cultural images.[24] When identity itself is fashioned (and incessantly refashioned) in relation to these transient cultural images, how can we speak of any kind of premedia, premediated body? What authentic body is left to preserve or liberate? I am not discounting the importance of coming to terms with the body's frailties and imperfections, but these narratives of the authentic material body unwittingly install another form of perfection (authenticity now) in place of physical perfection.

SURGICAL SUBJECTS

By the end of the nineteenth century, the cultural conditions were right for the near simultaneous emergence of three different cultural phenomena that have proved central in the Western experience of the self in the twentieth century. These phenomena were celebrity or star culture (including the cinematic apparatus itself along with fan culture), psychoanalysis, and plastic surgery. Richard Schickel traces the emergence of our current brand of celebrity culture from 1895 to 1920 (*Intimate Strangers*). Freud began writing in the 1880s and published what became the turning point for psychoanalysis, *The Interpretation of Dreams*, in 1900. As Sander Gilman has documented extensively in *Cre-*

ating Beauty to Cure the Soul, the modern history of plastic surgery is coincidental with and ideologically related to the history of psychoanalysis. "Curing the physically anomalous," writes Gilman, "is curing the psychologically unhappy" (7).[25] While Gilman has been interested in charting these two different routes toward personal fulfillment in a culture placing increasing emphasis on individual experience, I want to look at psychoanalysis as a cartography of the subject that is very much parallel to the mappings of the body of plastic surgery. Psychoanalytic developmental accounts of the human subject and the psychical agencies are elaborated within a culture with a particular set of assumptions regarding the relationship between identity and physical appearance. Moreover, star culture, with its circulation of two-dimensional icons as paradigms for modern identity, plays to and shapes the vicissitudes of this relationship among identity, image, mind, and body.

Theorist of stardom Barry King maintains that among the necessary ingredients for an idea of stardom to emerge is the centralization of production (e.g., Hollywood and mass, as opposed to local, culture). Of course, stardom can happen only in the context of a large audience that converges in the celebration of the iconic actor. Consider how necessary this institutionalization of star culture has been to the creation of a culture of cosmetic surgery. In order for cosmetic surgery to be appealing, not to mention a viable professional solution, enough of us have to agree on standards of beauty—not even on the standards themselves so much as on the idea of a standard, which is what the star often typifies. The star is a cultural standard of personality and appearance on which a mass culture can agree. Again, as important as the specificity of the star's traits is the degree to which the star stands for agreement—a consensus, if you will, of the general population's ideals. The star is both the standard and an instrument of standardization. The machinery for a star-making consensus, which includes publicity, typecasting, fan magazines, and so forth, was in place very early in the history of the cinema.[26] A culture invested in mass icons is more than willing to turn over our bodies to surgeons for the regulation and beautification of all that deviates from a standard we universally celebrate.

There are different names for what has happened over the course of the twentieth century, some of which are recriminatory and others wildly celebratory; whether hopeful, despairing, or cautionary, what all these accounts share is their emphasis on the visual media as the cause and/or effect of what we have become. Thus, those who worry about the negative effect of gorgeous body images on real bodies (many feminist cultural critics) are closely related in tone to those who blast the culture of the "pseudo-event" (Boorstin) or simulacral (Baudrillard). Visual media seem to stand for something fraudulent, a lure away from what really counts in life, or in print culture, or in the good old body prior to its reinvention through camera angles, airbrushing, and surgery.

> *The surgeon tells me: "Doing it for themselves—that has to be, in my mind, the prime reason psychologically for the patient to have surgery. If I hear, my boyfriend wants me to do this, I won't do it."*

While plastic surgery, star culture, and psychoanalysis may have been cultural effects of what I would call the increasing transience of identity, whether the transience occurs through relocation geographically or socially or economically, subsequently these effects have in turn become the cause of even greater changes in identity formation. The greater popularity and increased normalization of plastic surgery as a bodily practice at the turn of the millennium are the results of a population of people who identify with two-dimensional images as our most permanent form of "value." I will not pretend to say that this is a good or a bad state of affairs, caught as I am in the often contradictory flows of alluring and impossible images; but I will admit that it's hard. This book will describe and try to make sense of a culture in which surgery presumes to make people feel better about ourselves but often makes us feel worse. As I've told many of the surgeons I interviewed, I want to understand what it means to say about oneself: "I feel young, but I look old," or what

the surgeons are really saying when they insist that patients must be "doing it for themselves." Both of these statements suggest the experience
of a radical split between the "I" who feels and the "I" who appears in
the mirror as well as between the body that is for oneself and the body
that is for another. Plastic surgery functions as an apparent cultural solution to the very identity crises it embodies.

Most accounts of the transformability of appearance, unhinged from
nature, race, region, social class, and even anatomical sex, share a similar perspective regarding the politics of these changes. While such options may seem liberatory, critics observe, they are deeply conventional.
Thus, Elizabeth Haiken argues that the surgical reworking of visibly
ethnic features to free people from ethnic stereotyping is at heart a
disingenuous excuse for fitting into a highly conventionalized notion
of "American" appearance (*Venus Envy* 186). Susan Bordo worries that
many self-proclaimed, postmodern, body-liberating strategies are deeply
disciplinary, oppressive, and narrow. As she puts it, "Madonna's new
body has no material history; it conceals its continual struggle to maintain itself, it does not reveal its pain" (*Unbearable Weight* 272). We are
applying the "facade of individuality to an essentially conformist environment," writes Stuart Ewen (*All-Consuming Images* 232).[27] Style, he
argues, emerged as the surface-image of change to disguise the interminable reiteration of the same. It is a way of maintaining intact the
practices of consumer capitalism.

While I agree with these views on the rigidly conventionalized practices of beauty and style, I am going to offer a slight twist—from the
perspective of what it means to shape-shift surgically. At the same time
that we dutifully carve the aesthetic regime into our bodies, the practice
of plastic surgery radically disrupts our desperate efforts at fixing a stable
relationship between appearance and character or even at locating that
elusive entity known as "self." Unsurprisingly, the surgeons disavow the
cultural effects of their practice. They speak in the most conventional
terms about everyone's right to be good-looking and how important it
is in modern society to keep up appearances and on and on until you

would think they were the most slavering guardians of the good old "self" instead of its worst nightmare come to shatter it into broken glass.

A prominent plastic surgeon wrote in an editorial: "Plastic surgeons are, after all, exterior decorators (perhaps the psychiatrists are the 'interior decorators' of medicine)" (Goldwyn, *Operative Note* 44). This notion of the "spaces" of subjectivity, acted out by the very practice of plastic surgery, this distinction between inside self and outside self, offers us a way to rethink the "location" of the self. Where does this self come from—inside the subject or outside, from the culture? Moreover, where is the self located—in the mind or in the body, or does it shift between them? Who "chooses" to have surgery, and what does it do to them, to us, once they/we go through with it? Does it reshape the inside self as surely as it does the outside? These are "geographical" problems of subjectivity that the *process* of plastic surgery activates at the same time that its practitioners deny any such agenda. Throughout this book I will try to complicate these dichotomies of mind and body, appearance and self, in ways that press us to rethink how what we call "I" originates and unfolds in both embodied and incorporeal ways. In addition to discussing plastic surgery procedures (especially reconstructive) that aim to alter the personality along with the body, I will give illustrations of people whose ongoing search for the body beautiful on the operating table (addiction) suggests that the self who wants surgery is never appeased or really changed by the repeated interventions in his/her body. Such are the very contradictory outcomes of surgery, just as those who practice cosmetic surgery contradict their own "stories" of what they can offer to patients by way of life improvement.

Ultimately, it is unclear how the self is forged in an appearance-centered culture. When we are received as attractive by the world, are we internally changed? What is the difference between being born disfigured and subsequently "repaired" and being disfigured by an accident after perhaps many years of having felt "normal"? Although it may seem apparent that the character of the developing self (especially in the newborn) is more radically influenced by congenital factors, when we see adults who are permanently altered internally by disfiguring accidents, the difference between congenital and environmental factors becomes less sharp, and the body seems to have ongoing shaping effects on the psyche. Such effects are bidirectional. Just as the traumatically altered body impacts the psyche, the person who seeks cosmetic surgery as a solution to bodily concerns already lives very consciously on the surface, a surface that is felt as the origin of our identity. This mutability of self has an increasing purchase on the cultural imaginary.

THE LURE OF THE TWO-DIMENSIONAL

The assumption shared by people writing about the cosmetic surgery phenomenon is that many of us, women especially, are influenced by the combination of pervasive images of impossible bodies and the cultural chokehold to maintain ourselves at all costs, as we engage in the social work of keeping up appearances.[28] Apparently, these coercive forces of both consumer culture and beauty culture converge to prompt a good number of us into surgery in what amounts to ritual masochistic submission. No doubt there is much truth in these perspectives, but I want to extend the discussion here to include the central question, Why is it that so many people would be willing to undergo surgery (i.e., be put at risk physically) for the sake of looking good? Surgery's difference from chemically mangling our hair, weight training ourselves into amenorrhea, bleaching, capping, and straightening our teeth, or interminable trips to the cosmetics counter to support a multibillion dollar industry that thrives on sustaining rather than curing our dissatisfaction is self-evident. Or it should be. Yet increasingly I find people (from scholars to surgeons to friends and family members) eliding the difference between superficial and surgical interventions in appearance. Critics of cosmetic surgery seem to appeal to the slippery slope theory: once you buy into the system's objectives, you may go to extremes; while the surgeons frequently offer me the pragmatic end of things: you wear makeup, you work out, this is another form of self-care.

Although it is mainly accurate to link the growing interest in cosmetic surgery to other beauty practices (after all, it's for the sake of looking good/better), it takes more than the social pressures of beauty culture to send people so willingly, desperately even, to an operating table. Consider the following comment regarding the safety record surveys of lipoplasty: "Earlier studies," reports Leida Snow, director of media relations for the American Society for Aesthetic Plastic Surgery, "had examined procedures performed prior to mid-1998 and had suggested mortality rates as high as 1 in 5,000." The results of a new study following mortality rates from 1998 to 2000 were impressive. As the author of this recent study puts it, "'Estimated risks as low as 1 in 47,000 translates to a remarkable safety record and means that patients can have a sense of security about elective cosmetic procedures.'"[29] While at first glance we should be relieved that the surgeons have swiftly and effectively acted to remedy such a dangerous situation, consider what we are talking about here. Life-risking surgery for smaller thighs or a sleeker abdomen. While now your chances of dying from your lipoplasty may be only one in forty-seven thousand, remember, as you sign those consent forms detailing all variety of associated risks, that you've made a choice, although largely disavowed, to risk death for beauty. I realize I'm sounding extreme about what seems to carry a very low risk of fatality—certainly no greater than crossing a street, anyone might rejoin. But this is for your thighs. How have we as a society found it so easy to take this step? According to the statistics of the ASAPS, in the year 2000 roughly two million people risked death for the sake of their appearance.[30]

Yet are those of us who have surgery really risking death? Do we think of this as an actual price we're willing to pay for beauty? I don't think so. Rather, people who have been raised to idealize and identify with two-dimensional images are well prepared to become surgical. It's easy for us to go under the knife, because it doesn't really seem like a knife after all, and transformations of our mortal bodies bring us closer to those image bodies we identify with in two-dimensional spaces.

Instead of concentrating as others have done so compellingly on how our mortal and imperfect human bodies are impacted by perfected, digitized, and surgical media images, I am concerned with the degree to which we identify with these images to begin with, thereby narrowing (at times even disrupting) the distinction between the human and the two-dimensional. This distinction is a critical one because, as deep identifications of the human psyche with the two-dimensional become a cultural pattern, the content of each image is almost beside the point. Thus, to claim that moderating media images by showing heavier, less pretty, less perfect-looking people would or could improve our body images is to reengage the fantasy, from another direction, that images can give us what we want or make us happy. It is the image itself with which we are infatuated, and whatever it pictures for us may in the end be irrelevant in the larger context of our general yearning for identification with the two-dimensional.

The beauty of images symbolizes what is now experienced as their essential lure, and plastic surgery is the cultural allegory of transforming the body into an image, an allegory that is deeply linked to the effects of celebrity culture. I find it impossible to discuss individual choice, therefore, around the issue of cosmetic surgery when the phenomenon seems to be so much more radically embedded in cultural strategies than a simple call to political resistance would address. Susan Bordo asks women to resist the cultural forces while Kathy Davis argues for women's agency *within* oppressive cultural circumstances. In her book *Reshaping the Female Body*, Davis maintains that women who have cosmetic surgery are taking control of their lives. By no means passive victims, they are agents in a culture that privileges the attractive. Debra L. Gimlin, argues for "the potential for female mediation" of our various beautifying rituals instead of being simply passive cultural victims (8). About cosmetic-surgery patients, however, she concludes: "Far more than the other women I studied, the women who undergo plastic surgery help to reproduce some of the worst aspects of the beauty culture, not so much through the act of surgery itself as through their ideological efforts to restore appearance as an indicator of character" (108). Concerned with the degree to which individual engagement in such practices influences other women to participate as well, Bordo writes: "I reserve my congratulations for those choices that are undertaken in full consciousness that they are not only about 'creating' our own individual lives but constructing the landscape of our culture" (*Twilight Zones* 16). While Davis believes that such a landscape preexists us and changing our bodies in order to be "happier" seems like a reasonable choice in the context of the current regime of beauty, Bordo is convinced that such putative agency is yet another form of submission; inasmuch as each gesture is culture-shaping, these women (unwittingly) *contribute to*, instead of simply mirror, a culture of cosmetic surgery.[31] In response to Bordo's injunction to interrogate cultural images instead of mindlessly submitting to them, Davis wonders how "any practices, feminist or otherwise, might escape the hegemony of cultural discourses in which the female body is enmeshed" (55). I would say there is a big difference between doing the work of analyzing the seductive cultural images, unraveling their combination of lures, and making one's own life/body a tribute to one's expressed politics. Is it even possible to resist if the drive to have surgery is already in place?

Let's be clear about what is happening here so we don't continue to harass one another about the relationship between our politics and our bodies. *No one* who wants surgery "resists" it. In many ways the wanting is partly the doing, inasmuch as you've already said yes to a whole host of surgery-related activities—that you would go that far, that you have already pictured your surgically reconstructed body part. Those who urge us to resist are never tantalized by a surgical solution in the first place, so they aren't resisting much of anything. Hence, there is no difference really between the "good" feminists who resist the seduction and the "bad" feminists who capitulate.

Why would there be a greater degree of cultural emancipation in saying no to surgery than in saying yes? Is there an outside to the cultural picture from which we can calmly assess the difference between our genuine desires and the distortions of consumer capitalism and gender normalization? Is the yes to surgery constrained by the "fashion-beauty complex," as Sandra Lee Bartky calls it, while the no to surgery is the supervening culturally resistant voice? Could the no be equally bound up in cultural fantasy? As Hilary Radner observes, "From a Foucauldian perspective, the 'resistant' body . . . is no less a product of cultural discipline than the 'dominated' body, the body of 'gender normalization'" (141).

We need to transcend feminist criticisms of body practices that can wind up being as shaming as the physical imperfections that drove us to beautify in the first place—as though some of us are superior to the cultural machinery while others desperately fling ourselves across the tracks of cultural desire. Through an extraordinary analysis of Jane Fonda's career, Radner shows how difficult it can be for women to be both successful and emancipated. We precariously carve out "a culture of the self in which the subject submits voluntarily to specific practices in return for certain economic and social privileges" (174). It's not always clear, of course, which practices constitute a kind of submission and which press the outer edges of the given system. Worse yet, sometimes the capitulation and resistance happen in the same arena. As Radner points out, Jane Fonda's incitement to women to overcome their anorexic/bulimic practices and take control of our bodies through working out ultimately became yet another disciplinary regime.

Most important, it is not always clear who is doing the choosing and what is being changed. Throughout this book I will be questioning just this order of events. To separate mind and body and designate mind as an agent over the body's material shape is to imagine we're all quite clear about the distinction. Moreover, as I will reiterate throughout, the very act of surgery, the expressed reasons for undergoing surgery or performing it, renders impossible that cartography. Despite its self-characterization as creating a harmonious interaction between mind and body, in reality the very practice of plastic surgery both represents and facilitates in a dramatic way the erasure of the mind/body dualism.

When identity formation takes place in relation to two-dimensional images, then we cannot help but partake of some of their characteristics. It's not as though children are raised in isolation within their nuclear families and then (once personality and ego are fully in place) suddenly rush across the family threshold into the potentially dangerous landscape of television and magazines and movies. No, these have been our shaping guides from the very beginning. I'm certainly not encouraging us to toss our televisions out the window and return to a prior, more "human" form; we're past that. We are immersed in visual culture to the degree that we become its embodied effects, so instead of condemning the images that are now constitutive in a more elemental way than, say, making us want to diet when we see skinny models, I would encourage us to consider the meanings, for both individuals and their culture, of these recent modes of identity formation.[32]

To identify with two-dimensional images by no means involves merely passive imitation. Psychoanalysts Jean Laplanche and J.-B. Pontalis define identification thus: "Psychological process whereby the subject assimilates an aspect, property or attribute of the other and is transformed, wholly or partially, after the model the other provides. It is by means of a series of identifications that the personality is constituted and specified" (205). In other words, what we call the self comes into being through a range of identifications. While it may seem as though we are being "taken over" in some way by the external object of our identification, we are also actively engaging that otherness and making it our own—assimilating it as part of our selves. As I will discuss throughout this book, because of certain characteristics of media images (their two-dimensionality, their transformability, their constitutive technologies), identifying with them may put us at risk for a lifetime of transformational identifications. Psychoanalysts have for some time been addressing the rise of narcissistic personality disturbances in the twentieth century.[33] As I will discuss in chapter 5, it is of importance that these disturbances are linked to the actor-psyche itself in a culture where actors are among the most venerated of public types.

In a culture fixated on becoming a celebrity, where we find an individual's "inner truth" through the apparatus of the filmic close-up, it's increasingly impossible to impugn perfect images as though they are entirely distinguishable from the ground-zero level of the self. It may well be that the only bodies that seem real to us are those witnessed by millions of people in movie theaters or on national television.[34] To imagine that there are people who could change the images if they wanted to is to misunderstand the embeddedness of the image producers in a cultural machinery that they don't run but instead merely service. For them, as well as us, the image and beauty are coextensive. The product becomes an excuse for the production of beauty; in advertising, beauty may seem to function as the lure toward the product, but at the same time the product is simply a road toward beauty.

More important, the power of the aggressivity released in response to idealized and impossible images leads to a deadly social side effect. People not reflected by the idealized images (practically everyone) imagine that if we were so reflected we would necessarily feel better about ourselves. Imagine the aggressivity multiplied by knowing that, for example, one's race is rarely represented and only insofar as it is mainstreamed for white aesthetic consumption. For many nonwhites in the United States, the reality of their missing bodies (especially the range of bodies) from the media landscape could lead one to believe that one reason it's easier to be/look white is that whiteness is more widely represented as aesthetically desirable. But this predicament is simply a reduplication of the central splitting between material bodies and two-dimensional lures. No one measures up—no one at all—this is the whole point, and it is exactly what leads to what I term transformational identifications. The racist aesthetic of media bodies only intensifies our faith in a two-dimensional solution.

Cosmetic-surgery patients and plastic surgeons seem to replay the only roles available in a fairly circumscribed plot. But just what is the plot these days, and how have its elements and characters shifted without our even knowing? While gender remains pivotal to the story, it's less important than it used to be. Even though the desire for physical perfection seems extreme, we seem to be more bound up in the transformative act itself than we are in the end result. When and why did we become surgical?

Although so many of us clamor for change in the current cultural circumstances that render human bodies inadequate and send us rushing to the plastic surgeon, we need first to determine what it is exactly that we need/want changed. In other words, what is the combination of social conditions and imperatives that have stranded us in a culture of cosmetic surgery? Is it interminable pursuit of the beauty myth? Is it a persistent acting out of gender? Is it disgust with and intolerance for the material body as such? In order for a cultural practice to grip us with such tenacity, it has to be fed, I will argue, from multiple directions—some pragmatic, like the profit motive of plastic surgeons in conjunction with wide-scale cultural fantasies: that a new body is something you can buy, that you even want a new body to begin with, that appearance changes your life. This book is in inquiry into the fantasies and practices that have forged such a culture.

THREE

The Plastic Surgeon and the Patient

A Slow Dance

AESTHETIC LANDSCAPE

The surgery lasted seven hours. The patient was a woman in her mid-fifties—in for a face-lift along with an endoscopic brow-lift, upper and lower blepharoplasty, and fat injections to her lips. She complained that her eyes seemed increasingly deep-set, and she disliked her forehead creases. She told her surgeon that she wanted to "soften her look." I entered the room just as the patient was going under. It's easier that way. Linking the surgical process to someone I've met makes it impossible for me to achieve an emotionally neutral, aestheticized distance during the operation.

Each time, I anxiously watch the monitor, scanning heart rate and blood pressure. I shudder when they are wrenched from their anesthetic sleep, the whole body heaving up and arching when the ventilator is pulled from the mouth. I worry that they won't be able to reconnect consciousness to their surgical bodies, that they will die. And then after, in recovery, left alone with the patient and family, I feel responsible, telling them the surgery went well—as though I have any idea, really. I suspect, with experience, I would get over this and would be able to separate more readily the human from the surgical field.

This patient's procedure took place in a large surgery room in a hospital. The staff was very concerned to keep me far away from any of the sterile areas, and nurses were busily relocating me. Two huge Sony television sets faced the operating table. These would be used for what is called an endoscopic procedure. The endoscopic unit, as Oscar M. Ramirez describes it, consists of "a camera, xenon light source, two video monitors," an endoscope along with "special [periosteal] elevators and manipulators" (639). The sheets were lifted from the patient, then redraped very carefully to avoid any pressure points of fabric, which could lead to blood clotting. During long surgeries like this one, blood clots are the greatest concern.

Another surgeon told me that she wouldn't operate for longer than five hours because of the degree of risk. "I just don't think it's a good idea. I think you put the patient at higher risk when you put them under general anesthesia for a longer time. They have risks to their lungs, they have risks of blood clots, so I really limit the surgery. I've had patients ask me if I'll do their breast implants and abdominoplasties at the same time, and I've said no." One of the problems surgeons face is that patients tend to prefer combining procedures—one big surgery, in other words. Cost is often the primary concern. If a patient were to have implants and a tummy tuck at separate times, she may not be able to afford the additional funds required for hospital and anesthesiologist charges; indeed, the total cost could increase by several thousand dollars, not to mention the additional recuperation involved, extra time off work.

The surgeon began by suctioning out fat from her belly for injection into her lips. He explained to me that there is some anecdotal evidence that the fat from some areas of the body is more volatile than fat from others, meaning that if you gain weight, the newly augmented lips might expand as well! The process of suctioning out the fat seemed so violent, plunging back and forth with the suction tube into her soft abdominal skin. "She's straining against me," the surgeon complained to the anesthesiologist, who was instructed to sedate her further.

The anesthesiologist, in perusing the patient chart, was not especially pleased to note that the patient had claimed to imbibe between four and five alcoholic beverages a day. I spoke with the anesthesiologist about her experience with this surgeon, for whom she had great respect. Two years earlier, there had been a fatality. The evening following her breast augmentation, a young woman rose to go to the bathroom and died from a blood clot. "Every now and then, these things happen," she commented, but I sensed that the memory continued to agitate her, this death of a young woman for no good reason.

As he plumped up her mouth, the surgeon explained that the patient suffered from what he calls incomplete oral closure, meaning that the teeth touch each other before the lips meet. He believes this configuration ages the face by forcing certain muscles to compensate; thus he plumps up the lips to supplement the deficiency.

He turned to the brow. The lights in the room dimmed when the two large television screens flared awake. I felt as though I were viewing an art installation, not surgery. A tight circle of light beaming down from the surgeon's headlamp contained the faces of the surgeon and the patient, and the paired screens glowed blue. The surgeon made two incisions in the patient's hairline, each approximately an inch and a half long. He gently pried the skin apart from the periosteum and, with a drill, made what he called a bone tunnel to define the endoscope's route; he then inserted a wire to make sure the tunnel went all the way through. A periosteal elevator raised the skin from the forehead. Hearing the scalpel rasp against bone unnerved me. In this aestheticized technological space of television screens and monitors soothingly flickering orange data and a table full of harmoniously arrayed metal instruments in an unrecognizable variety of curves and angles, body sounds seemed out of place. He then inserted the endoscope, a long thin instrument with a camera at the end, which gives one visual access to what would otherwise be out of visual range. Use of the endoscope allows doctors to make smaller incisions, because the scope reveals to them the underside of the face, otherwise visible only by rolling back the whole forehead. Many surgeons consider the technique revolutionary, but others think the results are less impressive than the old-fashioned coronal brow-lift or even aesthetically undesirable.[1]

I could not take my eyes off the screens. As the endoscope traveled beneath her brow, against the bone and periosteum, it first seemed to be speeding through a tunnel and then came out into a chamber of luminous wet colors—reddish pink tissue and yellow fat and white slivers of nerves. It looked as though they were filming under the sea. Art historian Barbara Maria Stafford, in claiming that the eighteenth-century "anatomical 'method'" of inquiry into the secrets of nature persists in the present, worries that "one result of the new noninvasive imaging technologies in the area of medicine is the capability of turning a person inside out" (48). She wonders: "Will this open-ended trend toward complete exposure give rise to the same sense of vulnerability, shame, and powerlessness that the eighteenth century associated with anatomization?" (48). Curiously, the displacement of the patient's body onto the television screen had the effect, not of turning her inside out exactly, but rather of disembodying her, transforming her into a visual landscape—not for beautification per se, instead for the sake of transformation itself. Thus, viewing the projection of her body into two dimensions in the very process of being surgically manipulated on the three-dimensional plane (after all, his scalpel was indeed beneath her skin) seemed to enact the process of the body becoming an image, becoming televisual even.[2]

While the television screens in the room certainly amplified this effect, I had a similar experience of the body's transformation into a two-dimensional aesthetic landscape when I observed a breast augmentation. The surgeon turned to a resident who was assisting and invited him to palpate the location of the nerve in the pocket he had created under the chest muscle. As the assistant inserted his fingers, nodding when he felt the nerve, I imagined what it would feel like—rubbery? dense? kind of like a coaxial cable? In that moment of my wanting to explore the surgical field further, the patient herself disappeared for me. Her chest was no more than a plane on which a surgical event took place. As the implants were filled with saline, they rose from the chest, reconfiguring its topography. This in itself was fascinating and seemed to have nothing to do with her bra size or what kinds of clothes she would wear postimplant. This had nothing to do with anything human.[3]

Surgery doesn't really seem to be about the body's interior, because the process, during which the inside becomes another outside, is ultimately topographical. There's no sense of revelation, the stunning moment of making visible what was hidden; rather, there's a realignment of what constitutes the surface.

The current patient's brow-lift was more difficult than expected and went very slowly. She had many little perforating vessels, prompting the surgeon to explain, "Even a drop of this [blood] in a scope looks like a river." Painstakingly he cauterized all the little vessels that were leaking into the tissues, forming rivulets. The room filled with the smell of burning blood.

Epinephrine locally injected into the face is supposed to stop most of the bleeding, but this patient bled continuously throughout the operation. During the face-lift proper, it took a long time for the surgeon to unmoor the skin from the fascia. At the end of this, almost her entire face had been undermined. He worked on one side at a time. Scrupulously he progressed through her face, rearranging tissue, restoring the substructure, in order to create a more youthful contour—but it wasn't until the end, when he pulled the skin back and stapled it shut, that I could actually register the result. The skin was taut and smooth; there was now a jawline where before there had been a swell of double chin. He turned over her face to the untouched, older side, like the painting in the closet.

TIMING

A few years ago, all 13 of the Lexington, Kentucky–area plastic surgeons (13 serving a population of just 250,000) joined in advertising the benefits of preventive face-lifts. "If you prefer a more harmonic relationship between your self-perception and outer image, you may prefer to tackle these concerns before they become too obvious. You may benefit from a facelift performed at an earlier age" ("A Case for Undergoing Facelift"). They urged people to consider treating facial aging earlier than before—as early as thirty-five in fact. They claimed that such early interventions will improve the result (younger skin is more elastic) and guarantee future results (future face-lifts). Moreover, the most recent surgical innovations are designed especially to effect changes on relatively young faces. One surgeon told me: "I think what's going to happen with this is you're going to see more of it being done but in a lesser amount. People are going to start having cosmetic surgery done like going to the dentist, because you know, every two or three years, you'll have a little endoscopic tightening done to keep up. Frequent smaller procedures done."

Face-lift surgery has traditionally been an option for well-to-do women in their midfifties and over. But, as this surgeon observed, things are changing and rapidly, especially given the increasing geographic and economic availability of these procedures. Equally important is the marketing of the "smaller" procedures that identify localized pockets of facial aging. When a patient is wooed with an eyelid lift claimed to erase five years from her face for only four thousand dollars and a short recovery period—in contrast to twelve thousand for the whole face and a longer convalescence—this patient is necessarily more motivated to start early. Add this divide-and-conquer and pay-on-the-installment-plan approach to the fact that women are trained from early on to experience our bodies in fragments, and one can see how easy it was for surgeons to tap into this market.[4]

The contradictory information from the surgeons can feel alarming, however. Many surgeons say the risk is in letting it go too long. Past the point of no return. You bring your face to the surgeon, and wearily he shakes his head and tells you he only wishes that you had come to him sooner. One surgeon compellingly explained to me the advantages of early intervention: "So you do it early and often. It does make a difference, because the person always looks good, and you never really need that horrendous megaoperation to rearrange everything. The most difficult problem I've got is some lady that comes in here at seventy with a real baggy neck and she's a wreck. And she's expecting to look fantastic with one operation. It's not going to happen. It's like rehabbing a house. But with the subperiosteal midface-lift, that's changed the ball game a little bit. I don't do early face-lifts anymore—I'll do an early midface-lift, because I can do it without a scar." Another surgeon pointed out that it's when you wait too long that you get the "wind tunnel" effect: "When they're reasonably young, like fifty years old and still have pretty good elasticity in their skin, you can get nice results without pulling them too tightly. When they get older and the elasticity is gone, then the only way a plastic surgeon can tighten them up is to overtighten them." A number of surgeons asserted that very early (but more minimal) interventions require maintenance. It's more subtle, less surgical-looking, but has to be fine-tuned with some frequency. At the opposite end were the surgeons who claimed that you should have one big operation (everything at once) and thereafter fine-tuning every couple of years.

Nevertheless, some surgeons cautioned that early face-lifts could potentially adversely affect someone's aging down the line: "You have to be careful not to start operating on people too young because of the effect long-term. The younger a person starts this type of surgery, the more potential effect it has on their aging. So it can be good and bad." Indeed, by way of criticizing one another's techniques, surgeons are now claiming that the wrong kind of face-lift makes the patient look strange after a few years. One surgeon explained to me (very convincingly) that they all look good at first, but five years down the line, the patients who had the wrong kind of face-lift look "weird." Either way, one worries. What if you wait too long and wind up looking frozen and pulled? What if you start too early and wind up looking oversurgical as well? What if you have a subperiosteal procedure, and it ages unevenly? What if you expose yourself to greater risk by undergoing more frequent procedures? What if you do a deep-plane on the superficial musculoaponeurotic system (the SMAS) and experience permanent nerve injury? One person I interviewed had lost all feeling on large areas of her scalp and face. Still, she loves the way she looks and is happy with her surgery.

What kind of face-lift and when—this feels like the highest risk of consumer decisions. Several patients I've interviewed have looked to me for advice on what to do and which surgeon to patronize. They understandably imagine that all my research has enlightened me. "You know all about this stuff, so when you're old, you can find the right surgeon. You're going to have the best doctors in the world." The very feeling that such expertise is possible can become a compulsion that links the quality of surgery to one's consumer expertise.

What if you order the wrong operation at the wrong time from the wrong surgeon? What if your surgeon finds out that his wonderful new technique, which he tried for the very first time on you, has an undesirable side effect? I think of what one surgeon explained to me about cheek implants: "The hard thing stays right where you put it; it never moves. Soft tissue moves; you end up with a deformity that's very, very typical. If you look at [a famous actor's] left side, you'll see it. He had implants put in a year or two ago, and there's a bulb on his left cheek. The rationale is at twenty-one, you can take a model and make her look like she has higher cheek bones. Fine. That's fine. But as she ages—compare twenty to forty or fifty—she will look very bizarre." But then so much of what I read suggests that cheek implants are just the ticket to supplement the atrophying contours of the aging face. Does cheek augmentation then necessarily require a series of maintenance surgeries to keep the implant correctly positioned under the skin? Would this lead to an endless cycle of surgeries? One false step . . .

The technical innovations in face-lift surgeries are designed for younger people.[5] As I've shown, the endoscopic approach gives the surgeon visual access without having to make a more extensive incision. As one surgeon expresses it, "Young people don't like scars." The results on young people also look better than results on older patients. The younger patients look—well, surprise—younger. Surgeons like to show and publish their best results. I have speculated that one of the reasons surgeons want to operate on younger people is that they have grown accustomed to seeing young face-lifts in their professional journals and conventions.

The surgeons refer (globally) to "the aging deformity," which they micromanage through particularizing a series of interrelated, but at the same time separable, "deformities" of the aging face and neck. Reading through plastic surgery journals makes me feel simultaneously subdivided into pieces of age and extraordinarily confident in the surgeon's ability to divide and conquer. Let me present the signs of aging along with their scientific names (a consolation really) and what you can do about them, because aesthetic age is reworked into a medical riddle like smallpox or polio, and, apparently, merely by isolating the cause of each aging symptom, you can find a cure shortly thereafter.

"Global characteristics of aging are that the face closes up on itself in the central region" (Krastinova-Lolov 22). A surgeon entitles his article "The Armamentarium to Battle the Recalcitrant Nasolabial Fold," as though aging has become some menacing foreign invader at the same time that it's "recalcitrant," like poor people who won't pick up and leave the gentrified neighborhood (Guyuron). Nasolabial folds are the creases that run from the corner of your nose to your mouth. Then there's eyebrow ptosis. One surgeon criticizes the "concept of 'brow elevation' as the essential mechanism to correct both brow ptosis and upper eye deformities" (Daniel and Tirkanits 605). Whether simply to trim the upper lid or lift the whole brow to restore a youthful line—such is the nature of the debate. The problem seems to be that the surgically lifted brow is almost invariably higher than the authentically youthful one.[6] There are submental fat pads on either side of the mouth and malar fat pads on top of the cheek. "Toward the end of the third decade," a surgeon writes, " the fat starts to slide forward and down, as the overlying skin loses its elasticity" (Owsley 464). You end up with hypertrophy of platysma (the neck) or, worse yet, the "senile" upper lip. One surgeon claims that "the lengthening and shape deformities of the upper lip are the most important senile alterations" (Guerrissi and Izquierdo Sanchez 1187).

THE PLASTIC SURGEON AND
THE PLASTIC SURGEON'S WIFE

When I asked a surgeon what he thought of the recent trend in young face-lifts, he immediately responded: "I encourage it." He explained that the bony structure of one's face matures by sixteen in women and eighteen in men. "Now, if you can argue that age twenty-five is maturity and you had exactly the right amount of skin coming from the brow down to the first fold and exactly the right amount of skin coming to the eyelashes . . . and that was normal, then is it normal to allow time to change it, so that the skin begins to slide down over the jaws and the bags begin to show? Well, that's not the way it was when it was twenty-five, anymore than when I painted my house it was natural for me to let it gradually deteriorate. I keep it up—repair and maintenance." Now, notice here that he effortlessly invokes a very recognizable (and for the most part predigested) brand of middle-class morality—nice middle-class people aesthetically maintain their homes. As Lakoff and Scherr point out: "It is sometimes suggested in the popular media that a woman has a virtual moral duty—to herself and those who must behold her—to remove those wrinkles and bags, tuck that tummy, raise those breasts" (171).

Moral duties, with their competing agendas, confront us on all sides—which shall we choose, of which "moral" shall we be an example? I think this surgeon's analogy, however, culled from the ostensibly benign mainstream American discourses of cleanliness, community membership, and self-improvement, is shifting in a slightly different direction—toward an utter reversal of the received definitions of his categories. Specifically, when he yokes surgical maintenance to "natural" upkeep, something has changed. Certainly "natural" insofar as it refers to physical appearance has never been a neutral term. But I still think that a large number of Americans would disagree that it is natural to have one's face surgically rejuvenated, nor would they think it abnormal to age without intervention (recall that he questioned whether it was normal to let your face age). What becomes clear in this surgeon's account is that the body is normal only when it is at the apex of its youthful maturity—and again, maturity as defined in a very aestheticized way.

Given the elaborate aesthetic criteria devised by plastic surgeons to provide for one another the measurements and contours of youth, increasingly fixing in their mind's eye this blueprint of the correct face, it is no wonder that they begin to pathologize aging. Certainly their professional vocabulary suggests as much. It is significant, moreover, that the surgeon interviewed uses "normal" and "natural" interchangeably. In part, his aesthetic standards are encroaching on psychological assessment. If you let yourself "go" as it were, then you are not a fit, or normal, psychological subject. You lack self-esteem, you let yourself go to pieces, your paint chips, the signs of wear and tear remain unattended to. You might be cited. You might be fined. You might be condemned.

"When patients ask at what age they should have a facelift, I say I think the average age that a plastic surgeon's wife has a face-lift . . . early forties, late thirties. Why? Because a plastic surgeon's wife is sitting there and has immediate access. My wife had her eyes done when she was thirty-seven, her face done when she was forty-three. She's fifty-five now. Now, if you look at photographs of my wife back when she was thirty-five, [you see] there is very little change in her. You do little things because there's not much wrong. My wife first started seeing these little folds right down here and just the beginning of a little sliding of her jawline, because she has a real strong jawline. That's her picture right over there." At this point in the interview, the surgeon took down from his wall an eight-by-ten photograph of his wife. He put it in my lap and, as I looked down at a slightly out-of-focus picture of a woman with a stylish black hat and a debutante jawline, I thought back to what he had said earlier about a plastic surgeon's wife "sitting there"—that's the way he put it—and I wondered vaguely about how sad it was, really, that someone could not just "sit there" and age. I wondered how it would be just to sit in a chair, say, at your dining room table, seated opposite the man who would, with his highly trained eye, appraise what happened to your face yesterday—the gentle trace you had when you went to bed the night before now deepened into a full-fledged wrinkle, or the depressions in your chin that he had, with his precise aesthetic unforgiving gaze, noticed happening all along but had been too discreet to mention until now.

Mr. Ghengis, one of Ruth's plastic surgeons in Fay Weldon's *She-Devil*, observes that he's never married because "he knew he would, sooner or later, succumb to the urge to make his wife more physically perfect, and that once he had achieved perfection with her he would lose interest. It was the journey, so far as women were concerned, that satisfied. The arrival was anticlimax" (252). I thought about Mr. Ghengis as the surgeon cheerfully continued: "Now, that's the type of person I'm married to. She is a very, very striking and attractive woman." I nodded politely as I looked down at the framed picture in my lap. He leaned over my shoulder directing my attention, perhaps the way he directed his wife while he stared over her shoulder as they both watched her looking back, baffled at her incontinent, sinful aging, from her place, her rightful place, her only place—in the mirror.

"There she is at age forty-five [let's not even ask why he keeps a ten-year-old photograph of his wife in his office], and she has already had what she thought underneath here was beginning, and a little bit of slide under here. It was *so little*, so minimal that people who talked to her said, 'I don't see anything wrong with you. Why are you having anything done?' Right? . . . And I would argue that then she shouldn't have anything done, but she could see it and I could see it. It was there." It—aging—was there, sagging between them over the breakfast table, solemn, unspeakable, but so powerful in its effects. To be called an it makes the aging process a monster from another planet, an alien being rising up within one, taking over one's normal, natural body, rendering one an eyesore, a blot on the community.

I looked at her and felt a little chilled by her presence in my lap with her husband speaking over my shoulder, and for a moment I panicked about whether I had let things go too far—because he warned me about what happens when you let things go. The major concern, he cautioned, is that if you wait too long, surgery will effect a radical change. "If you begin to see some of these changes occur, isn't there some value, in terms of preserving self-image and preserving a certain amount of personal satisfaction, in intercepting them as they occur? Is there some sort of requirement that you have to reach a certain age when this is *really* becoming very noticeable?" Note how rapidly he assumes the language of liberation, of freedom of choice—"is there some sort of requirement"— in contrast to all those body police who would regulate appropriate ages for face-lifts. "For somebody to wait until their fifties and sixties for all these changes to occur and then have it *changed* is to me a problem. . . . I think they have to go and get reidentified with themselves. . . ." Indeed, one risks psychic trauma. But the psychic trauma I was experiencing was the tremendous desire he tapped in me, because, despite how appalling I found his account on many levels, I was nevertheless almost entranced by the promise he held out of never having to age, never having "to pay," as he put it.

Somehow, I believed him, that if I put myself in his hands he would put me on a program of repair and maintenance. He would monitor my face for changes and notify me when the time was right. And then I flashed forward to the operating room table, where I would gaze up into his knowing, expert, soothing face as the anesthetic began to sweep through my senses, as he leaned over me with his purple pen, marking off the sites of aging on my face, landmarks for him after he's cut the flaps and is trying to link the nether-face to the surface-face. And I have the dizzying recognition of how—when he tethers back my SMAS and tugs the malar fat pads to get at my nasolabial folds, and he delicately suctions the submental fat pad (because I imagine all this, every detail, as he reassures me that no one has to pay, and everything will come out right, and he will never have to perform a full face-lift on his wife again, because the basic structure has been reset for life by his deft surgeon hands)—I have the relief of knowing there is someone out there who can harness for me, hierarchize, put in order my otherwise out-of-control chaotically aging body. The cultural critic and the cultural narcissist responded to him in waves, at times simultaneously, at times at odds, but it was finally apparent to me that they are ultimately, for me at least, interwoven—that my cultural criticism chastens my submission to the beauty industry but by no means contains it, and my narcissism genuflects at the feet of my shame and guilt.

A PHASE APART

Many plastic surgeons operate on their family, in marked contrast to other medical specialties, where it's considered ethically questionable and emotionally high-risk for, say, a neurosurgeon to operate on her or his partner. One surgeon assured me it is only the most famous surgeons (the prima donnas) who operate on their wives, because, as she put it, "they claim no one else is good enough!" From my own research, however, I learned that many men are operating on their wives. One wife showed me her eyelid work before I interviewed her husband. Other surgeons mentioned operating on wives or other family members. Was it simply, I wondered, that plastic surgeons are so especially egomaniacal (more so than other surgeons) that they unthinkingly transgress the most hallowed codes of the medical establishment? But I have no reason to believe this is so. Rather, when the male surgeon operates on his female partner, it has more to do with the inherent gender dynamics of the plastic surgery encounter itself.

What do the patient and the doctor find in each other? Their relationship is clearly only a step removed from the more boldly erotic maneuvers of the plastic surgeon and his wife. What does the patient want from him? What does he want to do for and to her? Freud described men and women as "a phase apart" developmentally, which leads to very different styles of object love. While the psychoanalytic view is certainly not the truth of the sexual relation for all times and places, psychoanalysis nevertheless provides some insight into contemporary experiences of sexual difference, because it's an explanatory narrative forged by the same social forces.

Freud offers a picture of men wanting to love (actively) while women want to be loved (passively).[7] In general, Freud avers, women love according to the narcissistic model. In his essay "On Narcissism: An Introduction," he enumerates four types of narcissistic love: A person may love: (1) what he is himself; (2) what he once was; (3) what he would like to be; (4) someone who was a part of himself. What men love in women, claims Freud, is the vicarious experience of their own forfeited narcissism, or self-love, that they felt as a child along with the attention they received from their caregivers when they experienced themselves as the center of the world.[8] Women, in contrast, as a result of their "castrated," hence anatomically damaged, bodies, regress to what Freud called "secondary narcissism."[9] They become fixated, in other words, at the level of the damaged body; their investment in personal beauty is compensatory. Consequently, instead of finding fulfillment in the active form of the object relation, in loving another, Freud argues that women love best to be loved.

If we follow Freud's model, then women experience their love lives on the surface of their bodies (passive objects of a man's overvaluation). Interestingly, Freud notes that it is generally the most beautiful women who are thoroughly narcissistic. What might he mean by this—that the most beautiful women are the most perfect accomplishment of feminine narcissism? Would the material beauty of the woman suggest that her compensatory gain is "real" rather than a mere substitute for the missing penis? If women experience love on the surface, where their beauty happens, men love on them this surface, which is literally the place where the infantile narcissism is relived.

In a significant reversal of Freud's version of male and female styles of loving, Edith Jacobson observed that it is men who remain fixated in the narcissistic position. When the small boy imagines, according to Freud's Oedipal schema, that he will be castrated if he goes on desiring his mother, he gives her up. For Jacobson this suggests that the boy's narcissistic investment in his penis supersedes object love. Women, conversely, experience object love. Where Freud has men actively loving and reliving through women their own lost narcissism, Jacobson shows women recuperating their lost ego ideals (banned by cultural imperatives regarding women) in the men they love. Either way, the depicted heterosexual couple finds in one another (projects onto one another) a combination of disavowed traits and repudiated goals. Crucially, Jacobson's account would suggest that the male version of loving and being loved happens on the surface of the body as well—the love for the penis supplanting the object relation. The deception at the heart of Freudian accounts of sexual difference, then, would be that the overvalued penis has nothing whatsoever to do with the body's *appearance*.

Cosmetic surgery has been a means for acting out and keeping in place the cultural expectations surrounding male and female narcissism. It sustains ("proves," in fact) the pervasive cultural fantasy that women care more about their bodies while men care more about their talents and abilities. Moreover, what they value in one another is precisely that attribute (men's skill, women's bodies) they are believed to have. The patient thus dutifully identifies with the ego ideal of the surgeon. How he sees her becomes how she wants to be seen. The surgeon, meanwhile, identifies with the surface narcissism of the patient. Specifically, he identifies with her need to preserve her beauty just as he had to preserve the integrity of his body/penis.[10]

MEN ACT AND WOMEN APPEAR

"Men act and women appear," famously claimed art historian John Berger (47), a point restated countless times by feminists who have absolutely concurred. Indeed, a short course in art history, certainly a history of the nude, would indicate in no uncertain terms that women pose for male artists. But what happens when the artist himself is in the habit of "appearing"?

Plastic surgeons are celebrities in their own right. Indeed, one surgeon I interviewed prominently displayed on his waiting room wall the published gratitude of one of his celebrity patients. Surgeon to the stars Stephen Hoefflin doesn't tell the names of his patients, but somehow we know anyway. Meanwhile, Dr. Hoefflin has posed for a weight-lifting magazine in which his photo rivals any of the "after" poses his star patients assume. Just as Dr. Hoefflin has transformed the faces and bodies of celebrities, these very same celebrities have transformed Hoefflin into one of their own.[11]

Florida surgeon Daniel Man has coauthored a book entitled *The Art of Man: Faces of Plastic Surgery*. And, yes, the pun on "man" is intentional, because it is specifically Dr. Man's "art" (including his surgeries and his paintings) that is center stage. Although the book initially professes to be another informational book about plastic surgery with a series of candid accounts from actual patients, the emphasis turns out to be on what Man himself can accomplish.[12] Part of what makes Man especially skillful, we learn, is his ability to "read" the inside of a person: "I try to envision the inner person, the inner beauty, and the potential that are lying so close to the surface. When I look at her, I visualize a finished work of art that truly expresses how she feels inside" (Man and Shelkofsky 34).

This transposition of the site of "appearance" from the generally female patient to the generally male surgeon makes sense in light of a culture in which *both* men and women are invested in making an appearance. If the distinction between men acting and women appearing

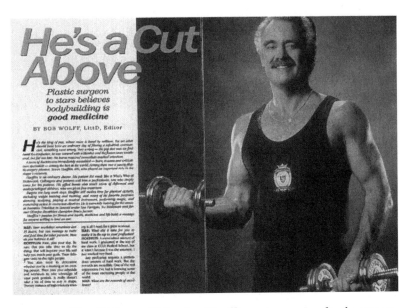

Figure 1. "Doc Hollywood," Stephen Hoefflin, enjoys posing for the camera ("He's a Cut Above," *Muscle and Fitness Magazine* Feb. 1996).

seems true enough, one might argue that it is true only insofar as the masculine form of making a good appearance was discovered in "acting." Moreover, let us follow Berger's point to the edge of the pun implicit in the term "act"—which could mean acting the *part* of an agent. While the nineteenth and twentieth centuries were largely successful at distributing convincing social roles for men and women along the narcissistic continuum of making a certain kind of appearance, the late twentieth century seemed to be underscoring the passively narcissistic quality in both men and women.

Although cosmetic surgery seems to be the culture's last bastion of this difference between men and women, in which women supinely submit to the Pygmalion touch of their male creator/surgeon, it is also the arena where such an apparent difference is rapidly disappearing.[13] Figure 1 shows Hoefflin's body. When he is not improving the photogenic-

Figure 2. Surgeon as artist, Dr. Leon Tcheupdjian.

ity of his patients, he remakes his own body in the image of a magazine photograph. Figure 2 shows how another plastic surgeon promotes himself as an artist and a sculptor. To express your own aesthetic requirements to him could interfere with his own need to express his talent. Try telling the artist that you don't like the nose he's drawn for you.

In his 1976 low-budget horror film, *Rabid*, David Cronenberg both phobically and parodically envisions the heterosexual plastic surgery dance gone awry. Female accident victim, Rose (played by famous porn star Marilyn Chambers), is treated for her life-threatening burn injuries at a nearby plastic surgery clinic, the Keloid Clinic. The clinic's founder, Dr. Keloid himself, performs a radical surgery whereby he grafts dermis tissue onto internal organs, thereby saving the patient but at the same time unfortunately transforming her into a kind of flesh-eating monster. Her new alimentary organ, however, is not her mouth but rather a sharp penislike organ that emerges from an anus-shaped cavity under her arm, near a graft site. This is a very special penis that not only penetrates its victims but sucks their blood. Radically remapped in both gender and function, this body signifies danger to the heterosexual regime.

Plastic surgery thus culminates in the very gender confusion it was all the while meant to suppress. By superficially confirming the conventional cultural roles of masculine surgical activity and female passivity, plastic surgery can deny the very identity it expresses between masculine and feminine forms of narcissism as well as the always rather tenuous problem of sexual identity itself. Now the scalpel is in the other hand or the penis grows from the other orifice, as it were, and Rose is the recombinant nightmare fallout of plastic surgery's otherwise carefully orchestrated reproduction of the heterosexual order.[14] Focusing on the explicitly sexual nature of Rose's bloody encounters, Cronenberg humorously implies that surgeons need their knives in order to get off. Less humorously, he seems concerned about what will happen once all boundaries dissolve, once patients become surgeons, once women become men. Recognizing in the heterosexual plastic surgery ritual the very gender threat it's trying hyperbolically to disavow with its scalpel-wielding men of science and its fragile, vain, supine, and unconscious female bodies, Cronenberg projects world chaos as the horrific consequence of transgressing this particular fine line.

PROJECTING THE BODY

Cosmetic surgery offers us an extreme and therefore instructive example of the relationship between the sexes. Eighty-five percent of board-certified plastic surgeons in this country are men; in 2000, 89 percent of the cosmetic-surgery patients were women. Male cosmetic procedures treat mainly hair loss and prominent ears, although the statistics are changing. The 1998 gender distribution for cosmetic procedures shows significant increases in the overall percentage of men seeking surgery—including such procedures as abdominoplasty, botox injections, and upper arm lifts. Since then, however, the numbers have remained approximately the same. Women still constitute the overwhelming majority of cosmetic surgery patients. The distinction between the mastery and activity of the male surgeon and the prone materiality of the female patient who offers up her body to his surgical prowess is almost too obvious to belabor. But it is important to see this relationship as an ongoing allegory of the relationship between cultural stereotypes of men and women—between male instrumentality, activity, and agency and female passivity. In the surgical relationship, men perform and women are acted upon, intervened in—as though created anew by men who correct Mother Nature.[15]

Dr. Robert Alan Franklyn, who was one of the surgeons pioneering breast implant surgeries in the 1950s, desperately forges a distinction between God and Mother Nature, who has abandoned "her" creatures to ugliness: "My goal was to help the embarrassed, self-conscious woman Nature had neglected" (21). This is a tenuous line navigated by the surgeon-figure who genderizes God (father) and nature (mother) in order to align himself with the father and against the faulty capricious mother. Franklyn's predicament, having to effect a split between "bad" and "good" progenitors, is illustrative of how hostility to nature is related to a distaste for femininity itself. By insisting upon this split between God and Nature, the plastic surgeon can pretend to be doing God's work:

"Gradually, surgeons had gotten over the idea that you should stay the way you were born 'because God made you that way.' God made cosmetic plastic surgeons, too. He must have had work for them to do" (30). Indeed, the God/surgeon position is venerated *because* of his marked contrast to defective femininity.

In the 1941 film *A Woman's Face*, the burn-scarred protagonist, Anna (played by Joan Crawford), is surgically restored by a plastic surgeon. Just as he is about to unbandage his "creation" after her final operation, he hesitates: "Now, as I was about to say, I unveil my Galatea. Or my Frankenstein. . . . Tell me this, Miss Holmes. I'm worried . . . If this operation's a success, I've created a monster. A beautiful face and no heart." Note the film's fantasy that he's "created" his patient, from the outside in. The story suggests that Anna's misdirected life (she's an evil-tempered thief) is due to her damaged appearance.[16] Now that her face is being made beautiful, her inner beauty will have a chance to surface and thrive. But what if, as the doctor frets, she's evil through and through? Then her evil will be (dangerously) masked by the seductive *appearance* of beauty. The audience knows, however, that such a turn of events is unlikely when the surgeon is the progenitor of the woman, the "good" father in contrast to the bad father, who caused her injuries in the first place. As her former lover complains, the surgeon has "changed my partner into a dove . . . soft and weak and full of love for her fellow man. . . ." In Freudian terms, now that her feminine narcissism is allowed to flourish, she can assume her proper femininity.

The position of plastic surgeons is in many ways untenable when you consider that they have to serve some higher truth (whether it be God or simply an overarching universalized Beauty) at the same time that they are gratified (who wouldn't be?) by their own power to effect major changes in people's lives. And then of course there is the problem with women falling in love with them.[17] One especially handsome surgeon admitted that, yes, occasionally women fall for him, but he has ways of managing it; possibly his strategy is to keep mentioning his wife, as he did with me during our interview. He shifted nervously in his seat. He glanced away. "It's not a problem for me," he said. "Maybe for others."

This surgeon and others have made it clear that there is often a direct cause and effect relationship between the surgery and the woman's finding a marriage partner. Maybe there's a slippage—might he become confused in her mind with the fantasy partner he enables her to "get"? He changed her life; she loves him for that. Who can blame her? And who can blame the surgeon for giving Nature (that wayward and selfish mother) such short shrift? A plastic surgeon's nurse told me that many women make appointments with him simply because they have decided to marry a plastic surgeon. I asked her how she could tell. "Before they even meet him, they want to know if he's married." I am incredulous—why would they choose a plastic surgeon in particular? "A good income," she speculated, "a good provider." I wondered if more was involved. I suggested that there was a certain transferential relationship onto plastic surgeons—the father-god who would be the final arbiter of woman's value. So "good provider" was the literal index of her value on the open market.

The story of the plastic surgeon falling in love with his patient has tremendous purchase on our imaginations. In *A Woman's Face*, Dr. Siegert falls in love with and marries Anna—his beautified creation.[18] It took the talented plastic surgeon to recognize all along her inner beauty, which he then "matches" on the surface.

> ANNA: You couldn't love me. . . . You don't think for a moment that I've changed from what I was, do you?
>
> DR. SIEGERT: No.
>
> ANNA: No, of course not. Oh, you don't think I've changed. [seeming upset now]
>
> DR. SIEGERT: Not a bit.
>
> ANNA: You still think I'm the most terrifying, ruthless, cold-blooded creature you've ever known?

DR. SIEGERT: I didn't say that.

ANNA: Oh, yes, you said it once.

DR. SIEGERT: That wasn't you. It never has been you.

In a 1996 made-for-television movie, *A Face to Die For*, a surgeon transforms his severely injured patient from plain to beautiful (a ringer for his dead wife!), then proceeds to fall in love with her. Both surgeon and patient fantasies are engaged simultaneously—his power to produce such miraculous transformations and her power to win the love of the master-aesthetician. His love for his creation proves that she is perfect—in his eyes and hers.

One surgeon whom I interviewed imagines he has harnessed the patient's transference to effect deeper (psychical) transformations in his patients. "I've done a lot of training in Eriksonian hypnotic techniques, and there's a lot of personal change that you can get people to go through at this time. I can get in there and work with some of the dials in the inside during this window of opportunity and return the TV set to the patient. It's just amazing. It exceeds what the surgery itself has done. Of course, the surgery gets the credit. It's a very powerful transference."

Clearly what we have here is a case of countertransference as well. The surgeon is participating in the patient's fantasy of him as the one who can save her simultaneously from her imperfect body and her negative body image. What also seems significant is his investment in his ethical responsibility to use his special skills with caution: "It is necessary under the circumstances to do no more than basically touch in a psychic sense (anything more than that is clearly invasive), but if you don't do that, you can't do what you have to do. This happens on all levels. Women who come in for breast implants or liposuction—at first I can barely get her to take her clothes off, and at the end I can't get her to put them back on. It's great, because how many people can they show it off to? It's very powerful, but it absolutely requires that I be totally well behaved during the whole thing—anything other than that is inexcusable. This would be *way* outside the standards of medical conduct." It seems so potentially erotic, to have access to a power you consciously restrain. Back and forth he goes between his own unimpeachable conduct and the transgressive possibilities. So much power over the vulnerable female body. So much responsibility. Now that she loves you . . .

But our love can so easily slide into hate.

> *"Surgeon-to-the-stars Raises Concern,"* reads a headline. *"The plastic surgeon who sculpted Michael Jackson's face and rejuvenated Elizabeth Taylor, Joan Rivers and Phyllis Diller is accused of disrobing, fondling and ridiculing anesthetized patients."* (Allen)

Hollywood surgeons typically choose to be Hollywood surgeons. "They hire publicists, personal managers," one surgeon explained to me. He talked about Stephen Hoefflin, the Hollywood surgeon par excellence, whose recent wedding included his star patients and a sizable chunk of the plastic surgeon community. Hoefflin is a star.[19]

Hoefflin was charged with sexually abusing his patients under anesthesia as well as charging for surgeries he only pretended to perform (he was ultimately cleared of all charges by the Medical Board of California). The Hollywood community (Phyllis Diller, Joan Rivers, Michael Jackson, and Elizabeth Taylor among them) were depicted by the tabloids as "staggered." It seems to me inevitable that Hoefflin, having become a star among stars, would eventually become the target of an inflamed cultural imaginary regarding plastic surgeons in general—as someone who licentiously plays with bodies and toys with our narcissistic vulnerability.[20] The scandal about Hoefflin taps into three paranoid responses to the plastic surgeon:

1. We fear he will go too far—hence the story about model Angie Everhardt's boyfriend, Sylvester Stallone, talking the surgeon into making her breast implants much bigger than she had requested.[21] We worry that once we turn our bodies over to the surgeon, he can do what he likes with us. We fear the very power we repose in him to change our images.

2. We fear he will ridicule us. The stories about making fun of Elizabeth Taylor's aging body (Kettle) and ridiculing the size of Don Johnson's penis tap into our anxiety about the plastic surgeon as the ultimate arbiter of beauty and value (Whittell, "'Doc Hollywood'"). What does he *really* think of me? If I think he is good enough to make me better looking, then I must also think he is discerning enough to pick out all my physical flaws.

3. We fear being taken. The allegations that Michael Jackson repeatedly paid for surgeries that were faked (the medical staff turned the clock forward) play into our fears that cosmetic surgeons are only the most recent version of medical fraud (Whittell, "'Doc Hollywood'"). Like the quacks purveying worthless nostrums from their traveling wagons, plastic surgeons seem to be on another kind of cultural wagon ride through the desperate and undiscriminating crowds of aging baby boomers and movie-star wannabes.

WHOSE BODY?

John and Marcia Goin bluntly call the surgeon's overinvestment in his own aesthetic the Pygmalion Effect. "Whenever the surgeon's motivations are to produce the best possible postoperative photography rather than the happiest possible patient, the Pygmalion Effect may be at work" (*Changing the Body* 115). While there is a recognizable difference between surgeons who tell patients what they need and those who try to accommodate patient expectations, I suspect that the Goins were overly optimistic in distinguishing as dysfunctional what is in truth an inextricable component of the practice. Many surgeons consider themselves artists.[22] Realistically, how would the person who feels motivated by an aesthetic aim suppress her or his own creativity for the sake of what would then feel patently like a consumer service?

Although every surgeon I've interviewed has insisted that he or she tailors the operation to the individual, most of the articles I've reviewed suggest otherwise. In my interviews I always showed a series of photographs taken from the article of a famous surgeon known for his "aggressive" management of the nasolabial fold area. All the women start out completely different, yet they all end up looking somewhat alike, now sharing an eerie surgical sisterhood. While most surgeons confessed that they had some reservations about the results, at the same time they said they admired this surgeon, and one even insisted he would send his grandmother to him. One surgeon, Oscar Ramirez, whose technique invariably results in high brows, goes so far as to claim that the brows in his postoperative photographs aren't as shockingly high as they appear to be: "Although, during the analysis of postoperative photographs it may seem that the brows are elevated too much, in real life it does not seem to be the case and I have not had any patient complaining that their brows are too high" (657). The women surgeons I interviewed felt that persisting in a single technique one considers "the best" is more a masculine style than a feminine one. But when I review articles by women surgeons, they seem to be equally committed to an overarching aesthetic that shapes all the faces and bodies on which they operate. As Alec Wilkinson writes, the face-lifted face "will reflect the doctor's style, not the person's, and people with a certain discernment will be able to identify a particular surgeon's hand at work the way someone of another kind of discernment is able to walk into a fancy apartment and call out the name of the decorator" (119).

In Ovid's version of *Pygmalion*, a sculptor falls in love with his own statue, which is an idealized version of a female body. His prayers are answered, and the statue comes to life. In the case of plastic surgery we find two significant revisions of the Ovid story. First, the original medium is flesh, not stone. Second, the goal is not for the idealized art object to become accessible flesh and blood. On the contrary, she is reworked into a photographable state. Her trajectory in other words is from life to art, three dimensions to two. Wives, patients, it doesn't matter—in the end we are all reduced to photographs, and the surgeon is our superphotographer who will correct all our worst angles, capture in the right light the most fleeting glimpse of our perfection. A recent advertisement for the American Society of Plastic and Reconstructive Surgery (fig. 3) gives us a contemporary Galatea, flung back like a Victoria's Secret model, presenting herself to whom? Her surgeon?

Nathaniel Hawthorne's 1843 short story "The Birthmark" perfectly condenses the transferential relationship between husband/scientist and wife/patient with the culture's increasing interest in the photographable surface of the body. Brilliant scientist Aylmer, having devoted most of his life to his work, comes out of his laboratory long enough to marry a beautiful woman named Georgiana. It is made clear that she is the only woman who sufficiently rises above the rest of frail and defective womanhood to fulfill his exacting aesthetic requirements. This close-to-supranatural woman nevertheless has one refractory flaw—a hand-shaped birthmark on her cheek—what today we might call a port-wine stain and try to remove with laser surgery. Although well pleased with his wife, Aylmer is nevertheless tormented by this birthmark until Georgiana, realizing how repulsive he finds her, begs him to use his scientific arts to remove it. He manages to remove the flaw, but in so doing kills his wife, for this little hand on her cheek represented, as she explains to him, "nature's hand" on her.

The question of where the apparently superficial defect has its origin is central to this story in which the scientist needs to pursue the body's hidden interior in order to conquer its surfaces. "Know, then," Aylmer exclaims to his wife, "that this crimson hand, superficial as it seems, has clutched its grasp into your being with a strength of which I had no previous conception" (278). We learn that Aylmer is especially interested in the new optical phenomena of his day. In his effort to entertain his wife with the "light and playful secrets which science had taught him among its profounder lore," Aylmer puts on for her an optical show. "Airy figures, absolutely bodiless ideas, and forms of unsubstantial beauty came and danced before her, imprinting their momentary footsteps on beams of light" (271–72). Emphasized implicitly is the contrast between Georgiana's mortal embodied substance and the "unsubstantial beauty" of her husband's realm. "The scenery and the figures of actual life were

Life Is What You Make It.

ACTUAL ASPS PATIENT

When it comes to PLASTIC SURGERY you want to make the right choice.

Choosing the right plastic surgeon is all about trust. You want to find a plastic surgeon with skill and training to help achieve your goals.

This symbol is what to look for. The symbol for the American Society of Plastic Surgeons.

Every member is board-certified by the American Board of Plastic Surgery.

Our surgeons are uniquely qualified to perform cosmetic and reconstructive surgery on the face and all areas of the body. So you can't make a better choice than an ASPS plastic surgeon.

Questions? Call for your "Make The Right Choice" Guide to Plastic Surgery.

AMERICAN SOCIETY OF
PLASTIC SURGEONS

1-888-4-PLASTIC (1-888-475-2784)
www.plasticsurgery.org

Figure 3. Advertising the benefits of surgery—a modern-day Galatea. Courtesy of American Society of Plastic and Reconstructive Surgery.

perfectly represented, but with that bewitching, yet indescribable difference which always makes a picture, an image, or a shadow so much more attractive than the original" (272).

Here, as though in anticipation of Jean Baudrillard's account of the simulacral, Hawthorne is capturing the falling away of representation from its material referent. When the image supersedes the original, the image becomes the model for the original to emulate. Ovid's story imagines this possibility, the supervention of the idealized model, but sees no point ultimately in the representation unless it can become real. In Aylmer's Pygmalionesque fantasy, he is aiming to elevate Georgiana's inferior material substance into the highly controlled frame of a picture.[23] Indeed, Aylmer's form of science seems to be a special form of *aesthetic science*, and, from what we see, his work is more allied with the emergent technology of the daguerreotype than it is with the natural sciences.[24] "He proposed to take her portrait by a scientific process of his own invention. It was to be effected by rays of light striking upon a polished plate of metal. Georgiana assented; but, on looking at the result, was affrighted to find the features of the portrait blurred and indefinable; while the minute figure of a hand appeared where the cheek should have been" (272). This episode reverses the story's conclusion insofar as the hand supplanting the beautiful face is an ironic refusal of Aylmer's photographic goal to make the body permanent, immortal, two-dimensional; here the body exceeds the image, whereas by the end the image will overwhelm the body.[25] At the same time, Aylmer's psychical fixation is reproduced intact—all he sees is the hand. The very daguerreotypic process of fixing the image to the plate thus seems like a metaphor for the man fixated on beauty. Roland Barthes has described the experience of becoming a photograph as that of "a subject who feels he is becoming an object . . . I am truly becoming a specter. The Photographer knows this very well, and himself fears . . . this death in which his gesture will embalm me" (14).

Throughout the story, Georgiana reposes utter faith in her husband—even though she fully recognizes that his experiment will result in her death. But she cannot live, she maintains, as an object of his repugnance: "Danger is nothing to me; for life, while this hateful mark makes me the object of your horror and disgust,—life is a burden which I would fling down with joy" (268). Georgiana, pursued by numerous other suitors, nevertheless submits willingly to her husband's vision of her. She concurs that the birthmark that never troubled her before is a deformity and needs correction. She is like the plastic surgeon's wife who shares her husband's perspective on her aging. As the surgeon put it: "She could see it and I could see it." In their taxonomy of personality patterns at risk when undergoing cosmetic surgery, Goin and Goin have pathologized just this type of "passive-dependent" personality. These people "tend to deal with the rigors and stresses of life by leaning upon a commanding figure, someone (or sometimes something) who will guide, nurture, and defend them. . . . Passive-dependent patients are very easy to recognize during the initial consultation. Their most arresting characteristic is their total, almost obsequious relinquishment of responsibility to the surgeon who is, after all, usually a complete stranger" ("Psychological Understanding" 1127–28). These patients sound very much like Georgiana, who puts herself unreservedly in her husband's hands; they sound like the plastic surgeon's wife, who takes for granted his position as guardian of her surface beauty. Indeed, the Goins seem to be overlooking the culturally prescribed submission of women to men. The very transference that leads to male plastic surgeons operating on prone female bodies, a transference in which the patient's "passive-dependence" on the surgeon would be prerequisite, is denied and pathologized in the Goins' disingenuous account.

As I've learned from several surgeons, it can be the wives themselves who put pressure on their surgeon-husbands to operate, a curious reversal of the male surgeon's gendered aesthetic authority. One surgeon claimed that he puts off his wife by reminding her how many weeks of recovery it will take before she can return to working out at the gym. Another surgeon expressed concern over his wife's passion for surgery. What does it mean for these surgeons to be haunted by the very aesthetic machinery they've set in motion? How is it that they have become servants to their wives' unappeasable demand? Has something been subverted in the received order of male agency and female passivity? Or, like Georgiana, are the women merely acting out with a vengeance the "choice" to have surgery—a choice which is no choice?

The perceived flaws of the female body could prove metaphorically as fatal as Georgiana's cure—to her life on the heterosexual marriage market. As Alice Adams puts it in her important discussion of the relationship between gynecological and cosmetic surgeries (breast surgery being where they most clearly intersect):

> It is particularly difficult to separate the interests of heterosexual women from those of men, not only in societies where clitoridectomy is one of the prices women pay for the privilege of being considered marriageable, but also in the United States, where the catalogue of potentially mutilating practices is limited only by money and where an approach to whole-body perfection, through dieting, exercise, and surgery, makes some women far more competitive than others on the heterosexual market. (76)

That Georgiana manages to be married despite her physical flaw belies the obvious reality that women's physical appearance plays a central role in their heterosexual desirability; indeed we could even go so far as to call the turn of events a reversal into its opposite of the "real life" version. Aylmer would have been repulsed by the mark before marriage.

Barbara Johnson reads this as a story about curing femininity itself. While it is true that the birthmark seems to be a symbol of what is deeply disturbing about feminine sexuality, I would add that femininity isn't being cured so much as relocated—reinscribed on the very surface where it was believed to linger all along in its narcissistic reverie.[26] That the birthmark is where Georgiana's mortality lies suggests that woman's vulnerability is in her surface appearance, because it is where she *lives*. It's on the surface that she is a woman, which is what makes her different from men. It is why she is the perfect subject for a painting, or a photograph, or a magazine layout. This suggests that even though the hand is intended to represent her depth/humanity, her being/femininity (after all, they are the same) resides instead on her surface.

Paradoxically, even though her surface *is* her depth, it is life itself that interferes with Georgiana's surface beauty, at least from Aylmer's perspective, which is why he must kill her. The tragedy for Aylmer is that when Georgiana is dead, unlike a photograph, she cannot remain permanently beautiful. Aylmer's fantasy is that he can unmoor this surface from the depth of her body, her subjectivity. Compare Hawthorne's account of the tension between the surface and the depth of the beautiful female object with the face-lift patient, whose superficial face must be wrested from what feels like the "real" aging interiority of the underlying tissues. Moreover, like Aylmer, the plastic surgeons learned that beneath the surface there's yet another surface—and another—and that they must address all these surfaces in order to effect long-term change at the most superficial level. "When analyzing the aging face," writes Sam T. Hamra, "one must be aware of the deep anatomic components that create the superficial topography of the aging face" ("Composite Rhytidectomy," 313). For many years face-lifts were simply superficial skin lifts; you made incisions, pulled back the sagging skin, cut off the excess and sutured it all back in place. But this was unsatisfactory, many realized, in the long term, as the momentary tightening gave way within a year or less to more sagging. The truth of aging, they found, lay deeper. Since the 1970s, with Tord Skoog's paradigm-shifting explorations with the SMAS (the superficial musculoaponeurotic system) and Paul Tessier's introduction of what he called the "orthomorphic subperiosteal facelift" to intervene in the earliest signs of aging, "skin shifters," as they have been called, are, like Aylmer, pursuing beauty to its hidden recesses.

Many articles on face-lifts these days argue over just how deep one must go. In 1974, Tord Skoog, of Sweden, "described a method of face-lift that elevated the platysma and lower face without detaching the skin and advanced it posteriorly to move not only subcutaneous tissue but also the deeper 'foundation' structures to provide a more predictable and long-lasting result" (Larson 208). Oscar Ramirez holds that the very deepest plane, the subperiosteal, which is virtually against the bone, "allows a better optical cavity than the subgaleal or subcutaneous plane of dissection" (641). Moreover, "the bony landmarks and fascial attachments to specific areas of the bone help the surgeon to get oriented more easily during the subperiosteal dissection as opposed to the subgaleal or more superficial dissection" (641). Sam Hamra, Daniel Baker, and John Owsley, to name some of the most influential innovators in face-lift techniques, argue back and forth over the finer points of both the plane of dissection and the direction of tension. Hamra calls his face-lift a "composite rhytidectomy," which is "a technique based on the elevation of a composite flap of the face. This is a bipedicle musculocutaneous flap that includes the platysma muscle of the lower face, the cheek fat overlying the zygomaticus musculature, and the orbicularis oculi muscle" around the eyes (317). John Owsley uses what he calls a "bi-directional" approach. What one learns from reading through the rhytidectomy literature is that the superficial aspect of appearance has multiple surfaces, all of them at one time or another adduced as *the* plane on which youthful beauty falls apart.

"We are all old," writes Wendy Chapkis, "for some of us it just doesn't yet show" (15). Kathleen Woodward has called the cosmetic-surgery solution "the aging body-in-masquerade" ("From Virtual Cyborgs" 165). "The surface of the body," she points out, "is cut and stretched to disguise the surface of the body" (162). Woodward's account of the double layer of surfaces is analogous to the plastic surgeon's discovery that there are really two supporting layers of the face. The prior failure to understand that the skin is merely a container of a kind for the underlying aging process—repeats almost intact the way we imagine the difference between appearance and essence.

Plastic surgeons' struggles with the geography of facial aging are prefigured by Aylmer's pursuit of the anterior origin of his wife's surface beauty. However, in contrast to Barbara Stafford's claim that we are turning ourselves inside out, the opposite is true I suspect: we're instead obsessively turning ourselves outside in, as we relocate the final truth in the surface. Just as plastic surgeons locate the proof of their deep anatomy in the superficial result ("my face-lifts last ten years," one surgeon assured me), the basis for prospective transformative surgeries is established two-dimensionally, through digital imaging equipment or even in the surgeon's freehand sketch, which serve as the basis for the transformation; they *inform* the "deep structure." And it's not just the surgeons who are pressing the transformation of the body into two dimensions. It's the patients as well who have engaged the cultural goal of becoming photographable.

In Fay Weldon's *The Life and Loves of a She-Devil*, protagonist Ruth, who is committed to transforming herself entirely into the image of her rival, Mary Fisher, brings to her plastic surgeon a photograph of Mary as the template of her future self. Moreover, Weldon's novel is an effort to invert the roles of master surgeon and supine patient in the plastic surgery ritual; Aylmer simply would have been another in the chain of men who unwittingly and helplessly advance Ruth's indefatigable purpose. "[Ruth's surgeon] was her Pygmalion, but she would not depend upon him, or admire him, or be grateful. He was accustomed to being loved by the women of his own construction. . . . But no soft breathings came from [Ruth]" (249). Ruth is compared to "Frankenstein's monster" (258), and electrical storms short out the power system on the eve of surgery. The surgeon blames the operation:

> "God's angry," said Mr. Ghengis, suddenly frightened, longing to go back into obstetrics. "You're defying Him. I wish we could stop all this."
>
> "Of course He's angry," said Ruth. "I am remaking myself."
>
> "We're remaking you," he said sourly. . . . (269)

Here the miserable surgeon thought he could create from scratch instead of function as mere midwife to Ruth, who has turned the received order on its head. Yet isn't cosmetic surgery indeed a form of obstetrics—or rather corrective obstetrics, remaking what came out wrong or inadequate the first time round?

Why would it be more desirable to remake a faulty body than to participate in an actual birth? We could say it's all about the surgeon's narcissism, his refusal to play second fiddle to woman's generativity, but instead let's focus on the end result. In cosmetic surgery all you have at the end of the day is a body, a different body, perhaps an improved body, but a solitary body, in contrast to obstetrics, which culminates in a relationship—parent and child. Instead of having children, Aylmer and Georgiana have medical experiments. Instead of going home, getting married, and having children in the "normal" way, as I will discuss in the next chapter, Victor Frankenstein removes himself from the human world and engages in solitary creation. In "The Birthmark," *She-Devil*, and *Frankenstein*, as well as in the practice of cosmetic surgery, what gets highlighted is the defiance of the "natural" order. What seems to be mangled, however, is not nature, as though there is some essential precious authenticity that requires preservation, but instead the object relation itself. Doctors turn into parents, and partners turn into surgeons—and what kinds of relationships are forged out of these wild refashionings? Ruth's surgeon, Mr. Ghengis, imagines growing bored with a surgically perfected wife—just as Victor Frankenstein rejects the creature he spends so many months building—and the plastic surgeon I quoted early in the chapter struggles to preserve his wife permanently at forty, as though to defeat not necessarily the aging process but the evolution of their relationship, evidence of shared history. There is no object loss, of course, but then perhaps there was no object relationship to begin with.

FOUR

Frankenstein
Gets a Face-Lift

A SURGICAL CURE

Plastic surgeons say they won't operate on patients in the midst of emotional crises. The loss of a parent or child, the commencement of divorce—these are among the "red flags" for the surgeon considering operating.[1] "The key is timing. If you're going to do it just after you found out that your spouse is leaving you—no. That's not a good time to do it, when they're just going crazy and they've finally stopped crying after five days, and they come in and say, 'I'm going to get an augment.' But, once all that is over it's like the grieving process, once you go through that . . ."

A number of surgeons mentioned their hesitancy around patients confusing intense experiences of grief and trauma with the urgency for some kind of aesthetic surgical corrective. They made it clear that these patients were, for a while at least, incapable of distinguishing between internal and external need, between the psychological and the cosmetic. What struck me was that the various traumas cited were typically about radical emotional separations of some kind. The loss of a partner through divorce or death. The loss of a parent or a child. I wondered if the surgical visit was motivated by the wish to restore through their bodies this connection to the love object.

But how does this happen that emotional disorders can be displaced onto the surface of the body—that feeling sad finds its physical correlative in a slack jawline or a bump on your nose? Moreover, while surgeons insist they won't operate on patients who are in the throes of emotional trauma, they do in fact make a practice of improving the body for the sake of better intimate ties. At the same time that surgeons claim wariness of patients who think they may find a mate as a result of surgery, they in fact hold out just this hope to people. Worse yet, the widespread practice and advertising of cosmetic surgery can make people feel as though no one will love them if they *don't* improve their bodies.

As many psychiatrists have observed about surgery and as Sander L. Gilman has discussed at length, the history of plastic surgical interventions in appearance actually can make people feel measurably happier. Often they do in fact go on to have better relationships. Image-changing surgeries typically effect personality transformations as well:

> SURGEON: I did a rhinoplasty on my partner's daughter who was very withdrawn. She had his nose, and it just didn't fit her. Then after I did a rhinoplasty, her dad has told me how she's president of the class, she's getting dates all the time. It's not that I really changed a person, but I changed her outlook. Now she's popular—that makes it all worthwhile for me. I certainly don't ever bill aesthetic surgeries as being able to change somebody's life; in fact, I tell them, "This is not going to change your life." But sometimes it does.

Sometimes it does. I asked a surgeon straight out about whether or not the surface change can transform the personality.

> AUTHOR: Is it possible then to make an improvement on the "surface" that actually leads to internal difference?

SURGEON: Oh yes. What I like to assess is if a patient's life is significantly altered by the thing they consider problematic. Are they aware of it every time they pass a shop window, or do they cringe every time they look in the mirror? Is it dominating their lives, in other words? If a physical change that they're interested in can be achieved, then I think you're doing a lot for that patient as an individual. You may not be doing a lot in terms of the change in the face or the nose, but you're doing a lot for the individual. So it's not the physical problem; it's how they feel about it. That's always true.

AUTHOR: But it is also true that they might be received in a different way by the world once that physical change is made?

SURGEON: Yes, what the external world sees is the change in their well-being. They don't say, "Gosh, you've had a nice face-lift"; they say, "You look well! Did you have your hair done?"

Some surgeons believe that we create our appearance from the inside out. I show a surgeon a picture of a forty-year-old woman who appears much older. She has aged unusually rapidly, and I ask about possible causes. The surgeon responds: "Sad psyche. I believe people create their appearances. Entirely. Absolutely."

AUTHOR: If people create their appearances, though, then why do they go to plastic surgeons?

SURGEON: Well. They can't all do it with the certain power and intention that they like.

AUTHOR: So, if it's true that the aging woman of forty is representing on her body her inner personality, that she's draggy and downtrodden [I was quoting him here], what good does it do to operate on her? Why bother?

SURGEON: We try to determine ahead of time whether somebody really will appreciate their results. There are people who get a premature recurrence. The complexity of it is that you can do one of these operations on one of these kinds of people and make them look quite spectacular. And you can see all of a sudden their whole life changes; they brighten up and have a whole new future.

Repeatedly what surgeons have told me they love about surgery is exactly the way these operations can turn around people's lives.

SURGEON: I do a fair number of lower body lifts. I did one woman who had lost 290 pounds. She went and had bypass surgery and was able to lose all this weight, and she ended up with a lot of excessive skin. The lower body lift on her was able to trim that skin. She was severely depressed, was seriously thinking of committing suicide. Since her surgery, she's turned around. She's studying biochemistry, of all things. We're very careful about this, because we would be very, very hesitant to operate on somebody who thought that through changing their physical appearance they could resolve all their personal problems. Having said that, let me tell you that I have seen so many people who, having had plastic surgery, literally turned their lives around, either through improved relationships or careers.

AUTHOR: Is it because they feel better about themselves or because they look better?

SURGEON: Both. I think the way we come across is a matter of self-confidence, and self-confidence is affected by your appearance.

But if self-confidence is affected by your appearance, then it's largely appearance, isn't it? Isn't this the chilling reality that surgeons are revealing at the same time they are trying hard not to stray too far from what's culturally acceptable to say?

SURGEON: I can think of one person who is a wonderful lady. She was a graduate student, very bright, very articulate, had a really ugly nose, big nose, no chin. And she's one of these people where, because of that, you couldn't see the rest of her. After the surgery, I used to love when she came in, because she'd say, "My god, it's really transformed my life." In the past, she would go to parties, and no one would pay attention to her. Now she goes in and she's the center of attention. And that's been wonderful for her. She's still the same person, hasn't changed at all. Just the change in her appearance has changed her social life.

While the eighteenth-century physiognomists believed that the lineaments of face and body reveal character, in the twentieth-first century many of us are convinced that internal feelings and even character can be transformed by interventions on the surface.[2] Such a conviction is central to the practice of plastic surgery.[3] Famous plastic surgeon Maxwell Maltz boasted that "changing the physical image in many instances appeared to create *an entirely new person*. In case after case the scalpel that I held in my hand became a magic wand that not only transformed the patient's appearance, but transformed his whole life" (6). His theory swung both ways; he became equally well known for his series of self-image improvement books that emphasize our ability to transform the outside through positive change on the inside.

Cosmetic surgery is so statistically normal by now that many of us take for granted the practical benefits of surgeries once considered the arena of the psychologically unbalanced—or the rich and famous. Before the 1970s, mental health professionals generally believed that cosmetic-surgery patients suffered from some kind of pathology and were better off treated with therapy than surgery.[4] Michael Pertschuk argues

that now that such surgeries are common, "a patient group more representative of the general population may be requesting these procedures"
(12). It is now the interface patients (interface surgery involves extreme
changes like narrowing, lengthening, or shortening a face—hard-tissue
changes in other words), suggests Pertschuk, who represent the psychologically more disturbed sector of the patient population. Today, the literature suggests that cosmetic surgery more often than not can provide
"internal" relief—even in the most diagnostically "disturbed" group of
patients. Consider the following example of a woman with classic symp-
toms of dysmorphophobia:

> W. L. was a 35-year-old woman with a history of rhinoplasty, chin
> implant, blepharoplasty, and mandible contouring by two prior plas-
> tic surgeons. Although W. L. was somewhat pleased with these facial
> changes, she felt that these operations had not achieved her goal of
> "thinning her face." Her perceived deformity was certainly not no-
> ticeable to the casual observer. She exhibited marked social with-
> drawal and depression. . . . Through a bicoronal scalp incision, bilat-
> eral resection of the zygomatic arches, contour reduction of the
> malar bones, and partial resection of both temporalis muscles were
> performed. Follow-up 3 years later revealed markedly improved psy-
> chological and social functioning. W. L. has felt no further need for
> surgery. (Edgerton et al. 605)

As someone who finds such interventions extreme, I cannot help but
wonder what finally made W. L. happy. What in that final width-reduc-
ing craniofacial surgery sufficed for her? Clearly through surgery she
had achieved a "match" between her ideal image and the reflection in
the mirror—surprisingly, if we insist that the surgery was internally motivated by some gaping narcissistic injury. How did plastic surgery find
and repair such an elusive target? Who knew a scalpel could excavate so
very much—touch one so deeply? "Her self-consciousness and depression cleared and she has returned to a full and active life" (602).[5]

What and where is the route from psyche to body and back again? Sanford Gifford believes that "the majority of candidates for cosmetic surgery have externalized their inner conflicts in a concrete body part" (22). Why would you imagine a face-lift could soothe grief over a child's death? When people crave emotional relief through surgery, the psychiatrists read it as a displacement of the internal wound onto the sense of a surface "defect"; when people feel "healed" by their surgery, psychiatrists shrug and say the displacement fantasy worked. Never for a moment do they suspect that the problem may be curable through the body because the pain is in fact located on the body. And I don't mean the pain of the perceived "defect"—the too-big nose or the weak chin or the flabby stomach—I mean the pain of the internal wound itself. I will argue that the reason plastic surgery can relieve emotional suffering is that, for the modern subject, the surface of the body and the body image are where object relations, both good and bad, are transacted, not only in the formative moments of our identity, but throughout the life cycle. This is hardly to reverse the received psychology and proclaim plastic surgery as the solution to all our tribulations and sorrows. Rather, I will suggest that it is because the body is so central to identity formation and primary object loss that, given the right combination of circumstances, emotional trauma can come to rest on its surface. In offering a psychoanalytic explanation of how the body image comes to picture object loss, I want to situate this story in the modern world, where physical appearance has a central impact on our relationships with other people. Thus, the early process of identity formation, when we arrive at an experience of the "self" through the body, is repeatedly revivified, not only in the major transitional periods of adolescence, maturity, and old age, but also in our daily encounters, when smiles linger on us or abruptly turn aside.

LOSING LOVE

In his 1915 essay "Mourning and Melancholia," Sigmund Freud tries to account for the psychic similarities and differences between the mourning that takes place after the loss through death of a love object and what he calls melancholia (what we now term depression), which neither seems overtly linked to object loss nor diminishes over time.

> In melancholia, where the exciting causes are different one can recognize that there is a loss of a more ideal kind. The object has not perhaps actually died, but has been lost as an object of love (e.g. in the case of a betrothed girl who has been jilted). In yet other cases one feels justified in maintaining the belief that a loss of this kind has occurred, but one cannot see clearly what it is that has been lost, and it is all the more reasonable to suppose that the patient cannot consciously perceive what he has lost either. (245)

Most important, the object loss associated with mourning is entirely conscious in contrast to the at least partly unconscious experience of object loss leading to melancholia. While in the case of mourning, the loss of a real object in the outside world has occurred, in melancholia loss is not always so identifiable. "An object-choice, an attachment of the libido to a particular person, had at one time existed; then, owing to a real slight or disappointment coming from this loved person, the object-relationship was shattered" (248–49).

Hostile feelings toward the abandoning object are redirected toward the subject's own ego. Thus the individual endures a double burden of pain—both from the sense of loss (often unconscious) and from what subsequently becomes an attack on her or his own ego, which now stands in place of the loved object. In the case of the "jilted girl," superadded to internalized aggression would be the sensed insufficiency of the self to hold on to the object. One part of the ego (the superego) stands apart critically, while the other part of the ego identifies with the lost object, leading the person to feel at war with her- or himself.[6] Thus, depression can arise as a result of the part of the self identifying with the abandoning object. So compromised is one's self-love by what amounts to self-loathing that one can become suicidal. "If the love for the object—a love which cannot be given up though the object itself is given up—takes refuge in narcissistic identification, then the hate comes into operation on this substitutive object [the ego], abusing it, debasing it, making it suffer and deriving sadistic satisfaction from its suffering" (251). It is precisely because of the identification with the object that Freud considers the impulse sadistic rather than masochistic—this sadistic hatred is really directed against someone else.

People who are in the initial stages of divorce could fit Freud's description of melancholia. They may feel simultaneously abandoned by the love object (hence insufficient) and enraged. It is as though what was loved in oneself is now lost along with the loved object. As I will show, it makes sense that the surface of the body can become a scene of the internal conflict and its resolution. To repair the defective body (standing in for the vilified ego) could be seen as denying the object loss.

Melancholic mourning for the object can begin very early in the course of identity formation. Melanie Klein universalized a depressive position in all infants: "The infant experiences some of the feelings of guilt and remorse, some of the pain which results from the conflict between love and uncontrollable hatred, some of the anxieties of the impending death of the loved internalized and external objects—that is to say, in a lesser and milder degree the sufferings and feelings which we find fully developed in an adult melancholic" ("Psychogenesis of Manic-Depressive States" 286). It is only through unification of good and bad objects, real and imaginary, external and internal, that the small child begins to overcome its sadism, anxiety, and aggression. "Along with the increase in love for one's good and real objects goes a great trust in one's capacity to love and a lessening of the paranoid anxiety of the bad objects" (288). All splittings (of the ego and objects) are resolved, in other words, in an integrated experience of the self and object world. We can see in Freud's account of melancholia, then, a regression to the panicked splittings of infancy, when it's no longer clear where the danger and abandonment come from.

For Donald Winnicott, it is the mother's care and love that holds the infant together; any loss or withholding of this love in the first few weeks of life threatens the infant with "annihilation" ("Primary Maternal Preoccupation"). The normal process of ego building for Winnicott involves a series of maternal deprivations that are compensated for. Whereas too much deprivation leads to "madness," in the normal cycle of deprivation and restoration "babies are constantly being *cured* by the mother's localized spoiling that mends the ego structure. This mending of the ego structure re-establishes the baby's capacity to use a symbol of union; the baby then comes once more to allow and even to benefit from separation. *This is* . . . [a] separation that is not a separation but a form of union" ("The Location of Cultural Experience" 97–98). *It is because it can fall apart* that the self becomes autonomous. It is in attempting to repair or recuperate what was in the midst of falling apart that the child learns to take over for itself the functions of the mother. What is striking about Winnicott's account of the baby's coming into being through the building of a solid ego structure is that this process happens as a result of a series of threatened failures. This is due to the paradoxical nature of separation from the mother into an individual. It is only through being thoroughly attached to someone else (e.g., its caregiver) that the child is able to internalize the capacity to take care of itself and, thus, eventually become a successfully separated and autonomous self. Yet, at the same time, it is only through a series of controlled losses that a permanent "union" between the child and its mother can form—this is a union between the child and what becomes the "internalized" mother.[7]

But everything seems so very precarious—it would be so easy really for the structure-building process to go awry, for separation to feel like permanent object loss, for the permanent internalization of the primary caregiver to feel more like the separations and deprivations on which it is based. It can begin to seem as though attachment itself is the culmination of habits of mourning—of repeated object losses. This process of mourning, then, leads to what we come to experience as our identity. Becoming human involves a constitutive process of separation from primary caregivers;[8] individuality is achieved through primary loss, and the body becomes the site of mourning. Otto Fenichel, one of Freud's early adherents, suggests that "primary identification," which is the basis for ego formation, "can be conceived of as a reaction to the disappointing loss of the unity which embraced ego and external world" (101). Freud's adult version of mourning charts a similar path of separation through incorporation.[9] As Abraham and Torok summarize Freud's thesis: "The trauma of objectal loss leads to a response: incorporation of the object within the ego. . . . Given that it is not possible to liquidate the dead and decree definitively: 'they are no more,' the bereaved become the dead for themselves and take their time to work through, gradually and step by step, the effects of the separation" (111). It seems that throughout the life cycle, any experience of loss/abandonment can lead to an incorporation of the lost object. It is clear that some of these incorporations of the mourned object take place on the body's surface.

A surgeon who specializes in correcting severe craniofacial anomalies in infants often confronts an implacable conviction of disfigurement in apparently normal and attractive patients. He gave me an example from his practice: "The individual was twenty-one or twenty-two at the time, and she felt fat and wanted liposuction. She was not fat, but she just felt so bad, and she was so insistent that I said, okay, fine. Although I was very reluctant, I did it. And afterwards she still wasn't satisfied." Eventually he learned that the young woman was adopted and had recently contacted her biological mother, whom she was scheduled to meet for the first time. Her obsessive concern with a physical defect was a way of unconsciously localizing and correcting the imagined flaw that had led the biological mother to abandon her as an infant. Now that her body had been tailored more nearly to the mainstream cultural aesthetic (or so she imagined), her biological mother might look on her more favorably. Surgeons do not like operating on this kind of patient, because they have a high rate of postoperative dissatisfaction. (One surgeon goes so far as to make prospective patients take a personality test.) Such dissatisfaction, surgeons believe, is inevitable when patients are driven to the surgeon to correct internal rather than external defects. At the same time, as I've pointed out, these surgeons are in the business of improving the internal conditions through interventions in the external appearance. This particular young woman, who was trying to recover a nonexistent relationship, illustrates clearly how her internal sense of abandonment is experienced as physical disfigurement. The surgical intervention is intended to restore to her both the body worthy of a mother's love and the mother herself—now imagined as ready to embrace the no-longer-defective child.

The analyst Margaret Mahler studied what she called the subphases of attachment and individuation of the small child, from the fourth or fifth month to the thirtieth through the thirty-sixth month. According to Mahler, we experience two births; the first is biological, and the second is psychological. Like Winnicott, she remarks that "the child is continually confronted with minimal threats of object loss (which every step of the maturational process seems to entail). In contrast to situations of traumatic separation, however, this normal separation-individuation process takes place in the setting of a developmental readiness for, and pleasure in, independent functioning" (Mahler et al. 3–4). Once again we have a strong sense that the price paid for becoming autonomous (human) is an ongoing but manageable experience of object loss. It's as though psychoanalysts imagine an idealized form of object loss that is never too painful, that moreover masquerades as permanent union through the final internalization of the outside object. Thus mourning is warded off on one level, even though on another level it seems to become wedded to individuality itself.

Mahler notes that one's body image is deeply bound up in the attachment and separation experiences of these early months. The "holding behaviors" of primary caregivers do much toward creating the frame of the external world in relation to which the child creates its internal "self" and outer boundary. Mahler accuses one mother of "overstimulating" her little girl physically at the same time that she "did not seem to have enough tender emotion for her children" (Mahler 441). Mahler believes the consequence in this case is a "narcissistic hypercathexis of the body ego," meaning that the surface of the body (which has been overstimulated) is consequently overinvested with concern and attention by the little girl (441).[10]

Like the young woman who imagined that a perfectly carved body would regain the love of a rejecting mother, so many people (mainly women) in the middle of a divorce believe they have been left because they have lost their young and attractive appearance. While we all recognize the error in the young woman's fantasy, we aren't so certain when it comes to the middle-aged divorcée. One surgeon told me that the cosmetic surgery business in Dallas took off as a result of the late 1980s economic crash: "When the crash came, everything that went along with exciting marriages crashed with exciting marriages. We had the highest divorce rate in America. So, you have a terrifically high population of women who got dumped for all the wrong reasons. And many of them have come from other parts of the country; now, they're left here with children, and their parents are back at home, [which leaves them] no support group, no support whatsoever. Some of these procedures that we do are really good—they have the world at their fingertips. They look terrific; they may not have a lot of money left, but they certainly have a lot more of the stuff it takes to get another guy." They felt horrible, they lost everything—love and money; plastic surgery restores to them the necessary tools for retrieving both. The abandonment is experienced as a surface phenomenon; they are no longer love-worthy, because they no longer invite loving gazes. Beauty itself can be seen as the ultimate vehicle of attachment: losing it will lose you the love you had; regaining it will find you love again. Just as the child is held together provisionally in the mother's eyes and embrace, the operating table is the place where the surgeon-as-mother will repair the discarded and fragmented body. Just as you mourn the loss of the object, you mourn, most important, the loss of the self loved by that object, the self that was attached. Paradoxically, the table where your body is split apart, your face torn asunder, is the table where you will once again be made whole. You attempt to make present on your body your missing beauty/love.

In 1923, Freud wrote what would become central to the subsequent development of body-image theory: "The ego is first and foremost a bodily ego; it is not merely a surface entity, but is itself the projection of a surface" (*The Ego and the Id* 26). The ego is where the outside touches the inside, where the body's location in the world intersects with the mental representation of "self." What is experienced as the psychical ego is founded on the shape of the body, which is critical to understanding how one's body image can vary according to emotional changes. The analyst Paul Schilder published his book *The Image and Appearance of the Human Body* a little over a decade later and considered the origin and effects of the body image, which he defined as "the tri-dimensional image everybody has about himself. . . . The term indicates that we are not dealing with a mere sensation or imagination. There is a self-appearance of the body" (11). The development and shaping of this body image happen along much the same lines as the psychical apparatus evolves: "We take the body-images of others either in parts or as a whole. In the latter case we call it identification" (138). Most important, the body image is variable, always in motion. As Schilder asserts: "The important conclusion we may draw is that feeling our body intact is not a matter of course. It is the effect of self-love. When destructive tendencies go on, the body is spread over the world" (166). It is self-love that makes the body intact and holds it together. Because of the narcissistic investment in our body, we can mourn it just as we mourn love objects. Certainly, when we imagine someone experiencing catastrophic injury from burns or amputations or any other radical change to the body's surface and shape, we realize that a grieving period would occur for the loss of the intact body and body image, that you would emotionally part with your lost body in increments. The loss of your youthful body can similarly induce an experience of protracted mourning.[11]

But what does it take to bring the body together to begin with? "The emotional unity of the body," writes Schilder, "is dependent on the development of full object relations in the Oedipus complex" (172). The emotional unity of the body seems to be dependent on the psychic reconciliation of feelings of love and hate, desire and aggression, feelings that emerge in relation to parental objects.

Writer Lucy Grealy, who lost a third of her face to cancer when she was nine, explains that while growing up she took for granted that her "ugliness," as she termed it, was an insuperable obstacle to finding love. Becoming interested in reincarnation as an adolescent, she decided she had chosen this difficult path: "Why had my soul chosen this particular life, I asked myself; what was there to learn from a face as ugly as mine? At the age of sixteen I decided it was all about desire and love" (180). Suppressing desire was necessary for one who had, as she believed, no chance to experience love—because of her disfigured face, a face imaginatively "chosen" for just this purpose.[12]

One patient I interviewed had had a face-lift at a relatively young age in order to "recover" the five years she believed her mother "stole" from her through abuse. It was not clear whether she thought she had aged more rapidly as a result of the abuse or if the face-lift just symbolized compensatory life. Another woman explicitly felt that she had aged prematurely because of her abusive parents. Her damaged face seemed to betray an internal damage that somehow was repaired along with the rejuvenation procedure. Undergoing surgery in order to heal childhood abuse suggests that the surface of the body enacts the object relation itself. The mirror reflected to these women the image of their tortured histories with their parents. But instead of choosing image-changing operations like a rhinoplasty or chin implant or any other surgery that effaces the identity of the abuse victim, they chose restorative surgeries—as though to begin again, to have a fresh start/birth. Actress-comedian Roseanne claims that her extensive cosmetic surgeries were meant to overcome the abuse (by parents and husbands) she glimpsed on her body's surface. Her rhinoplasty, moreover, was intended to wipe from her face the sight of her "father's nose." Psychologist Joyce Nash worries that the surgery, on the contrary, could revivify early feelings of pain and that the surgeon could become identified with the abuser (91). This was very much the case with one patient I interviewed who had a severe reaction to the surgery, including the follow-up care and recovery period. The surgery that was supposed to be restorative was identified (at least for a time) with the very condition (damaged childhood) it was supposed to be curing.

That mourning is constitutive of the original body image suggests why cosmetic surgery can serve as an answer to the loss of love. Jacques Lacan's theory of the "mirror stage," first published in 1949, illustrates how body image emerges out of the vicissitudes of attachment and loss. The mirror stage occurs between the ages of six and eighteen months. The child assumes a self-image (internal) on the basis of its relationship to a mirror image (or the mother, or another child). Thus, the image of the self comes from the outside—it is a picture upon which the psyche is modeled. This picture is indeed picture perfect. It is better than the infant, who from its own perspective of motor uncoordination, clumsiness, fragmentation (what Lacan calls a "body-in-pieces" [*corps morcélé*]) recognizes in the image the accomplishment of a perfect body, one whose parts all hang together in a coherent, stable unity. This is the future that the infant will pursue through its own body and through a "self" modeled upon this fluid, intact, pulled-together image.

Lacan emphasizes the temporal dimensions of this process; the unity with the mother is *"retroviseé,"* as he puts it—a unity only imagined as such after the fact. Similarly, the body-in-pieces is an idea that (literally) takes shape around the idealized gestalt in the mirror, which simultaneously depicts a lost unity (with the mother) and a future bodily intactness. That this image both precipitates and substitutes for the lost attachment is what I want to stress here. The mirror image can mobilize the sense of object loss; it pictures the child without the mother. At the same time it compensates for the dawning experience of separation by appearing on the infant's horizon as a substitute formation. Building on

Freud's description of the relationship between the bodily and psychical ego, Lacan holds that the image (literally a projection of a surface) is internalized as "I," the blueprint for the psychical ego. This means that the gestalt in the mirror, the picture of the unified body, *presents itself as the solution* to the lost relationship with the mother, a relationship that it nevertheless emblematizes. Inasmuch as this phase is a central part of the separation and individuation process, it leads to a mourning for a unity that is now reflected as the pulled-together surface of the body. The body thus comes at once to stand for and compensate for the lost unity with the primary object.[13]

Inscribed on the very surface of the body, therefore, is the image of that lost attachment. One's assessment of the relative beauty or ugliness of that surface might stem from the quality of the attachment it supplants. Lacan writes: "The image of his body is the principle of every unity he perceives in objects" (*Seminar*, book 2: 166). The general regard of symmetry as a central ingredient for "beauty" by social scientists, biologists, and plastic surgeons alike might be an example of the projection into the outer world of our earliest relationship to this idealized body image, which we try to match as nearly as possible. But we can never match it, claims Lacan, a failure that is a prototype for the failure of "perfect complementarity on the level of desire" (166). One reason we cannot match the mirror image is that literally we see ourselves in reverse.[14] Another is the way in which the mirror image is experienced in relation to the body's felt insufficiency; it presents the future (to be achieved) and a past (that has been lost) but never the present. Finally, the image is *internally* a mismatch in that it pictures simultaneously a restored attachment and the constitutive separation of the self. Possibly the achievement of beauty is compensatory in that it can "fake" the symmetrical match between the subject and the image.

This is all just internal, however, and while we can see how deeply connected the body image is to feelings of love and attachment, how might we be affected by being received in the (outside) world as beautiful or plain? There's only so much the history of our early object relations can tell us when we consider, realistically, that our physical appearance actually has a significant impact on our lifelong object ties. Besides that, our physical appearance changes, and our body is the landscape where those changes unfold. Does this body take over for family ties? Does it become our home? [15]

THE LOST BODY

"Many times if it's a very severe abnormality we'd like to begin working as soon as possible — certainly within the first year of life," explained a surgeon who specializes in reconstruction. "The parents will have a different relationship with this child. I've seen it with several parents that have children with severe craniofacial anomalies — at first they're shocked, and the initial feeling of the mother is guilt — something she did caused this child to be born this way. Then they go through a period of rejection — they don't want to look at the child. But when we start discussing what we can do, they become more involved, they notice that this child actually has some features that they haven't looked at — you know, the child can smile, the child can utter initially some babbling. This way the child will have a sense of bonding, and the parents in turn become the child's advocates — not only their biological parents." (interview with surgeon who specializes in craniofacial deformities)

Beginning life with damaged bodies, possibly shunned by parents who guiltily fret over what they might have "done wrong," born with eyes on opposite sides of the face or a flat plain where there should be a nose, features out of order, skeletal structure underdeveloped or gone entirely awry — these children are carried to the plastic surgeon to be put together, to give them a chance at what Mahler calls that second, "psychological," birth. The surgeon rapidly intervenes to make them look human enough to love. As the child becomes more "human" in appearance, the parents relate to it as human.[16] The loss of love is prefigured on their bodies, even before the parents set eyes on them. MacGregor et al. describe a not uncommon pre-1970s hospital event: "When Tommy was born, Mrs. Jonson was not allowed to see him after delivery. Her questions were left unanswered until the next day when a student nurse told her that he was 'deformed'" (15). The disfigured body resulted in an enforced separation from the mother.[17]

A surgeon discusses outcome: "In the great majority of cases, they will not look normal, but they may go from bizarre, hideous, to someone who is just ugly or not very pretty or not cute, but more normal in appearance." They will no longer be monsters, in other words. But is this enough? Is being ugly yet another version of monstrous in a beauty-obsessed culture? Another surgeon was more frank: "You turn monstrous into very ugly. Is it worth it? Sometimes I think a bump on the head at birth may be the answer."

We flinch at his casual inhumanity—killing newborns who aren't perfect. Where might it end? we wonder as we imaginatively hurtle through the Hitlerian possibilities. But in a culture where perfectly beautiful people chronically visit the plastic surgeon for fine-tuning (of a lip, an eyelid, that line that just appeared last weekend in your rearview mirror), "just ugly" might feel intolerable.

One surgeon marvels over the results of craniofacial surgery in young children: "What a wonderful way to establish a life," he said and urged me to "look at what we're able to do by intervening at such a young age compared to what it's like if you see that child later, unrepaired—the damage it's created." I never asked whether "it" was the child or the disfigurement. There is just such a convergence of the "it" in Mary Shelley's novel *Frankenstein*, between the creature and his ugliness. The disfigurement leads to violence. Another way of putting it is that the creature's psychical internalization of his monstrous image leads to his behaving monstrously. The damaged child could eventually do damage to his environment, thereby becoming the very thing apprehended by the horrified parents. Psychiatrist Norman R. Bernstein discusses how the disfigured appear and are treated as less human: "If people are deformed, they may be converted into *things*, and treated in an altered manner. The *contents* of an individual who is visibly marred are devalued, and the person has to struggle to avoid being discredited as an object." There are different forms of being objectified, it seems. "The very beautiful are also converted into *objects* by onlookers, but they do not share the negative or frightening tone set by deformity" (131). The very beautifuls' objectification can actually win them love and attention, in contrast to the disfigureds' experience.

But where do we locate the original "damage"? I knew a woman who considered her lovely daughter's cleft palate surgery unsuccessful. No one but the mother "saw" the residual damage on her daughter's face, the scars of surgical intervention as well as the traces of the original defect. Living inside her mother's vision of her, the daughter, too, saw herself as materially damaged. Where did her damage come from, and was it internal or external? Why was the mother blind to her daughter's beauty?

"The initial feeling of the mother is guilt." Perhaps the mother of a congenitally deformed child took medication or smoked or drank. But these are just ways of attributing concrete causes to what is psychically more elusive. Isn't it the sense that some secret defect has reached the light of day through one's child? Haphazard genes well up to expose the imagined parental deficit. The plastic surgeon, then, is meant to correct the parent's flaw as much as the child's. The child *is* the flaw made flesh.

One man reported his childhood obsession with the tip his nose, to which in desperation he once took a penknife, hoping to pare down the overgrowth of cartilage. But the bleeding stopped him right away. This man's mother chronically dwelled on the physical flaws of others, thereby deflecting attention from her own sense of damage. Of significance, the nose he attacked was identical to his mother's.

Whether or not emotional abandonment occurs, the threat of such loss is inscribed on these damaged bodies from the day they are born. Born into a culture where appearance has a considerable influence on our destiny, the congenitally disfigured can appear brazenly to emblematize the constitutive loss from which all our body images derive. The love taken away or withheld can feel like dismemberment, but the child's body can also represent to the parents their own (secret) fraudulence. Perhaps they are just beasts in disguise.

The child's damage can rise up like the return of the repressed parental heritage in defiance of the assimilative efforts of Jews, Lebanese, Asians, Africans. Generations of damage are reawakened and suppressed with yet more trips to the surgeon's office; the surgeon oversees the family morphology. There are many families whose members all patronize the same surgeon. He is the guardian of their ethnic and racial secrets; he processes their faces through mainstream "American" prototypes. He double-lids Asian eyes, narrows and upturns black and Semitic noses. Only, the next generation of children will reveal all. As the eponymous scientist laments in H. G. Wells's late-nineteenth-century novel *The Island of Doctor Moreau*, the beast-flesh grows back. Moreau surgically transforms animals into human beings, but the beast-flesh is relentless, and ultimately it will outstrip his paltry efforts at cosmetic retooling. The child can seem to the cosmetically assimilated parents like a dreadful (and dreaded) genetic reversion.[18]

Moreau explains: "As soon as my hand is taken from them the beast begins to creep back, begins to assert itself again" (Wells 76). What makes these bodies human in the first place is the touch of the creator; without the constancy of that touch, the flesh dissolves back into disarray. These creatures, when they revert, aren't simply animals. It's as though they fall to pieces, riven by a multitude of appetites that surge through and wreck the internal unity of what in the novel is called "the Law," barely, only transiently, achieved through formal physical coherence. Once the hand of the creator leaves them, however . . .

An extreme version of what abandonment looks like, these animals can't even retain the image of mourning (the incorporated lost object) that their human shapes signified. When we, too, begin to fall apart, when, as Schilder says, our self-love is at an ebb, do we resort to the plastic surgeon as a kind of makeshift object relation? Can the surgeon rescue the human from the path of the beast-flesh—aging, ugliness, becoming unlovable?

Conversely, aesthetic operations can be read as attempts to separate from family members who are either disliked or dangerously engulfing. "The possession of father's nose, mother's hips, or grandmother's hair, will carry with it an emotional agenda based upon feelings about that specific family member. Having a nose that resembles a loved and admired relative will often generate quite positive feelings about one's body image. The reverse may be true when the resemblance is to a relative who is hated or despised" (Goin and Goin, "Psychological Understanding" 1131). Sometimes the surgery is intended to efface the traces of the bad or reviled object, as in the following story reported by a psychiatrist:

> A 22-year-old single man, an Arts student with a protuberant jaw, was referred for assessment as the reasons for his requesting surgery were unclear. When the author saw him he expressed no personal dislike of his jaw nor was it a source of embarrassment or self-consciousness. In fact, he was relatively satisfied with his appearance and was not aware of it interfering in his social relationships. It emerged that an important impetus for the surgery came from his mother who had frequently expressed a dislike of his jaw and had initiated his seeking surgery. Due to his father's infidelity, his parents had divorced when the patient was an infant and his mother continued to despise his father. Careful questioning revealed the patient's jaw resembled his father's and that his mother had pressured him into surgery. (Schweitzer 251)

In order to experience an unambivalent connection with her son, the mother needed to eliminate from his face the phantom of the rejecting object. From the son's perspective, his face seemed to sustain an invincible attachment to his father, which he was being asked to forsake.

Analyst Didier Anzieu tells of a patient who, in her desire to feel entirely separate from her mother, imagined herself trapped in her mother's skin—which was shrinking. Anzieu diagnosed Marie as having a borderline disorder; her skin experience was about the confusion between the maternal skin and her own. "You must get rid of this maternal skin," he urged her, "so that a skin of your own can grow. . . . You are like a sloughing snake that abandons its old skin in order to have a new one" (*Psychic Envelopes* 3). Marie's fantasy of her shrinking skin was a metaphor for her relationship with her mother and her struggle to differentiate her own ego from her mother's. In cases where the ethnically marked mother presses her daughter to change her "skin" in order to detach visibly from the family ethnicity, how might the surgery become a metaphor for self-invention? Moreover, how might we who were pressed in this way to be not-Jewish or not-Asian or not-black experience our identities in relation to both the culture and the family?

Elizabeth Haiken points out that records of Jewish rhinoplastic patients from the midcentury United States repeatedly give voice to the desire to be "seen for themselves" instead of as stereotypes *(Venus Envy).*[19] An African American surgeon asks his nonwhite patients to bring in pictures of "liked or disliked features of family members" in order to get a sense of how "realistic" are their surgical objectives (Matory, "Addressing the Needs of the Hostile Patient" 21). When the body itself is, as Anzieu puts it, a "psychic envelope," what we do to it, our interventions in its contours, necessarily reflects our sense of identity. Moreover, these changes can lead to entirely new familial structures. In a Jewish family where all the noses remain "ethnically" identifiable save your own, you cannot help but experience a physical sense of separation from your own cultural roots. Your body becomes emblematic of separation itself. You are the one becoming-American. You float on a wave of assimilation that takes you away from a past; you are the ultimate self-created American subject.[20]

When I attend family functions, almost all the women's noses are surgically altered. It is the nonsurgical noses, then, that stand out as refusals of the family identity—an assimilated identity. We are borderline Americans, marked by our refusal of the reality of our heritage as we pour ourselves into imaginary bodies. How many generations of babies will be pruned? In order for the daughter to look like the mother, the daughter must be escorted to the mother's surgeon.[21] A new family ritual.

THE GEOGRAPHY OF APPEARANCE

Plastic surgery happens in a culture where we are impaled on the effects of first impressions. Such views reflected and were fed by the physiognomic literature of the seventeenth, eighteenth, and nineteenth centuries: Johann Caspar Lavater, author of *Essays on Physiognomy*, and others dwelled on the legibility of character through surface manifestations.[22] That appearance could induce character was an emergent cultural conviction being directly countered by these seemingly reactionary physiognomic accounts. As Richard Sennett has discussed, by the eighteenth century it was already easy enough to transform one's identity through fashion, mobility, and urbanization, through which anonymity afforded all sorts of social options. Class lines blurred because one could assume the costume of a higher rank if one played one's part convincingly enough: "If the oil merchant's wife or anyone else could wear a *chemise de la reine*, if imitation was exact, how would people know whom they were dealing with? . . . the issue was not being sure of a rank, but being able to act with assurance" (69). As cosmetics and dress in the nineteenth century became associated with the effort to disguise one's true appearance, one could find manuals that would enlighten men about how to "read" the authentic female body through the contrivance of fashion.[23] Photography as well participated in fixing the relationship between character and appearance. Alan Trachtenberg remarks that, from its inception, photography was used in the service of solving the nineteenth-century "obsession" with the origins, cultivation, and representation of character (27). "Photographers adopted the notion that the exterior of a person might reveal inner character, and conventionalized it in a sentimental repertoire of expressive poses" (28). These poses created as much as they reflected material and social accomplishment. As I will discuss at length in chapter 6, photography was among the central tools for accomplishing successful visual identities.

At the same time that this ability to transform value through appearance had the merit of releasing people from the burden of heritage, those who were born with a deformed or less attractive body might be ostracized to a degree less likely in a close-knit traditional community, where ties are based on birth and family connection more than on face value. One famous surgeon was strikingly candid with me about the real-life consequences of his work: "If you want to go out and be attractive to somebody else and start a new life, you've got to face facts—the way you look has a lot to do with whether you're going to attract somebody else. To me there's nothing wrong with that. Let's be pragmatic about the fact that if a woman ceases to be attractive physically, it affects the physical, intimate relationship. I've seen women who have not had particularly good relationships or haven't had a relationship with men for a long time, and I make them look younger and prettier, and they go on to get married and have wonderful, stable relationships. There's absolutely no question that the face-lift helped them. We live in a real, physical world."[24]

As he spoke I felt older, uglier by the minute. I felt the interview time eating into my last remaining years of feminine value. I wanted him to tell me the truth; it was a relief, really, to have this surgeon be so outspoken about the impact of appearance in the culture. Nevertheless, I was plunged into the doubt that he articulated but did not create. I wondered how he saw me—what he would do to make me look "younger and prettier." He spoke with such authority. Yoked to his honesty is a kind of fiction about the transformative possibilities of plastic surgery. You can change her life. You can make her someone whom someone else would be willing to love. More to the point, if she isn't succeeding on the dating/marriage market, it must be because she's not attractive enough. That's the most unsettling part of his account, isn't it? The self-evident undesirability of the woman who isn't young-and-pretty. Young-and-pretty. You can't have pretty without the young. As a feminist, I am indignant. Outraged. As a member of the culture, I cannot help but stumble.

I asked him: "Because they measurably really look better, or because they feel better about themselves?"

"Both. People want to pretend it's all psychological, it's just how you feel about yourself. That's not true. You know when you meet somebody at a party, you're more attracted to them if they're good-looking. And the more good-looking they are, the more you want to be with them and get their ideas and interact with them." He paused, perhaps in recognition of the implications of his argument or his sudden recollection of just who was interviewing him. "That's not true if somebody's particularly interesting and charismatic and intelligent—if you're bright you go beyond those things." I felt as though he was speaking directly to me then. To avoid offending me, he interjected this point about "intelligent" people—like English professors? I see—the idea is that smart people don't need face-lifts to be loved? What a relief.

"But there's no question that the way you look has a lot to do with the kinds of relationships you form. They don't just do better in this life because they feel better about the way they look; they do better because they in fact look better. And I've learned that not just from my aesthetic patients but from my reconstructive patients too."

We spoke about the case of one young woman whose face and life he entirely overhauled. She went from plain to noticeably pretty. I've seen the photographs; there's no question that plastic surgery made her a different person. "Their personality changes. When the world reacts to you as if you're a pretty, attractive person, your personality changes, you evolve, you become a different kind of a person, your self changes. It's not something that is cast in stone." He dismissed Freud's notion that our personalities are shaped entirely by the time we are six or seven. "I think our personalities are somewhat malleable for a long time."

Here, he was expressing the *Frankenstein* perspective on the origin of personality. You become how the world sees you. What happens when the Frankenstein situation is reversed and the attractive person becomes

ugly or damaged in some way? There has been much work on the change
in the body images of people who as attractive adults suddenly undergo
disfiguring accidents of some kind. Norman R. Bernstein, who emphasizes that acquired deformity is more traumatic than congenital, illustrates as much with the "case of Alice":

> A 30-year-old woman had been injured when a kerosene lamp
> turned over on a camping trip with her boyfriend. Her face, breasts,
> neck, and hands were grossly scarred. She had been a perky cheer-
> leader who loved to flirt and greatly enjoyed her femininity and
> good looks. After the injury, she hid from curious and shocked
> stares, only occasionally venturing out in public. Once, in a depart-
> ment store, a middle-aged man glanced at her and said, "Oh, I
> thought Halloween was over." The patient felt ashamed and demol-
> ished. She stayed in hiding for months; ultimately, she took a job at a
> radio studio where she saw little of the public. "I am no longer a
> woman. I am a thing." This was her damaged self-concept, and she
> could not elude it. Her boyfriend had left her when she came out of
> the hospital. She had lost her ability to be what Burns (1979) calls
> "love worthy." (141)

This is a story I read with an overflowing sense of how easy it is to lose
what you think you have or own in the way of your appearance—instantaneously. The description of her prior to the accident says so much
about how we link appearance to personality. She is called a "perky
cheerleader"—even though she is thirty years old! She was typecast before, and now she will be typecast after, as a "thing," a monster.

In referring to a case of a traumatic injury, the surgeon discussed
above slightly contradicted his previous account of the malleability of
personality. He told me about a beautiful young female patient who had
been hideously disfigured. "I get people like that all the time. It's very
difficult. Some deal with it better than others. Some of them are remarkable in their psychic resiliency, and other people become devas-
tated by it. A lot has to do with the family and the family support; a lot
has to do with whether there's antecedent depression. If somebody gets

injured and there's a background of depression before the injury occurs, those people don't do so well." My question had been: "In the case of very attractive people—people who have been received in the world as attractive and thus for their entire lives have taken for granted positive attention—what happens to them when they suddenly and traumatically change from attractive to unattractive or even monstrous?" How do they respond to their faces in the mirror? Are their personalities rewritten along the topography of their distorted faces? Doesn't the answer lie in where identity is located? When he talked about antecedent depression, I thought of Freud's melancholic. Isn't the loss of your own face a kind of object loss that throws the ego's very foundations into question?

This surgeon told me two incompatible stories about the origins and location of personality. In one account, identity happens on the body's surface, and if you're good-looking outside you will be a happy person. In the other account, identity is internal, and if you are "strong" enough, what you call "you" can withstand having your beauty stripped from you overnight. The internal "you" will survive the destruction of the face you called your own. This second story was ultimately upbeat, the individual triumphing over adversity. It was in direct conflict with the first account, however, insofar as they were different stories about the relationship between the outside and the inside.

Nevertheless, they became identical stories when I looked at them from the perspective of the surgeon's role. About the beautiful but radically damaged woman, he claimed: "I'm going to make her pretty good. I'm good at this. I'm going to make her a good-looking nose because she has a fabulous, beautiful nose. I'll make her attractive. So once she has makeup on, she'll be pretty." The women in all cases—the aging, tired-looking woman, the homely young woman, and the disfigured woman—can count on the surgeon to improve their chances at happiness. Some will get married; some will find romance after a devastating divorce; some will be able to walk into a restaurant and "pass" (very briefly) as normal. It will all be the same surgical story of improving the quality of life through improving the body.

I want to return to this question of the location of identity, however, and its degree of malleability, as the surgeon put it. Most important is his claim to disagree with Freud's conviction that personality is set early on in life. Is it comforting to imagine that there are people whose egos remain undisrupted? Certainly, I felt happier with the story of people whose inner character surmounted the tribulations of bodily damage. This is the same hope I carry with me every time I read *Frankenstein* or watch yet another film version; secretly, I hope that this time blind old De Lacey will rescue the creature and that his family will "see through" the surface to the virtuous and kind inner self, and thus the creature will be saved from his future of criminal malignity. "When I contemplated the virtues of the cottagers, their amiable and benevolent dispositions, I persuaded myself that when they should become acquainted with my admiration of their virtues they would compassionate me and overlook my personal deformity" (115). I imagine a world in which a young burn victim can enter a restaurant and no one stares—where she isn't thrown utterly onto the resourcefulness (and mercy) of her plastic surgeon. But I am fated to be disappointed by the De Lacey family, by the world, by the creature, by my own preoccupation with physical appearance.

It is not that I sentimentally long for inner value to be recognized over outer; it's more personal, less altruistic. I always wait nervously for the story to disprove the link between my appearance and my value. As the surgeon matter of factly observes, *"They don't just do better in this life because they feel better about the way they look; they do better because they in fact look better."* It may be, however, that there is something in between these radically conflicting accounts of character surpassing the body and the body's formative influence over character. The treatment and effects of prominent ears in children may offer some insight into the origins of character in a culture that simultaneously dichotomizes and conflates mind and body.

Children with prominent ears typically are teased by other children for looking different. Multiple experiences of being teased about one's appearance lead to shyness, even introversion and low self-esteem. Thus far, insurance companies have been covering the costs of correcting prominent ears because it's been linked to mental health. Increasingly, however, insurance companies are protesting that this is a purely aesthetic surgery and cannot be justified as medically necessary. Plastic surgeons argue, conversely, in favor of the psychological necessity for heading off at the pass an encounter with the world that is bound to prove traumatic for the vulnerable young child.

Prominent ears are a good example of how a physical disadvantage can shape personality. Or are they? I mentioned to one surgeon how unfair it would be if, in the wake of insurance companies' refusing to cover this surgery, only the well-to-do could afford to have their body images rescued. He expanded upon my point: "The ones who are privileged need it the least psychosocially, because their environment will protect them to a large extent, prominent ears or not, whereas the children who are less socially fortunate will suffer more." As several surgeons remarked to me, prominent ears haven't unduly stressed Prince Charles.

It is certainly true that the socially privileged need not concern themselves as much in general with their physical appearance. While they may be the ones for whom cosmetic interventions are most affordable, they are also the least in need of the image building and sustaining supplied by making an attractive appearance in the world. The socially privileged have advantages that shield their self-esteem from the rude and inquisitive opprobrium of strangers. And while it is clear that someone with the devastating scars of facial burns would be reviled as much when they are rich as when they are poor, the role social privilege plays in boosting self-esteem suggests that the more your identity is dependent on first impressions, the more appearance matters.[25]

The consolidation of high self-esteem through community profile, family status, and personal achievement would certainly confer on the individual the sense of an identity impervious to the assessment of casual encounter. I should imagine a similar situation holds true for children from close-knit communities where identity is forged more through community ties than it is from the caprices of fortune in the schoolroom or a summer job. If you are Jewish and grow up in a Jewish neighborhood where people keep their racial traits, then your appearance will have the advantage of always confirming for you your relatedness to your people. Your physical traits confirm connections with your own group instead of separating you from the rest of the culture. What becomes concerning then is how much more physical appearance matters in a culture of fragmented communities, of unanchored nuclear families whose members move vast distances from one another, each isolated in finding his or her way through anonymous clusters of people who know nothing of that person but what they can see up front.

Geography plays a role in the story of surgery on many levels. When I interviewed surgeons, I showed them a series of photographs and asked for their commentary. I showed them the photograph of the "unnaturally" aged woman of forty whom I referred to in an earlier chapter. I asked the surgeons what they made of this accelerated aging. Almost unanimously they attributed it to the sun in conjunction with a certain set of genes—an Irish or Scottish heritage surmised one surgeon, not suited to high sun exposure in, say, the southwestern United States. Another way of saying this is that her body is in the wrong place. There is a marked incompatibility between her geographic identity and her genetic identity that is expressed in her skin's prostration before ravaging environmental elements; without the protection of a dose of Mediterranean or eastern European DNA, the body succumbs to the foreign elements of the new land. Sander Gilman discusses aesthetic surgery as part and parcel of "liberal societies [where] it is often imagined as the transformation of the individual, such as the immigrant, into a healthy member of the new polis" (*Making the Body* 20). Thus, the refractory body that falters in the wake of a geographic misalignment is a reversal of all that's hoped and expected around such euphoric transformations. Place suddenly seems more like a barrier than a frontier. The mark of transition is inscribed onto her body, her historically recent ancestral route across the Atlantic. Her prematurely aging face becomes a metaphor for cultural and geographic mis-fits, and her surgery is yet another more powerful attempt to acclimate her body to her otherwise hostile space. Surgery recuperates the failed transformation.

Frances MacGregor, a medical social scientist who wrote extensively on plastic surgery, describes the case of a Jewish man who underwent a rhinoplasty not, as he claimed, "'in order to pass for a Gentile, but just because [he wanted] the subject [Jewishness] dropped" (MacGregor et al. 102). He wanted to look the part of those who possess cultural supremacy in his family's adopted nation. His postoperative reaction to his transformed appearance underscores this theme of reinscribing national appearances on one's dislocated body:

> For a moment he couldn't speak—his eyes widened—he turned
> pale. Then he exclaimed, "My God! I look like an Irishman! . . .
> I look like someone I know—and I *like* him, *too!*" Saying that he
> felt weak, he sat down but rose repeatedly to look at himself. Fasci-
> nated, he was examining his nose when his brother arrived. He [the
> brother] looked at Arthur, sat down, and—trying to cover his sur-
> prise—said measuredly, "It's a good job." Later he said privately
> to the interviewer, "Now I'll tell you how I really feel. You see,
> I'm a Jew and I'm not ashamed of it, but it's a shock to have your
> brother look like an Irishman—not that I have anything against the
> Irish." (103)

I recall once again the surgeon's observation that people with sup-portive families have an easier time adjusting to disfigurement. This isn't simply about emotional support; it's about the structure of one's identity, at what level "you" happen. And if "you" happen daily, evanes-cently, on the surface of your body, then you are always in danger of be-ing torn apart.[26]

We each bear the geographic history of our family. In the United States, most of us have descended from nonnatives. Our skin color, the shape of our eyes, the proportion of our limbs, these are the traces of other places and climates. They signal bodies in transition. Interestingly, the science of physiognomy became increasingly important as people became more mobile and they could no longer take for granted the ancestral nuances of those whom they encountered socially.

Sociologist Anthony Giddens uses the term "distanciation" to describe the increasing sense of global proximity across tremendous distances now collapsed in all sorts of ways through technology. While there are many positive aspects to forging a global community, what are the emotional consequences of technological intimacy? Certainly, we can sustain physical separations more successfully at the same time that, paradoxically, our social communities burgeon. Kenneth J. Gergen worries about what he terms the "growth in social connectedness," meaning the countless relationships occasioned by computers, telephones, televisions, and so forth (60). What happens to the body as a result of such reconfigurations of intimacy? Didier Anzieu asserts that now that the sexual is no longer repressed, "the repressed of today is the body—the sensory and motor body. In the era of the third industrial revolution, the revolution of information, nuclear energy, and the video, the repressed is the body" (*Skin for Thought*, 64). Is it in our effort to recuperate this body, to make it one with the "program" of technological euphoria, that we subject this body to surgical improvements? Anzieu continues: "in our society, in which the language of machines and the mass media has become so predominant, in which long-distance communications have been perfected, generalized, and automated, and in which the production and possession of ever more sophisticated manufactured objects in indefinite numbers are experienced as obligatory, physical and affective closeness is being unlearnt . . ." (64). This tactile body, the body that in a sense comes into being in the arms of other human beings, the infant's skin made alive through close contact—this body, laments Anzieu, is being repressed and supplanted by forms of communication that ironically assert distance and division, the not-touching of electronic communication, the subversion of necessary proximity by rendering distance apparently invisible.

Like the sleight of hand involved in distanciation, plastic surgery is a technology of the body that compensates for object loss even as it signifies it. Consider in this light the young woman I discussed earlier who, in preparation for meeting her birth mother, liposuctioned her thighs. This was a compensatory strategy in all respects, from remaking her body in the image of what she imagined her mother would love, to the implicit transformation of the surgical touch into a maternal one.

HAUNTED BY THE OBJECT RELATION

Mary Shelley's 1818 novel, *Frankenstein; or, the Modern Prometheus*, thematizes how with increasing geographic mobility and industrialized responses to changing human conditions experiences of attachment and separation can be inscribed on the body itself. Often reading like a travel narrative as we follow both Victor Frankenstein and his creature around Europe and ultimately the North Pole, *Frankenstein* illustrates what can happen to a body stripped of context and origins. The novel abounds with paradoxes. In order to "give birth" to his creature, Victor Frankenstein needs to cut himself off from family and friends, including his fiancée, Elizabeth. Although he puts together what he imagines to be a superlatively beautiful creature, Victor finds his creation's appearance loathsome from the moment the creature opens his yellow eyes. Most important, such paradoxes are inherent, Shelley indicates, in a culture that finds the body an instrument that interferes with human ties rather than facilitates them—and turns to science to correct the impasse. Mortal bodies die and leave us; hence we need superbodies designed to outstrip nature.

Shelley repeatedly shows that the absence of intimate ties and family connection is inextricably linked to the creature's experience of his appearance: "I was dependent on none and related to none. . . . My person was hideous and my stature gigantic. What did this mean? Who was I? What was I? Whence did I come? What was my destination?" (113). In part, *where* he is is *what* he is; or, more specifically, the monster travels in pursuit of intimate connections, just as Victor travels to elude them. Moreover, as a result of choosing professional (worldly) accomplishment over family ties, Frankenstein loses his own family, one by one, to the monster that represents both his ambition and his dislocation.

Authored by a woman whose mother had died ten days after giving birth to her and who, shortly before writing the novel, had lost her own eleven-day-old baby daughter, *Frankenstein* can be read as the story of how the denial of mourning and separation (as well as the confusion between intimacy and loss) are imaged on the body's surface. This is an early-nineteenth-century body that has become the cultural register for dislocation, mobility, and assimilation. Separations between parent and child, abandonments, loss of love, these experiences now take place within the larger context of the counterimperatives of the close-knit extended family[27] versus an increasingly mobile culture in which families can separate not only spatially but also socioeconomically.[28]

Yet the novel most significantly concerns the refusal to mourn the body of the love object—and thus body itself becomes a kind of haunting, a perpetual return of that which can be neither mourned nor incorporated. Reworking Freud's account of mourning and melancholia, Nicholas Abraham and Maria Torok describe the psychic mechanism of incorporation as a refusal of mourning, a denial that the object has been lost to begin with.

> When, in the form of imaginary or real nourishment, we ingest the love-object we miss, this means that *we refuse to mourn* and that we shun the consequences of mourning even though our psyche is fully bereaved. Incorporation is the refusal to reclaim as our own the part of ourselves that we placed in what we lost; incorporation is the refusal to acknowledge the full import of the loss, a loss that, if recognized as such, would effectively transform us. (127)

In contrast to "introjection," which they define as a psychic process that entails "broadening the ego" (112) and, moreover, which happens in full recognition of absence and loss, "incorporation" defends against the loss. This constitutes a refusal to separate from the love object. No mourning is necessary, because no loss is consciously accepted. This, for Abraham and Torok, is what leads to melancholia, which they define as the giving up of part of oneself in the object. Consequently, the object takes the ego along with it—into what Abraham and Torok call "the crypt." "Reconstituted from the memories of words, scenes, and affects, the objectal correlative of the loss is buried alive in the crypt as a full-fledged person, complete with its own topography" (130). This "person" is made up of the lost object along with the portion of the ego attached to and identified with the lost object. Frankenstein's creature seems to be the "person" in the crypt come out of hiding, the embodiment of what was supposed to remain entirely isolated from the rest of the psyche. It is this structure that leads to the "double" effect in the novel, whereby so many of the creature's actions can be read as an acting out of Victor Frankenstein's repressed aggression.[29]

The creature is the amalgam of bits and pieces of dead and lost bodies; he is the living image, in other words, of the lost object and, crucially, that which was intended to be buried now reanimated.[30] "I collected bones from charnel-houses and disturbed, with profane fingers, the tremendous secrets of the human frame. . . . The dissecting room and the slaughter-house furnished many of my materials . . ." (39). It is perhaps because his function is to deny that anyone lost anything (that Victor Frankenstein lost his mother, that Mary Shelley lost her child) that his aspect is all the more hideous. Victor now has to encounter close up in his creation not only the very picture of what he has disavowed but also the very structure of his disavowal:

> How can I describe my emotions at this catastrophe, or how delineate the wretch whom with such infinite pains and care I had endeavoured to form? His limbs were in proportion, and I had selected his features as beautiful. Beautiful!—Great God! His yellow skin scarcely covered the work of muscles and arteries beneath; his hair was of a lustrous black, and flowing; his teeth of a pearly whiteness;

but these luxuriances only formed a more horrid contrast with his watery eyes, that seemed almost of the same colour as the dun-white sockets in which they were set, his shrivelled complexion and straight black lips. (39)

The paradox here is that the monster, who is meant to overcome object loss, becomes instead its image. Victor's pathetic efforts to render beautiful this body constitute a denial of its proper psychical function as the openly mourned and accepted corpse. This paradox overlaps with yet another—the creature's physical ugliness is an image of object loss that happens as a *consequence* of his ugliness. In other words, as I will elaborate below, his ugliness is both the literal cause and the figurative effect of his abandonment by his "parent." That the creature who was supposed to deny or overcome object loss becomes instead the agent of destruction points to the aggressivity central to the refusal to mourn. The hated lost object, in the guise of the creature, rises up to restore the object relation he is psychically accused of abandoning in the first place. In the end, all they have is each other, chaser and chased, Victor and his creature—and we get a deep sense of the endless reversals obtaining in the parent-child relation over who is abandoning whom.

The best way to avoid object loss, it seems, is to avoid the object relation in the first place. What feels for Victor so monstrous about the creature is that he not only demands real object relations (in contrast to the temporizing Victor, he wants a wife, for example), he also makes Victor as unattached and isolated in reality as he always has been emotionally, despite his protests to the contrary.[31] Tantalized by the domestic picture presented by the De Laceys, the creature wants some of that for himself. As he reports to Victor:

> Other lessons were impressed upon me even more deeply. I heard of the difference of sexes; of the birth and growth of children; how the father doted on the smiles of the infant, and the lively sallies of the older child; how all the life and cares of the mother were wrapt up in the precious charge; how the mind of youth expanded and gained

knowledge; of brother, sister, and all the various relationships which bind one human being to another in mutual bonds.

But where were my friends and relations? No father had watched my infant days, no mother had blessed me with smiles and caresses; or if they had, all my past life was now a blot, a blind vacancy in which I distinguished nothing. (97)

Indeed, the creature turns Victor's house into a "house of mourning" to emphasize the loss that he has been designed to figure and (re)produce. In a rage, the creature vows to Victor: "'I will be with you on your wedding night!'" which Victor mistakes as the intention to kill *him* instead of Elizabeth. Since the creature already has established a pattern of killing people close to Victor rather than killing Victor himself, it is surprising that Victor mistakes his true meaning. But to be "with you on your wedding night" is also a parody of attachment and separation. At least someone will be *with* someone; this is where the creature excels— the opposite of Victor who is with neither wife nor child. As the creature cries out upon Victor's destruction of his companion-to-be: "'Shall each man . . . find a wife for his bosom, and each beast have his mate, and I be alone?'" (140). Victor destroys the female creature when he imagines the two procreating, as though it's the very idea of successful intimacy that he finds abhorrent. As many commentators have remarked, it would have been simple enough to make a female without reproductive organs. Thus, this anxiety must stand for something else—sex or simply the object relation itself.

This isn't simply a story about a man's fear of intimacy, however—or a woman's fear of object loss or even childbirth for that matter[32]—because these readings need to be linked more directly to the creature's formative experience of his body, when he has a vivid realization of his insuperable separation from the rest of humanity.[33] His physical difference is the origin and symbol of his isolation. Note how he immediately internalizes his rejection.

I had admired the perfect forms of my cottagers—their grace, beauty, and delicate complexions; but how I was terrified when I viewed myself in a transparent pool! At first I started back, unable to believe that it was indeed I who was reflected in the mirror; and when I became fully convinced that I was in reality the monster that I am, I was filled with the bitterest sensations of despondence and mortification. (90)

Frances MacGregor has described how facial deformity has a more profound disabling effect on people than functionally disabling conditions such as blindness or a missing limb. The face is so important, she argues, because it is the central location of human interaction: "It becomes, in effect, a personal symbol by which one is able to bridge the gap between one mind and another" (MacGregor et al. 32). Similarly, it is the place where the "sense of selfhood is generally located" (31). But it is selfhood in relation to other people, selfhood as it is received and reacted to by others. The face is where the object relation is felt to be located and experienced. In terms of attachment behavior, then, the face assumes symbolic priority in governing how other people, including one's own parents, respond to one. Craniofacial anomalies trouble parent-child interaction much more than other congenital deficits. The creature is rejected because of his appearance: "No mortal could support the horror of that countenance. A mummy again endued with animation could not be so hideous as that wretch" (Shelley 43).

Gilles Deleuze and Félix Guattari argue that under capitalism, the face is at the center of identity and sign systems. What they term the faciality machine is particular to capitalism where one's face is read according to type. As they put it: "The face of a teacher and a student, father and son, worker and boss, cop and citizen, accused and judge . . . : concrete individualized faces are produced and transformed on the basis of these units, these combinations of units—like the face of a rich child in which a military calling is already discernible, that West Point chin. You don't so much have a face as slide into one" (177). The face is where identity and social function converge; in the context of capitalism, identity is subordinated to function.

Deleuze and Guattari make it clear that it was not always this way; they date the origin of this faciality machine in the "year zero of Christ and the historical development of the White Man. . . . Our semiotic of modern White Men, the semiotic of capitalism, has attained this state of mixture in which signifiance and subjectification effectively interpenetrate" (182). Under capitalism, the faciality machine flourishes insofar as our sign systems work in perfect concert with what we are psychically disposed to see. The concentration of identity in the face, then, is the script of capitalism that we might then read backward into a mirror stage, which, in this light, is the parable of how social identity is an appearance. Thus a face that appears ugly could signify the unworthiness of the individual. As I observed above, in *Frankenstein*'s context of industrial capitalism, class mobility increasingly throws individuals disconnected from substantial kinship networks on the mercy of their looks. In this sense, the creature's situation is representative—no friends or family to assign him value beyond what meets the eye.

Capitalist subjects reproduce themselves, create contexts for social identity. The melancholic structure of identity formation that I have been theorizing is deeply bound up in the way the face is the term of separation and hence of human legibility. Consider how psychoanalyst D. W. Winnicott revises Lacan's mirror stage to argue that the mirror is specifically the mother's face: "The bare statement is this: in the early stages of the emotional development of the human infant a vital part is played by the environment which is in fact not yet separated off from the infant by the infant. Gradually the separating-off of the not-me from the me takes place, and the pace varies according to the infant and according to the environment" (111). The locus of separation—where "me" branches off from "not-me" is where the infant's face encounters the mother's in a glance that is ultimately a mapping of the mother's version of identity formation (through the face) onto the infant's. Let us return, then, to Victor Frankenstein's account of his creature's face: "His yellow skin scarcely covered the work of muscles and arteries beneath; his hair was of a lustrous black, and flowing; his teeth of a pearly whiteness; but these luxuriances only formed a more horrid contrast with his watery eyes, that seemed almost of the same colour as the dun-white sockets in which they were set, his shrivelled complexion and straight black lips" (39). The place where the infant assumes its humanity, in other words, the face, is precisely where Victor rejects his creation; in an ironic reversal, this is exactly where Victor identifies his creature as *inhuman*.

Frankenstein is a case history of a new kind of surgical subject, for whom the relationship between appearance and character was a sharp reversal of the more conservative and generally held (physiognomic) views. At the same time that we seem to take for granted the effect of disfigurement here on relationships (both intimate and distant), we should consider that facial disfigurement may itself symbolize separation. Brought into existence by a creator who ironically uses this experiment to avoid *real* object relations with his family and friends, the creature's physical appearance becomes both the origin of his rejection and the result—a double-edged metaphor for Frankenstein's flight from intimate ties. Abandoned by his creator, reviled by other human beings, the creature glimpses in the water for the first time the ugly face that isolates him. Here we have an exact reversal of the mirror phase whereby the body pictures a (re)union of child and lost object—there is no such reconciliation in store for the creature. Nevertheless, recall my point that the imaged unity in the mirror is not only illusory; it also participates in the very separation for which it compensates. Yet here there is no illusion of unity reflected to the creature whose ugliness is the "real" separation (the truth) that the mirror phase denies.

Judith Halberstam reads the novel as the story of the horror associated with becoming human. I would add that it is an account of the terrible price of separation entailed in becoming human, and the creature reveals the experience of being "cut off," which is otherwise concealed and disavowed by the alluring image. The bits and pieces of corpses (both animal and human) that converge in the creature's body visually undo the unity they pretend to forge; they are the body as cut off, isolated. The body itself is where the separation is located—what is severed from the primary object, cut loose, "in pieces." From this perspective, our cultural investment in making the body more beautiful (an investment adumbrated by Frankenstein when he imagines he is creating a superior and beautiful race) is then no more than a defense against the body-as-crypt for the lost original connection.[34] Thus, any body is a dead body, and all bodies are in need of resurrection.

FIVE

As If Beauty

"That's what a star is . . . someone who is always re-creating themselves anew."

Joan Hyler, Hollywood manager, in "Altered States"

Brian D'Amato's updated *Frankenstein* novel, *Beauty*, makes clear the narcissistic side effects of celebrity culture. The narrator, Jamie Angelo, transforms aging faces with a combination of Artificial Skin, photography, painting, and, later, computer generations. He calls his craft "beauty technology": "industrial materials designed to imitate or . . . surpass nature" (39). He specializes in celebrities ("celebrity-makeovers," as he calls them) whose faces desperately need to measure up to the camera's intense scrutiny (127).

Jamie creates the template for his girlfriend's new face on the computer. She is not intended to seem quite real; that her beauty is unnatural is essential to its power. Nevertheless, the instant Jamie "releases" her to the public, she becomes a paradigm for others to emulate.[1] As D'Amato suggests, however, modeling oneself on two-dimensional images is inherent in movie-star culture itself. Plastic surgery is insufficient because it's limited by real flesh. Working with Artificial Skin (absolutely smooth, poreless) is like taking an airbrushed image and importing it into the domain of real life. This is plastic surgery's unconscious fantasy about itself, D'Amato intimates—to elevate the human into the celluloid.

"AS IF"

In 1942, the psychoanalyst Helene Deutsch coined the term "as if personality" to describe a particular set of patients unaccounted for by other diagnostic categories. Subsequently considered a subcategory of the borderline personality, the as if personality "forces on the observer the inescapable impression that the individual's whole relationship to life has something about it which is lacking in genuineness and yet outwardly runs along 'as if' it were complete" (75). While in "normal" development, the core sense of self is pretty much fixed by age six or seven, the as if personality never stabilizes. Consequently, this personality is extremely vulnerable to the influences of her or his external environment. As Deutsch puts it: "Any object will do as a bridge for identification" (77). This personality can "happen" only by way of identifications with others, identifications that keep shifting because there is no core personality discriminating and selecting. The identifications, in other words, are whole instead of partial. "The representatives which go to make up the conscience remain in the external world and instead of the development of inner morals there appears a persistent identification with external objects" (81). Instead of introjecting principles derived from parents and other adults and making them part of the permanent fabric of one's self, the as if personality simply drifts along, identifying with people as they come into her or his orbit, easily exchanging these identifications for others. With each substitution of new for old identifications, the as if personality transforms radically.[2]

Deutsch writes: "It is like the performance of an actor who is technically well trained but who lacks the necessary spark to make his impersonations true to life" (76). Deutsch unwittingly collapses the difference between "true" and "false" impersonations when she makes it clear that identity itself is merely a performance—which the as if's insufficiency reveals. Or, rather, some as ifs are more convincing than others. By performance I mean specifically the assumption of characteristics and behaviors of the person you want to be. For the as ifs, people they admire are a series of roles to explore. In this chapter I will argue that in idealizing and modeling ourselves on actors, people whose very profession involves constantly shifting identities, we are all prompted into quasi–as if lives. Moreover, because these actors with whom we identify are largely received by us in two-dimensional form (as screen images), our experience of identity is made not only insubstantial but also what I will call transformational. We as ifs are the perfect viewing subjects for the ever-unfolding pageant of movie-star culture. They represent for us both what we are and what (and where) we long to be.[3] It is this process of as if styles of transient identifications with two-dimensional objects that has made it so easy for us to become surgical bodies. Given conventional cultural expectations around the adaptiveness of heterosexual women, becoming an as if is only one step removed from normative femininity. Thus, women are necessarily more vulnerable to as if personality structures as well as cosmetic surgery. As this chapter will show, however, the cultural normalization of the as if structure of being means that men as well are increasingly susceptible to the transformational identifications of cosmetic surgery.

STAR CULTURE AND THE MAKING OF TWENTIETH-CENTURY BODIES

Those newly immigrated to the United States in the early twentieth century found in cinematic images the route toward personal transformation. Stuart and Elizabeth Ewen stress how the silent film could offer transformational images to people who were looking for access into a society with no other road maps, including linguistic ones: "For immigrants in a world of constant language barriers, the silent film was compelling and accessible. Silent pictures spoke primarily to urban immigrant audiences of women and children, themselves caught up in the social drama of transformation" (54). Film filled in the "fissures" of difference among people and was instrumental in creating a sense of mass culture. A central theme in this "training" technology was "metamorphosis through consumption" (Ewen and Ewen 68). Consumption, of course, was typically associated with women. Women learn to be more womanly, hence desirable (ironically), as they become world-class consumers of the codes of desirability/transformability. As I will discuss in the following chapter, physical metamorphosis was a central plot as early as Cecil B. De Mille's silent films. Gender conventions, the desire to transform/assimilate, and consumer capitalism converge in these allegories of becoming the right kind of Americanized subject. Moreover, the mythology surrounding star culture involves rapid serendipitous transformation. As the anthropologist Hortense Powdermaker puts it: "All actors stress the importance of breaks. These are emphasized more in Hollywood than anywhere else because of the lack of apprenticeship, or any specific path leading to success" (244). The Hollywood story par excellence is one of overnight "discovery," startling Cinderella-like ascensions into the public eye.[4]

The growth of star culture itself tells a certain story about the reconfiguration of identity over the course of the twentieth century. The reasons for and ways in which film stars became iconically central to the culture suggest a massive shift in how idealization and role modeling take place. In his excellent study of the emergence of the "star," Richard de Cordova breaks down the public's reception of screen actors into three phases: (1) discourse on acting; (2) picture personalities; and (3) stars. Originally, observes de Cordova, the actors were entirely secondary to the filmic apparatus, which was, in this sense, the central performer—what people came to watch. Within a short time, however, actors garnered more attention. This second phase, during which they became "picture personalities," offered by no means the same prestige as theatrical performances, however. Florence Lawrence, who starred in numerous Biograph films, became known as "the Biograph girl," just as

Florence Turner was popular as "the Vitagraph girl." They became known for a series of parts played in films and associated with particular manufacturers. Their identities were pieced together via the various roles they played, while their real names and real lives remained unknown and unpursued. It was only in the third phase, that of star, when their "real" lives became as important as their "reel" lives. From the beginning of the production of the film star, there was an inextricable connection between their performances and their personal lives. A high premium was placed on the stars' behavior in real life, which was expected to be of a piece with their acting roles. As de Cordova points out, however, almost from the beginning, movie stars became associated with sexual scandal. Their sexual secrets (who was having affairs, getting divorced, having illegitimate children) would soon become the stuff of audience fascination. Thus, early on we find audiences interested in undermining the very equivalence between real and "reel" lives they presumably demand.

The use of the movie star as social role model for the audience happened from the beginning. Lary May describes Mary Pickford's constant attention to her image both on-screen and off: "She was obsessed with maintaining this look of youth and purity. She never wanted her screen image to suggest that moving about in the rough and tumble world would taint this quality. So the star watched all her film rushes carefully, in order to detect any blemish or frown. As she explained, 'No woman can be a success on the screen if she dissipates even one little bit. The slightest excess, the least giving away shows unmistakably in the face and its expression. . . . I cannot remain up at night and have my face clear and shiny" (125–26).[5] For director D. W. Griffith, May writes, the condition of the skin told the story of the soul. No facial blemishes or defects of any kind were tolerated, because they intimated bad living and worse character. He would interview dozens of actresses before he found the quality of skin necessary to depict perfect virtue on the screen (75–77). Said Griffith: "'To me, the ideal type for feminine stardom has nothing of the flesh, nothing of the note of sensuousness. My pictures reveal the type I mean. Commentators have called it the *spirituelle* type'" (qtd. in Walker, *Stardom* 61).

Although Griffith's conviction of the self's legibility through surface appearance certainly has its roots in the eighteenth and nineteenth centuries' emphasis on physiognomy, he points the way to a new cult of the surface that screen images herald. For, if the face is blown up for all to gape at its slightest imperfections, it is also the highly altered product of special effects generated by the film apparatus itself.[6]

Pickford's concern with her "image" suggests that, as a medium, the cinema is inextricably linked to the production of images to live by and sustain. Think of her scrutinizing her rushes in her effort to preserve the image she sent out to the public—an image that sustained in the public imagination an idea of her as young, fresh, inviolate in the face of worldly depredations. It is not just that the pristine complexion translates into assumptions about character. If you do edit out the blemishes, then invariably complexion and character will come to be seen as one and the same; it is the fusion of the two that becomes the screen image. The entire technology surrounding screen images, moreover, becomes part and parcel of the cultural conceit regarding appearance and character— which is what made our relationship with screen images so pivotal for the twentieth century (as well as the twenty-first). In this manner, screen images are pressed into serving social functions. Mary Pickford's face becomes the model of femininity, and she becomes the guardian of her feminine image. Yet even as we read her account, it is clear that she, too, can no longer tell the difference between reality and film editing.[7]

What are the cultural side effects of this fascination with celebrities in general and screen actors in particular?[8] Why do we continue to be so intensely interested in the real lives of people whose talent lies precisely in playing roles? What, finally, might be the consequence of identifying with people who themselves seem to suffer from a high proportion of narcissistic and borderline disturbances? The multiple marriages, the instances of substance abuse, tirades on sets, and so forth, these are typical diagnostic traits of the borderline personality. The mere self-aggrandizing qualities of "being" a star and the lengths to which star culture goes to celebrate itself through numerous ceremonies, along with stars' uninhibited displays of their personal lifestyles, certainly indicate a profession tailor-made for the narcissistic personality.[9] As many theorists of narcissism have noted, the acting profession is perfectly consonant with the narcissist's craving for constant affirmation of his or her spectacular qualities. Moreover, the convention of the "discovery" of movie stars among otherwise quite everyday people is a fiction of specialness that shores up the narcissist's grandiosity. Because the actor possesses such a powerful identificatory influence on the culture, however, it is really beside the point whether or not actors are narcissists and borderlines. Rather, what they stand for culturally, the apotheosis of the two-dimensional image linked to the idealization of role playing, suggests a significant change in the structure of what we call the self.[10] This two-dimensionality is central to transformational identifications with film stars.

Psychoanalyst Eugenio Gaddini, in his reconsideration of Deutsch's "as if," theorizes that identification is preceded by what he terms an earlier state of "imitation," which takes place primarily through vision. Such imitations are fantasies of being or becoming the object through "modification of one's own body" (477). The "as if," he reasons, remains fixated at this preidentification stage. Judith Mitrani believes that such imitations take place in two-dimensional space. Without space between subject and object, there can be no development of what would be full-fledged object relationships. Rather, the imitative experience is like rubbing up against other surfaces. A famous literary as if, Dorian Gray, is remarkable for his extreme exchange of depth for surface. Upon seeing his beautiful portrait, the hitherto spotless Dorian expresses the wish that the portrait would age in his stead, which is exactly what happens. Not dissimilar to Mary Pickford's anxiety over diverse bad habits showing up in her complexion, Dorian's habits travesty the portrait in the closet while his body remains unscathed. More interested in the surface than the depth of other people, he falls in love with an actress, Sybil Vane, because of the brilliance of her performances. When Sybil returns Dorian's love, however, her acting talent subsides in favor of the real-life emotion that wells up in her; Dorian is instantly disenchanted by her revealed "depth." Her acting seemed to him the perfection of the surface self, which is exactly where Dorian himself lives. "Sybil Vane's 'tragedy,'" writes Rachel Bowlby, "is not so much that Dorian deserts her, as that she casts off the role of actress in the belief that she has found a fixed identity beyond her various theatrical parts" (23).

James Masterson opens his book *The Search for the Real Self* with a case history of a successful soap opera actress whose "real life" is constricted by an incapacity to experience her "real self." He calls her Jennifer:

> The popular, strong-willed character Jennifer played on television had become her professional trademark. . . . She wondered if the nature of acting required the actor to have an empty core at the center of his or her identity, a point many of her actor friends took pride in because they believed it allowed them to portray a wider range of characters. She feared that this trait would keep her from ever finding her real self, which in her heart she knew was a far cry from the hardboiled women she could portray so convincingly on the stage and television. (1–3)

Whether or not actors generally like to characterize their particular gift as stemming from an "empty core," it is certainly true that the definition of an actor, someone who professionally assumes the identities of other people, implies a lability of "self" if not exactly emptiness. As an actor, you are judged according to how well you wear the alternative identities of the other person.

One borderline patient describes her desperation to "crawl inside someone else's skin. It terrifies me to think of saying, 'This is me; this is my skin.' So I cop out on myself by being some other person, living with some other person's fantasy'" (Masterson 19). Although the "great" actor is known especially for the range of skins she or he wears, more often than not screen actors tend to be type-cast. "Jennifer," for example, routinely played independent and self-assured women, as though to wear the skin of her own ego ideal. An ongoing television part can leave us with the sense that the actor *is* this role.

Annie Reich described a patient she diagnosed as "as if":

> This girl, a European of Czechoslovak nationality, would feel herself
> to be "an American glamour girl," for instance, when she wore a
> sweater like the one she had seen pictured in an American magazine;
> or she would be a "sophisticated demimondaine" when she visited a
> night club. It is characteristic that there was no consistent content
> in these "ideals." They changed like feminine fashions and were
> influenced by anything that happened to come along. (307)

Later, unsurprisingly, this patient "had a minor success as an actress."

What kinds of identifications do we make with actors? They are very different in form and temperament from the identifications a reader makes with, say, a character in a novel, for the simple reason that identifications with film or television characters are *visual;* we react to them on the level of their physical images, to which our own respond, often even adjust, accordingly. Jackie Stacey offers a taxonomy of the range of imitations of and identifications with film stars of the 1940s and 1950s in her book, *Star-Gazing.* Some such identifications happen primarily during the viewing, says Stacey. Viewers describe themselves as having lost themselves in the star-ideal's role. Other identifications involve more deliberate comparisons or transformations on the part of the spectator. Many of the women in Stacey's study mention stars they most want to look like, despite the obvious differences. "'We liked to think we were like them, but of course, we couldn't match any of the female stars for looks or clothes. It was nice to have them as role models though'" (152). Where would the pleasure come from, then, if your own image was always held at arm's length? As Stacey reports: "Spectators often felt 'unattractive,' 'dowdy', 'plump' and 'gangly' by comparison. Stars are remembered through a discourse of feminine glamour in which ideals of feminine appearance (slim, white, young, and even-featured) were established and in comparison to which many spectators felt inadequate" (152). Nevertheless, many spectators either claimed traits in common with film stars or actively tried to imitate them. Stacey distinguishes between three extracinematic spectator practices: resembling, imitating, and copying. Resembling entails noting a trait in common and then "highlighting . . . star qualities in the individual spectator" (161–62). Imitating, for Stacey, refers to "behaviors and practices"—such as singing and dancing after watching a film (167); she contrasts this with copying, which refers to *appearances* and might involve choosing clothes in the style of a favorite star or changing one's hair color and other physical traits that indicate an embodied identification. It seems, then, that the central difference between various forms of identification involves the imaginary distance between oneself and one's screen idol. While some viewers acknowledge the enormous distinction between their own bodies and the star's, others strive to transcend the distance through actively incorporating the star image into their own.

BECOMING-CELEBRITY

When you can come closer to becoming a celebrity by having yourself surgically altered (imitating on the body what cameras and lighting do to the screen image), the identification becomes more complete; significantly this is an identification with a *process* (role playing) rather than with any particular person, thus necessarily putting any fixed sense of self at risk. John Frankenheimer's 1966 film, *Seconds*, explores the tension between the lure of "false" images and the feared loss of "self" in the image. The film concerns a secret organization that offers depressed middle-aged men a way out of their airless lives. Their deaths are feigned, and they are presented with new, young bodies—and lives to match. They are called reborns.[11] The company's guidance counselor explains his new circumstances to the protagonist, Arthur Hamilton, after a radically transformative wish-fulfillment-style surgery (he goes from bland, overweight, and middle-aged to Rock Hudson). Instead of a bank president, he will now be an artist:

> "You will be supplied with fresh paintings periodically. In time,
> you'll perfect your own style: surreal, primitive, impressionistic,
> whatever . . . you see, you don't have to *prove* anything anymore. You
> are accepted. You will be in your own new dimension . . . you are
> alone in the world, absolved of all responsibility. . . . You've got what
> almost every middle-aged man in America would like to have —
> freedom, real freedom."

But Tony Wilson (his new identity) finds out that this refurbished, superficially more perfect life is anything but free. Indeed, the rules are impossibly strict for someone who retains any affiliation with his original self. The integrity of his new role is vigilantly policed both by these employees and the other reborns. When on one occasion he slips and mentions his nephew, he is instantly reprimanded ("you don't *have* a nephew") by one of the company employees hired to facilitate and monitor his adjustment. To be a successful reborn, we learn, you can never slip and create a continuity between your present self and the past.

If the film's superficial moral lesson is that you can't escape your real self, there is a deeper current of suspicion over whether any such real self exists. *Seconds* suggests that all identities are simply roles that one plays more or less well. The very arbitrariness of these roles (making Wilson a painter regardless of native endowment) repudiates any notion of "true" or "core" self. Stifled by his policed environment, Arthur decides to give up his Tony persona and try again. As he explains to the friend who introduced him to the company: "California was the same. They made the same decisions for me all over again, and they were the same things, really. It's going to be different from now on. New face. New name. I'll do the rest. I know it's going to be different."[12] Arthur expresses his need for a choice: "It's so important. Choice." He rejected his original life because he felt as though he hadn't chosen it, but instead had unwittingly fallen into a tedious job and a loveless marriage; and the fantasy that remains undying in Arthur (as well as the roomful of men also waiting to try again) is that of infinite opportunities for self-creation. The impossibility of the very self-creation all these men crave is the dominant theme of the film.

What self are they after? Most psychoanalytic theories of the self hold that what is called the false self arises as a result of demanding and unempathic parents. Such parents are incapable of nurturing or even tolerating the child's true self, which could be at odds with parental needs. These reborns seem to be after an idea of core self that requires expression through lifestyle, professional identity, and appearance. Arthur complains about decisions being made for him—first by the caprices of life and circumstance, second by the company. This socially produced and monitored self, Arthur avers, is not who he really is. This is a conforming self who fulfills the objectives of the "company" (an allegory for society). Yet the film suggests that this imagined true self is simply another false self, a grandiose self fed by cultural fantasies about happiness and fulfillment.[13]

Most analysts of narcissistic and borderline disturbances not only acknowledge that these are the most common mental illnesses of our times but also point out that narcissistic personalities in particular may seem entirely congruent with wide-scale social objectives. One analyst observes with chagrin that "in a social climate where [narcissistic] characters tend to be almost institutionalized politically and economically, the grandiose self has a natural ally to support its already powerful claim to sovereignty" (Bromberg 463). Successful narcissists seem to garner all the best social supplies. It's difficult not to be envious. How, then, do the analysts diagnose, as though from the outside, what seems to be pervasive *cultural* discontent arising from narcissistic urgency? Considering the centrality of "individual entitlement" to the American ethos, Masterson asks: "Does the resultant narcissism contribute to a unique and healthy American character, or is it a pathological national flaw" (105).[14]

Masterson points out that highly successful narcissists rarely go into therapy: "Often he is in a profession that has considerable narcissistic supplies built right into it. If the narcissist finds the right niche in life, he can go for years without realizing that his life is empty at its core and that beneath the narcissistic glitter there is an impaired real self" (100). Not only do Masterson's misgivings sound suspiciously like the bad faith claim that even though the rich have a lot of material possessions, they don't really enjoy them, it is difficult to know how to pathologize (much less treat) the most successful personality type of our culture.

Seconds uncannily reproduces the psychoanalytic dilemma. Critical as the film is of Arthur's attempt to escape his true identity (read true self), we cannot help but feel that Arthur's "real life" is indeed as dismal as he thinks; we are also left with the sense of some element of role playing to all identities.[15]

The surgical transformation (from Arthur Hamilton to Tony Wilson), along with the requisite change in actors, undoes any sense of continuous or real self. In order for the fiction of *Seconds* to work, the audience must believe that the surgery is so powerful that the actor playing Arthur Hamilton really could be surgically reconstituted into someone looking like Rock Hudson.[16] Alternatively, our consciousness of the filmic process (in the sense that we cannot help but "identify" Rock Hudson as an actor instead of an authentic surgical outcome) might lead us to equate plastic surgery with acting. The surgery on Arthur Hamilton is highly explicit, and the camera's constant shift from the surgical diagrams to the flesh-and-blood face positions plastic surgery as the linchpin in the transition both from two dimensions to three and from one actor/role to another (see fig. 4).

More than a moral lesson on the vicissitudes of modern identity crises, *Seconds* aptly illustrates the culture's increasing identification with filmic representations of life and with screen actors. The best way to "become" Rock Hudson is to have him play you in a movie or on television.[17] This is the most successful, most complete form of cosmetic transformation. The ego ideal of cosmetic surgery—in other words, what surgery wants to be when it becomes a more perfect technology of

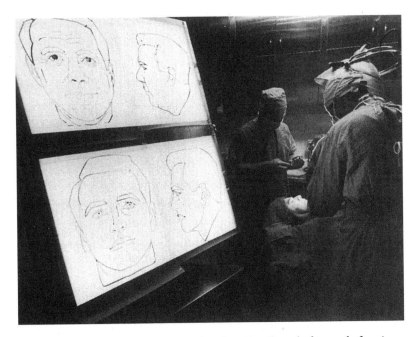

Figure 4.   Two-dimensional views of Arthur Hamilton, before and after, in *Seconds*. Courtesy of Photofest.

transformation—is acting: the exchangeability of one body for another, a real person for an actor. Rock Hudson's iconic effect in the film (as the choicest body) is achieved through his reputation as a heartthrob film star of the 1960s. It is Rock Hudson more than Tony Wilson who Arthur becomes.[18]

The notion of acting a part or comparing human identity to a form of acting is hardly historically recent.[19] As I have been emphasizing throughout, however, when our culture increasingly identifies with media images and goes so far as to measure the success of individuals against versions of success depicted in movies and television, the very idea of "acting a part" evades the semantically requisite distance between actor and role. In fact, the part can overtake the actor. More important, stars themselves outstrip their roles, which finally simply subserve the movie star's need to be a star—and the desire of the rest of us to identify with that brand of cultural triumph.

The addition of cosmetic surgery to the widespread cultural pattern of narcissistic identifications with screen images makes it all seem possible. While in films like *Ash Wednesday* and *Seconds* cosmetic surgery is presented as the exclusive domain of the rich and privileged and, perhaps as a result of its exclusivity, is depicted as all the more miraculous in its results, the current ready availability of surgery to "the average person," who is, moreover, the target of most advertisements, turns even the "everyday" body into movie-star material. The transformative effects of the identification give the two-dimensionalized self the sense that any old Arthur Hamilton can become a celluloid-quality idol.

The concern expressed among analysts over the sacrifice of the true self to the false reflects the culturewide fear of the loss of our individuality. Many different technological inventions, from cloning to genetic engineering to television and PlayStation, raise the specter of erasing altogether the distinctive and self-determined individual. We tell this story in so many different ways, it has become a convention in an ongoing battle with the equally powerful impulse to emulate culture ideals. As many of us feel increasingly swept away by screen images, we construct science fiction narratives around the loss of self. The films *The Invasion of the Body Snatchers* (1956) and *The Night of the Living Dead* (1968) could be read as prescient allegories of the intensification of the culture of celebrity, whereby we are all taken over by the exact same iconic movie stars. The "alien" or "zombie," then, is no more than the all-too-familiar idealized image, and we feel threatened by our own desire to be that image. That these films reverse the actual cultural trend (outside appearance keeps changing while the person remains the same) underscores the indeterminacy between inner and outer identities. The popular *X-Files* series repeatedly touched on the themes of shape shifting, alien invasion through impersonating humans, and large-scale cloning that fuses alien with human genes.

Is this story of aliens who look like humans an extreme version of the as if? They look like us—but they are not. Sometimes, they are identical, and the narrative objective is to figure out how to distinguish human from nonhuman, a curious disavowal of the underlying desire for the human to become celluloid. In the case of Frankenstein's creature, however, the problem is in the failure to achieve a fully human appearance. The creature's aggressivity is unleashed as a consequence of his formal insufficiency—he's on the brink of being/looking human but not quite there, making him feel all the more painfully his status as simulacrum. The simulacra of science fiction and fantasy often long to be fully human, even when they possess superhuman powers. Frankenstein fashions his creature to be the first of a "super-race," and so the creature turns out to be; he's bigger, faster, stronger, and, most important, much more resistant to the mortal frailties of the real human bodies he envies. Data, the android from *Star Trek: The Next Generation*, despite his extraordinary intellectual and physical capacities, despite his immortality, Pinocchio-like, wants to be a real human. These stories have a purchase on us because they convert ideal qualities (strength and immortality) into failings. They aren't "real." They are just "as if." It is the insufficiency of as if that, for the creature certainly, becomes a more critical failing than his physical power is valuable. Indeed, this superhuman strength of his, once linked to a series of atrocities, becomes yet another flaw or rather another token of his criminal proclivities. It is as though the ideal ego, the invincible and superior image in the mirror, is subordinated to the ego. The ego is now what the ego ideal seeks to be. In the as if circuit of self-creation, we find a bottomless pit of idealized possibilities that force upon the ego the interminable drudgery of shape shifting. This endless cycle could potentially lead to a concurrent and seemingly endless flow of aggressivity upwelling in each miserable subordination to yet another ideal ego—an aggressivity I will address in detail in chapter 7.

The way to compensate for and correct this ongoing experience of insufficiency, then, is to create stories in which the ideal ego is in the extraordinary position of wanting to be like *us*. Data gets an emotion chip, and Frankenstein's creature wants a girlfriend. Unhappy with his reborn life, Tony Wilson ends up revisiting his former home, nostalgic for the boring middle-aged identity he forfeited. This way we can forget who is superior to whom. Amazing, isn't it, to convert our mortality and vulnerability into the prize?

THE TALENTED MR. RIPLEY AND
ALL ABOUT EVE—AS IF IDENTIFICATIONS,
FAN CULTURE, AND PERFECT SKIN

In her essay "On Identification," Melanie Klein discusses Julian Green's novel *If I Were You* as an example of what she calls projective identification. It is about a man named Fabian, who is so unhappy with his current life and envious of others that he compacts with the devil to assume the identity of anyone else he chooses. Because Fabian literally projects himself into the bodies/identities of other people through whispering a magic formula to them, I suggest that this is an extreme version of the as if personality.[20] Projective identification could be considered the psychic mechanism by which the as if makes her or his transitions from one personality to another:

> One part of Fabian literally leaves his self and enters into his victim, an event which in both parties is accompanied by strong physical sensations. . . . We should conclude therefore . . . that Fabian's memories and other aspects of his personality are left behind in the discarded Fabian who must have retained a good deal of his ego when the split occurred. This part of Fabian, lying dormant until the split-off aspects of his personality return, represents, in my view, that component of the ego which patients unconsciously feel they have retained while other parts are projected into the external world and lost. (Klein, "On Identification" 166)

Like the protagonist in any wish-based fairy tale, Fabian continues to find out that none of the people into whom he projects himself are as good as he expected. Indeed, each personality comes with significant impairments. One is a pervert, another is burdened with a sick body, while yet another turns out to be a murderer. Each time Fabian projects himself from one body into another, he carries along with him vestiges of the recently discarded ego. Nevertheless, as he is increasingly separated from his original ego, he has difficulty recalling who he "was."

What does it mean that in cosmetic surgery the "other body" into which you project yourself is your own enhanced body?[21] Surgery gives you the feeling that you aren't stuck with the body you were handed. It's an almost miraculous realization of Fabian's dream of escaping his ugly and unfortunate self—of leaving one's body behind. A common account of surgery is that there is a feature by which the patient is enormously bothered until one day she or he makes the decision to get rid of whatever it is (fat deposits, baggy eyelids, bump on the nose) forever. It's a perceived flaw that haunts the person too many hours of the day, and she or he wants the flaw to vanish along with the emotion invested in it. It seems as though the as if phenomenon can happen on the body's surface, that you can imagine a perfect body, which you project yourself into— and then your experienced "self" follows the route forged by your altered body.

"I feel young but I look old" is the chronic lament. But what does it mean to declare a mismatch between this imaginary internal clock and the shocking reflection to which you just woke up? All the surgeons tell me this is the prospective face-lift patients' frame for their surgical stories. It only seems natural to want the look to be commensurate with the feeling. Moreover, the distinction invoked between the "real person" who "feels young" and the apparent vagrancy of their appearance reiterates the cultural cliché about inner and outer beauty—but with a twist. This time the inner feeling (youth/beauty) is used to justify clobbering the outside into submission. You have a right that the "real you" be seen, recognized. It's locked in there, clamoring to get out and announce itself. Plastic surgeon James T. Nolan writes of his patients: "Most of the people I see in my office . . . see that through cosmetic surgery they can match their exterior features with the constant youthful inside vision of themselves from which they form their originality and self-esteem" (15). Why is the inside vision, as he puts it, necessarily youthful? And why might it be linked to self-esteem?

If you felt old, would you reconcile yourself to looking old? Does anyone feel old—or if we do feel old would we long to etch that feeling on the surface of our bodies? By yoking itself to the rhetoric of internal value, plastic surgery has come to seem practical, a logical and valuable change to make. You need to have a match between the internal and the external, and since the "internal" apparently takes precedence . . . None of this, of course, is true. We exploit this rhetorical trick to disguise the truth—that we cannot feel young unless we look young. That the mirror tells us exactly how we feel. That it's in the desire to feel young again that people have rejuvenating surgeries. A surgeon told me: "When they see somebody in the mirror that looks more youthful, they actually behave as if they have more energy; they go out and do things more, they participate in life more, their self-esteem is better. Sometimes when you see somebody older and tired-looking, it's a self-fulfilling prophecy; you tend to act that way too." The appearance of youth is more compelling than any internal register. To change your surface appearance and then identify with it is exactly the *as if* style of transformational identification.

In questioning a surgeon about the relationship between an inner sense of self and outer appearance, I offered as an example a case of one female patient who had had fairly radical surgery. I wondered what would motivate her to have this kind of dramatic image-changing surgery. The surgeon responded: "Well, maybe she felt like that person before, but there was a discrepancy because she didn't look the way she felt. She felt like she was a pretty woman. She had a lot of beauty within herself. But when she looked in the mirror it didn't quite correspond. A lot of women do that."

There was much that was contradictory in his response. If she "felt like she was a pretty woman," certainly she saw with her own eyes that she wasn't—or why else have surgery? She may have wanted to be pretty, but she certainly did not feel pretty. The surgeon who did her work described her as very "aesthetically tuned in." She had come to his office knowing exactly what she wanted changed. This suggests that she had objectified her body and formed her preoperative observations from a distance, as it were. She was her own canvas. The mismatch between the body and the mirror involved her internal notion of what made a pretty face. When she viewed her preoperative reflection, she imagined it "as if" it were different.

Given the radical interventions they are making in identity formation, plastic surgeons are surprisingly conventional. It's why they have so much trouble answering my questions about where identity is located—in the mind or on the body? They cling to outworn notions of the received relationship between mind and body—even though their very practice undermines them. One surgeon told me: "What happens is that the person you see in the mirror doesn't look like the person you feel like. So that's the person you want to fool. You want that person to look like what you feel like you should look like." You want to fool the person looking in the mirror, not the person you see. You want the mirrored person to match your ideal projection of yourself. Who exactly *is* "you" in this story? His language betrays him. On some level he must understand the instabilities of identity he's both causing and perceiving—although he would never admit as much, because the practice of cosmetic surgery subserves such culturally conservative ends. But in reality surgeons are participating in forging as if identifications. They carve out identities on the surface of the skin—"skin-shifters" that they are. And, sleeping beauty that *you* are, you will arise refreshed from your anesthetic slumber, the bandages will be peeled, and with them you will shed your old skin for new. You will embrace this new you in the mirror—now you see what you were looking for.

In 1967, French philosopher Guy Debord wrote a scathing indictment of what he called "the society of the spectacle." In his attack on the society's intense concern with the surface of things over meaning and content, he claimed that "appearing" has become the supervening goal. We have traded in satisfaction in "being" for the desire to "have," and now "having" itself is only a matter of "appearing to have," a lamentable state of affairs that Debord attributes to the effects of capitalism upon the structure of human identity and relations (16). This structure articulated by Debord seems especially analogous to that of the "as if personality," whose "being" derives from the various personalities she or he comes momentarily to possess. While Debord seems convinced he knows the difference between being (a valuable person?) and having (the possessions it takes to make a certain social appearance), a culture based on as if identifications seems to unhinge a fixed distinction. It is only in such a culture that plastic surgery can become so commonplace. When "appearing" suggests what one both has and is, then identity happens on the surface, and the as if personality is the culture's most adaptive form of social functioning.[22]

The two films *All about Eve* and *The Talented Mr. Ripley* both center on eerily successful as if personalities who, much like Fabian, are able to steal the identities (or at least key attributes) of people they envy. Both eponymous characters, Eve and Ripley, start out lacking any sense of what we might call a core self. Rather, they are bodies in search of role models to emulate and replace. That Eve is an aspiring actress who seeks to supplant a star underscores the link between as if identifications and celebrity culture.

In the beginning of Anthony Minghella's 1999 *Talented Mr. Ripley*, Tom Ripley is mistaken by a steel tycoon, Greenleaf, for a former Princeton classmate of his prodigal son, Dickie. Tom is no Princeton graduate but rather the men's room attendant at a concert hall. But the mistaken identity occurs precisely because identity was mutable all along in this upscale crowd, where it is no more than a series of "acquisitions," like going to Princeton or having the funds to buy expensive art. These traits, which aren't about "being" at all but rather are illustrations of the degree to which "having" confers being, suggest that the lies and deception that will be practiced by Tom throughout the film were in place and culturally naturalized long before he begins to play that game.

Believing that Tom knows his son, Dickie, the tycoon hires him to bring his son back from Italy to his family in New York. When Tom is picked up by Greenleaf's chauffeur and handed a first-class ticket on a Cunard ocean liner, the viewer has the unsettling experience of what will be the ongoing visual motif of Tom's personal shabbiness in contrast with his sumptuous environment. He wears a worn tan corduroy jacket, and later we learn that he owns only one shirt, which Dickie's girlfriend Marge, in an excruciating moment, discloses to Dickie that he washes out every night. Unfortunately, clothes make the man, as they say, and Tom will eventually be unmade by his own threadbare ones, undermining his intense identification with Dickie. The worn jacket becomes a nagging source of visual anxiety that represents Tom's insufficiency, for Tom, Dickie, Dickie's friends, and the audience that shudders along with each moment of humiliation. It is not that the telltale clothes reveal the rupture of authenticity and the limits of posing; instead, much like the Princeton jacket, they reveal that it takes so little to assume the part—just the right jacket.

These jet-setting expatriated Americans are as a group undistinguished by their own accomplishments, but they wear their privileged identities as a glowing form of celebrity. They are known as the textile heiress and the son of the steel tycoon. Moreover, the transience of American democratic forms of class privilege makes it seem like mere play acting at aristocracy, bright and alluring identities cobbled together from financial success, the right schools, address, and all-around style.

Although initially charmed by Tom, whom he turns into a kind of honorary best friend, Dickie ultimately tires of Tom's adoration. It is when Dickie is insulting Tom that Tom beats him to death. Concealing the traces of the murder, Tom assumes Dickie's identity (he can forge signatures and can pass with his passport photo) and moves to Rome. The rest of the film follows Tom's amazing success at "being" Dickie Greenleaf.

In an ironic reversal, a number of people suspect that Dickie has killed Tom and is traveling in disguise with Tom's passport. This reversal is reminiscent of Mark David Chapman's confusion over who was the "real" John Lennon. As Richard Schickel writes, he "had identified so well with his victim that he apparently became convinced that he, Chapman, was Lennon, and Lennon was an impostor, a usurper of his life" (*Intimate Strangers* 21). "I'd rather be a fake somebody than a real nobody," blurts Tom—but this film explodes in our face these very categories. Tom certainly seems to be the most "authentic" character in the film, not only because we know and identify with his emotional world, but also because "being Dickie" seems to be no more than a set of easily imitable habits. You listen to jazz, practice his signature, comb back your hair, and act self-assured, and you can "become" this man Tom idealizes. Indeed, what is surprising is not that Dickie welcomes Tom so readily but that Tom falls in love with Dickie. What is it about Dickie that is lovable, ultimately, other than the way in which his existence is deeply linked to the structure of artifice itself? It is perhaps artifice with which Tom, the story's only "authentic" character, has fallen in love. It is Tom's demand for love in return that Dickie rejects.

Joseph L. Mankiewicz's 1950 film, *All about Eve*, tells a similar story of the erotic perils of the indecision between wanting to be and wanting to have the object of identificatory desire.[23] The title character, Eve, haunts the theater where her idol, the stage actress Margo Channing, is performing. Margo, charmed by the ardor of this fan, takes her in and employs her as an assistant. But Eve doesn't just want to be near Margo—she wants to *be* Margo, which she can achieve only through supplanting her.

In both films the longing to be the idolized person is distinctly homoeroticized.[24] Analyst Eugenio Gaddini distinguishes between *rivalry* as the "imitative-perceptive model (the object as what one would like to be) and *envy* [as] the incorporating-introjective model (the object as what one would like to have)" (477). It is the combination of imitation and introjection that becomes a fully articulated identification. Because they are "as if" types, Tom and Eve keep oscillating between the positions of wanting to be (imitating) and wanting to have (ingesting); it is the wanting to have that manifests as erotic desire.[25]

Eve Harrington's fan obsession with Margo Channing is constantly redirected from its obvious lesbian trajectory to heterosexual object choices. Thus, Eve ultimately makes a pass at Margo's boyfriend—as though in having him she will thoroughly have accomplished her identification with Margo. She will *have* everything that is Margo's (her celebrity, her boyfriend, her play) in her effort to *be* Margo.

Identification in the psychoanalytic sense can mean either identifying oneself with another or another with oneself (Laplanche and Pontalis 206). "Projective identification," writes James Grotstein, "involves the desire of the infant—or the suffering adult—to become invisible, to disappear, or generally speaking, to negate one's own existence. Such phantasies of disappearing usually come at a high cost to self-esteem, the sense of authenticity, and self-connectedness" (130). The second stage is "fusion with the other," but as Grotstein insists, "it is important to remember that in projective identification there is a self left behind or disavowed" (131). Leaving behind a former identity, refusing to discuss it, or transforming it altogether, these are the strategies whereby Tom and Eve disavow their own former selves in order to assume the mantle of new and improved models. Although not nearly as extreme a repudiation of one's former self, plastic surgery is characterized by a powerful disavowal of the former feature or the "real age" of the patient, who is explicitly leaving behind a version of the self.

Dickie becomes enraged when he witnesses Tom literally trying on his identity. Dickie walks into his bedroom to find Tom dressed up in his formal attire (minus trousers) and performing in front of a mirror. Although Dickie has repeatedly offered to buy, give, or lend Tom a jacket, he is infuriated to find Tom in this situation. It is as though Dickie suddenly understands that Tom is after his skin.

Didier Anzieu calls the original of the ego a "skin ego" to account for how skin itself has a shaping effect on the psyche. Like Freud's theory of the "body ego," the skin ego underscores the formative interaction of psyche and soma. Skin is experienced as the body's container, as what differentiates bodies from each other as well as keeps their insides intact, and this experience of the skin acts as a bodily basis for the emergent ego. As Anzieu puts it: "It is a mental image of which the Ego of the child makes use during the early phases of its development to represent itself as an Ego containing psychical contents, on the basis of its experience of the surface of the body" (*Skin Ego* 40). This skin ego originates in the skin imaginatively shared by mother and child. "This common skin keeps the two bound together, but they are bound in a particular symmetrical relation which prefigures their coming separation" (62).

Anzieu describes the child's narcissistic fantasy:

> The mother does not share a common skin with her child, but gives her skin to him and he dresses himself in it triumphantly; this generous maternal gift (she divests herself of her skin to guarantee him protection and strength in life) has a beneficent potential: the child imagines he is called on to fulfill a heroic destiny (which indeed, as a result, he may). This double covering (his own joined with that of his mother) is brilliant, ideal; it provides the narcissistic personality with an illusion of invulnerability and immortality. (*Skin Ego* 124)

In this fantasy, you have not only your own skin but also the mother's skin (or whoever possesses the best, most invulnerable skin), which she imparts to you because you are special; at the same time, wearing the two skins makes you even more powerful. Consider, then, how class privilege could create the sense of a double envelope of skin that is both your own and that of someone more powerful, a skin that blankets and contains you. Tom's experience of Dickie is of someone who keeps promising his skin and withholding it, like the most malevolent of mothers described by Anzieu: "In the masochistic phantasy, the cruel mother only pretends to give her skin to the child. It is a poisoned gift, the underlying malevolent intention being to recapture the child's own Skin Ego which has become stuck to that skin, to strip it painfully from him in order to re-establish the phantasy of having a skin in common with him" (*Skin Ego* 124). This account of not only the loss of the double wall of skin you briefly imagined was all yours but the loss of your own skin

Figures 5 and 6. The skin ego of celebrity. Anne Baxter as Eve, and Barbara Bates as Phoebe, in *All about Eve*. Courtesy of Photofest.

(your own separate identity) as well perfectly describes Tom's experience of rejection by Dickie, whose beaming affection once elevated him. Dickie takes away both the self-esteem he had loaned Tom and any self-esteem Tom had to begin with. "You're a leech," Dickie sneers at Tom, shortly before Tom kills him. "You bore me." His love, the skin of specialness with which he briefly encircles Tom, is no more available than the jacket he keeps promising and withholding.[26]

Although Dickie remains unwilling to give Tom the jacket-skin of identity he craves (of being "somebody"), the film grants Tom's wish.

That Tom, a murderer, manages to win the audience to his side in his besting of these rich, self-satisfied hoarders of the culture's narcissistic goods suggests that we are invited to identify with this story on the level of the skin ego itself. Dickie, who misleads Tom into thinking he will "share" his skin, and Dickie's friend Freddie, who ridicules Tom's class skin, his bourgeois tastes, his revealing jacket ("Imagine wearing corduroy in Italy," laughs Freddie), seem to deserve filmic deaths in compensation for the psychic death they have so nonchalantly inflicted on Tom.

Eve Harrington's intense identification with Margo is also figured through a skin that she fantasizes sharing. In a central early scene that is uncannily close to a scene from *The Talented Mr. Ripley*, Eve holds up to herself Margo's stage gown and takes an imaginary bow on the empty stage where Margo recently received real applause (fig. 5). Unlike Dickie, however, Margo is only amused and flattered when she finds her new charge trying on her identity. In a motherly gesture, Margo gives Eve one of her dresses, claiming after Eve has had it altered, "It looks much better on you than on me." This is exactly Eve's thought as well, that Margo's "skin," by which I mean everything that contains Margo, from her professional life to her wardrobe, will look much better on Eve. After meeting Eve, Margo tells her boyfriend, Bill: "Suddenly, I've developed a big protective feeling toward her. A lamb loose in our big stone jungle." Margo offers Eve her home and protection as a kind of motherly skin when Eve wants more—wants Margo's skin all to herself. That Margo won't divest herself of everything—her boyfriend, her career—makes her seem selfish to Eve, just like a small child who expects utter selflessness on the part of its mother. At the end of the film, Eve, who has now outstripped her idol, has her own acolyte, Phoebe, eager to make Eve the victim of her very own style of identification and emulation. The last scene of the film shows Phoebe trying on Eve's white satin cloak and holding Eve's Best Actress award, standing amid mirrors (like yet another layer of skin) that reflect to her from all angles the idealized woman's skin along with her celebrity (fig. 6).[27]

That clothing is a kind of skin we don to declare who we are at any given period of our lives or even to mark off one social situation from another seems at once banal and the most deadly illustration of our psychosocial experience. If clothing supplements the skin ego, or is simply a socialized version of the intrapsychic reality, that is one thing; but when clothing literally contains or holds together the otherwise unbounded subject, then human beings are ever in danger of becoming outdated or falling apart. Take this a step further and consider plastic surgery as proffering a kind of body clothing that slips out of fashion so easily that the tenuousness of identity seems to hang on the surgeon's arm. And perhaps this is part of the point of surgery, to recontain the leaking self, increasingly unprotected by the right face and body.

HOLLYWOOD SKIN

In Douglas Sirk's 1959 *Imitation of Life*, the agent Loomis hangs a mink over the shoulders of aspiring theater actress, Lora Meredith. He tells her that he is never seen in the company of a girl without a mink. Mink is the skin donned by stage actresses and those who want to look like stage actresses.

Hollywood skin, as it turns out, is sable. Hollywood, in *All about Eve*, is constantly referred to by Eve and others as a form of selling out, a commercialization and trivialization of the high art of the legitimate theater. It is because you have sold your art to the highest bidder that you can afford to wear sable. It is telling that the Hollywood actress who makes a late and brief appearance at Margo's party is seen only via the proxy of her sable coat, the ultimate token of the skin ego of celebrity. When Eve enters the bedroom holding the sable coat, her best friend, Karen, demands, "Hold that coat up!" Eve raises the coat. "Whose is it?" Karen asks her. "Some Hollywood movie star. Her plane got in late." From this moment on, the fur stands for the star herself.

> KAREN: Discouraging isn't it? Women with furs like that where it never even gets cold.
>
> EVE: (with a combination of assumed disdain and barely suppressed wistfulness) Hollywood.

Of course, at the end of the film, Eve herself is on her way to Hollywood, where actresses wear the superlative skin of sable, next to which a mere mink looks, as Karen puts it, like "an old bed jacket." When the sable coat brushes by her, aspiring actress Miss Caswell (played by Marilyn Monroe!) sighs: "Now *there's* something a girl could make sacrifices for." The Hollywood career, with its glamorous lifestyle and excessive attention, is summed up by the glossy folds of sable. It's *that* skin I crave, Miss Caswell implies, the one that will give me just the right feeling of invulnerable importance. Wrap yourself up in sable and feel truly loved. The sable is a metonymy for Hollywood, where love floods in from the multitudes. Eve imagines the love of a stage audience ("It's like, like waves of love coming over the footlights and wrapping you up"), but the Hollywood version would be a thousand times more gratifying. Alexander Walker describes the difference: "As an emotional response, it was different in kind and fervour from that which greeted stage celebrities. It was close and personal, yet dissociated and mob-like. It radiated love, yet turned the loved-one into an object" (*Stardom* 47). There is simultaneously more gain and more loss with Hollywood skin. For more love there are "sacrifices" to be made.

Spike Jonze's 1999 *Being John Malkovich* gives us an extreme version of the public desire to wear celebrity skin. People pay to enter a portal in order to spend fifteen minutes literally inside the actor. If actors wear their parts, what does it mean that we want to play the part of an actor? What is the nature of the skin they offer? Becoming-celebrity in this instance is the culmination of one's narcissism. When Malkovich enters his own "portal," he finds himself reduplicated everywhere, as though to exemplify the actor's narcissistic trajectory, which is necessarily a collapse back into the same—actor.

A casual glance at recent advertisements will show what selling power star skin has. Estée Lauder's "skin tone perfector" (a whole new class of cosmetic that is not foundation and not moisturizer) is called Spotlight. One advertisement shows Elizabeth Hurley outside what is supposed to be the marquis of a theater. Predictably, all eyes are fixed on this shining central figure, who raises one white hand to her pearlescent white face as though to touch the beauty of the image perfected as pure light— the spotlight itself. You are urged to buy this product and "show off your skin." No longer satisfied with just plain skin, we want to display it— to invite the admiring looks of the multitudes all turned on us as we radiate our star qualities. Avon's "brightening complex" is Luminosity, and it promises "a face that brightens a room," yet another ad offering the ordinary woman a miraculous transformation into "star"-light. Lancôme now has its own version, called Photogênic. I own something from Benefit called High Beam, which claims to be "for the starlet in you," because it "adds a soft gleam to the complexion." I have to wonder what I was thinking when I purchased such a product—why would I want my skin to gleam, and what would I do (moreover, what would people think?) if I *did* gleam? This is not a natural, dewy glow the cosmetics companies are holding out to us but rather a decidedly artificial actress-in-the-spotlight skin that we can squeeze out of a tube and make our very own, wrap ourselves up in a new alluring celebrity skin. The sales representative at my local Prescriptives counter explained to me what makes their line of "Magic" products so special: some of the formulas are adapted from those of screen makeup. Prescriptives has a line filler product modeled on the wax filler actresses use. She added: "The difference is that the wax strips get hard and fall out. We've found a way of keeping the look without the wax hardening." More recently, the makeup artist associated with "the natural look," Bobbi Brown, has joined other makeup companies in the renewed interest in looking celebrity. As her product packaging reads: "What Bobbi Brown did for the natural look with her Essentials Collection, she's now doing for color with her highly anticipated Coloroptions—an innovative color collection inspired by the dramatic looks created backstage in the theater."

Women's makeup has a long history of deriving from the formulas and practices of theater and film makeup. Because images of film actors' faces were more widely publicized than those of stage actors, their "look" had a powerful cultural effect on the female audience. In her book on the evolution of the American cosmetics industry and beauty practices, Kathy Peiss documents the crossover makeup (from screen to street) that used its screen heritage as an advertising pitch.

Max Factor—makeup artist to the stars—particularly exploited the movie tie-in. All advertisements prominently featured screen stars, their testimonials secured in an arrangement with the major studios that required them to endorse Max Factor. . . . Company representatives draped the glamorous image of the movies around their products. At movie matinees, they set up stands in theater lobbies, made up women on-stage, raffled cosmetic kits, and distributed complexion analysis cards with the names of local drugstores. (126)

Factor's "Pan-Cake" brand foundation was a product borrowed directly from film and stage makeup—as though to cement the fantasied assumption of the film star's camera-ready skin. Jackie Stacey points to the Lux Toilet Soap advertisement to illustrate the way in which identificatory relations with film stars influenced habits of consumption, especially among women. In 1955, Lux hired Susan Hayward for its ad campaign: "9 out of 10 film stars use pure, white Lux Toilet Soap," pointing out that "however much Susan may change character, one thing remains familiar: that fabulous *complexion*" (Stacey 4). Here the advertisement invokes simultaneously the star's changeability, from role to role, and the star's "star" substance, her movie-star appearance, literally, her skin.[28] While traditional foundation might seem "fake" to some, it clearly represents movie-star skin for the women who wear it. Ordinary women trying to "even out" skin tone and correct other visible flaws on the skin with foundation and concealers are imitating as nearly as possible the tricks of lighting and film makeup. We thus become objects of the filmic apparatus.

Ironically, concurrent with *Ripley*'s release was an *In Style* column showing us how to "steal" Gwyneth Paltrow's "look" from *The Talented Mr. Ripley*. The makeup artist, we learn, "gave Paltrow matte color for her character's excursions to Venice and Rome, using MAC Spice lip pencil and Max Factor Lasting Color lipstick in Rosewood" ("Steal This Look" 124).[29] Throughout the century, though, star identities have been attached to consumer products of all sorts, which suggests both the stars' entanglement in the workings of consumer capitalism and our desire to be/have the stars as an effect of our consumer identities. Within their films, actors were shown beside appliances that would then be used as oversized cardboard cutouts advertising the product.[30] Of course, there is a big difference between wanting to own a Maytag and wanting to dress like Gwyneth Paltrow, but somehow the star's image forms a link between the two consuming desires.

TRANSFORMATIONAL BODIES

Not only are we increasingly familiar with the surgical transformations of actors; it is as though the film screen justifies these transformations or renders them at once permissible and inevitable through its functioning as a site of transformation. Both the television screen in our homes and the movie screen, which can "become" whatever is projected onto it, are socially sanctioned sites of transformation, metonymically linked to the actors who perform within their frames. Television images hurtle from one to another, cutting between ice cream or battery or automobile commercials and upcoming scenes from a steamy-looking "thriller"—all vying with each other for my attention as I watch the television unfold yet constrain them behind its implacable screen. The very experience of viewing proves transformative for the viewer. We are transported into another sphere. We rise above our daily worries, our personal stories. In the relationship with the screen, the viewer is caught up in the process of limitless change and transformation.

To live in a culture of ubiquitous identification with celebrities means that the shape-shifting images of celebrities can have a profound and transforming effect on noncelebrities. A group of celebrities are well known for their surgical shape shifting—Cher, for example, who is widely criticized for having gone "too far," whatever that means. Figures 7, 8, and 9 show respectively 1995, 1996, and 2001 versions of Melanie Griffith in Revlon's "Defy Your Age" campaign. She looks like three different women in these ads. Most obviously, her mouth has been plumped up by the 1996 version, but there are other changes as well, though not as easy to isolate. I have shown these images to several plastic surgeons, and they disagree about whether Griffith has undergone

Figures 7, 8, and 9. Melanie Griffith for Revlon's ad campaign, in 1995 (fig. 7), 1996 (fig. 8), and 2001, with Halle Berry (fig. 9).

surgical alteration to her facial contours or whether, instead, the images are airbrushed. Regardless of what the actress has done (or not done) in the service of "defying her age," what might be the effect of these noticeable visual transformations upon female consumers?

When we identify with film stars, we identify at the level of the transformation itself. "The postsurgical Dolly Parton," writes M. G. Lord, "looks like the postsurgical Ivana Trump looks like the postsurgical Michael Jackson looks like the postsurgical Joan Rivers looks like . . . Barbie" (244). This shape shifting of the movie stars—from role to role, from body to body—is essential to their lure. They are the preeminent cultural icons, perhaps *because* they make two-dimensionality stand in for three. The surgical celebrity is simply an extreme version of what movie stars always are for us anyway. As I discuss in the following chapter, such identifications with stars and star bodies have destructive consequences as well.

W. Earle Matory, Jr., believes that the evident use of plastic surgery by black entertainers is the reason for the enormous increase in African Americans requesting cosmetic surgery (195). Of course, Michael Jackson instantly springs to mind when we think of black entertainers with high-visibility plastic surgery. And although we could read Jackson as an extreme example of a shape shifter who is unlikely to inspire emulation, what I find unsettling about him is the way in which he throws into relief "as if" patterns of the culture in general—both black and white.[31] Racial difference in Jackson's hands has become just another project for medical ingenuity—like, say, a port wine stain or oversized thighs. Although some characterize Jackson's multiple surgeries as a caricature of the phenomenon of racial passing through surgical intervention, it seems clear that Jackson is doing no such thing. First, while he may be turning himself whiter, he's not passing in any conventional sense, because not only do we know he's black (and he's certainly black-identified), but also we've followed his whole career of physical transformation. Moreover, it is Jackson's corporeal career that suggests no one *is* passing any longer and that the surgeries signal surgery as much as they do con-

ventional beauty. Jackson himself is surely the product of a very particular surgical aesthetic. Racial traits, then, are no longer what you hide
or reveal; rather, you keep them or go get them "fixed." While on the
one hand it appears that whiteness has successfully colonized the entire
physical landscape, on the other, whiteness as an identity is in danger of
disappearing altogether—now that it's just a another surgical outcome.

WHAT IF

"What if," pondered a gentle music-framed female voice on my car ra-
dio, "what if I had cosmetic surgery? Do you ever wonder 'what if'?" If
you do, you should make an appointment with this cosmetic surgeon.
"He will probably tell you that you don't need anything done—but just
in case . . . don't you want to know the answer to 'what if'?"

One way to find out what would happen *if* you change your face is
to have yourself morphed through video-imaging technology, which
first became popular in the late 1980s.[32] "Clinical video imaging is best
used by creating a standard frontal and lateral patient image. The physician and patient then discuss the reconstructive options during software
modification to forecast a desirable surgical plan. The preoperative and
modified images are then loaded, side-by-side, for comparison" (Mattison 387). Alterations are "drawn" on the photographed face with a stylus and pad by means of a software paint program. Right then and there
you can see the answer to "what if." Instead of picturing your postoperative result through other faces (examples from the surgeon's previous
work), you can see yourself immediately—as if you were another. Nor
are hand drawings satisfactory, because it remains "difficult for most patients to imagine what they might look like postoperatively" (Thomas
et al., "Analysis of Patient Response" 793). I suspect people growing
up in the context of late-twentieth- and twenty-first-century technology don't find hand drawings adequately representational. Where better
to fulfill the destiny of transformational identifications with celebrities
than through a video-imaging process that uses a stylus in place of a

scalpel? Is the surgery the cause or the effect of this fantasy whereby one collapses into the very screen image with whom one identified in the first place?

Unsurprisingly, video imaging is a sensational marketing tool. As one writer claims, patient confidence in the surgeon is enhanced; even better, many want additional procedures after viewing their projected computerized transformation.[33] The face can begin to seem like an ever-transformable canvas. I attended the "Seminar on Facial Plastic Surgery," run by an otolaryngologist affiliated with my university. Not only did the presentation covertly encourage multiple procedures at once (offering discounts), but afterward the audience was invited to go upstairs and see how they would look with computer-generated alterations.[34] A small cluster of people enthusiastically waited in line, excited by the possibilities of what the computer could do for their faces. They expressed no doubts about the ability of the surgeon who had access to such amazing technology. And this is my point—their confidence in the surgeon is increased by their investment in the video-imaging technology. As far as patients are concerned, the projected image *is* the postoperative result; the face is airbrushed into beauty. When we are coaxed into identifications with airbrushed, digitized, two-dimensional screen images (from print to television to film), we are identifying on the level of the technology itself. The "end result" pictured optimistically on the video screen turns you into the very two-dimensional image that was always at the other end of your cosmetic-surgery dreams.

More than the surgeon's personal expertise, they are trusting his prosthetic link to technological transformation whereby he can convert flesh into image. No blood, no sliced skin, just software. The performance artist Orlan, who has staged a series of "live" plastic surgery operations in her effort to assume the features of eight famous paintings ("She will fuse into one facial image the chin of Botticelli's *Venus*, the nose of Gerôme's *Psyche*, a Fontainbleau Diana's eyes, the lips of Gustave Moreau's *Europa*, and the brow of Leonardo's *Mona Lisa*" [Wilson et al. 13]), entitled one of her performances *Ceci est mon corps . . . Ceci est mon logiciel . . .*

This is my body . . . This is my software. In her computer-generated projection of the composite finished project, we see that she has elided the difference between the digital and the flesh.

But such elisions can have awkward consequences. Many patients have felt that they were misled by the "perfect" images on the computer screen when their flesh-and-blood faces don't exactly match. In fact, Mattison's excessive enthusiasm for this technology allows him to imagine that the actual postoperative result on one young woman was "close to" the preoperative video image. Let's just say that the patient may have felt (justifiably) let down. Most of the surgeons I interviewed won't use this technology or do so only rarely because of exactly this problem with patient expectations. As Gorney reports, after several lawsuits, surgeons were advised to have patients sign carefully worded disclaimers. But the disclaimers can only minimally, if at all, diminish the expectations projected onto the fantasy image on the screen—you with the "perfect" nose or your chin realigned or all the bags and folds beneath your chin miraculously waved away. A surgical nurse told me that often patients absolutely cannot grasp the limitations of their individual bodies or surgical technique. Thus, they expect surgery to make them look magazine-perfect—even though, as the nurse observed, such photos are all digitally retouched to the extent that no real body could measure up. Video imaging conspires with patient fantasies of being able to transcend both corporeal and technical barriers. The Adobe Photoshop wand breezes across your nose, through the tenacity of cartilage and bone, and presto, there's Jodie Foster's nose conjured right in the middle of your face—magic. Repeatedly, surgeons complained to me about the expectations of patients accustomed to these airbrushed images.[35] Yet, I try to point out to them that the widespread demand for cosmetic surgery is very much dependent on these transformational identifications.

While most surgeons conceded to me that they couldn't utterly transform someone ("you can't make an ugly woman beautiful," I heard perhaps too many times), several surgeons did make surgery sound close to miraculous. One surgeon sang the praises of the lower body suspension surgery developed by Ted Lockwood. As he put it: "Happy is a tummy suction or tummy tuck; ecstatic are these body changes. Ecstatic. Ecstatic is when you can get into a size six and you've been a twelve all your life. I'm sitting here doing these procedures, and I'm thinking to myself, this didn't happen. You can't get these bodies this good." I complained that the extensiveness of the scars seemed to outweigh the benefits of contour: "They look like they've been cut in half and sewn back together." "I know," the surgeon replied, "but the body looks fabulous!" Which body was he talking about? Moreover, he pointed out that "99.6% of your adult waking life is in clothes; 99.9% of your ego trip and your body image is in clothes." He insisted that the husbands of his female patients are ecstatic with the results as well and have had no complaints about scars that eventually turn white. And besides, what is the big deal when "the trade-off here is basically for a woman to have a fabulous body and wear lovely clothes, which make a big difference to that aging body? It's a zero trade-off. They're a little bit beyond in-the-backseat-of-Chevrolet dating and worrying about somebody finding the scar around their tummy."

But, of course, it is a trade-off nevertheless, as the surgeon could not help but reveal, no matter how enthusiastically he extolled the radically transformative qualities of this surgery. What is strikingly illustrated in his description, moreover, is that this particular surgical body is made for clothing, not for parked Chevrolets. It is not about sexual encounter any longer—it's about making a certain kind of appearance in the world. It is at the level of this "image" that one can appear to be miraculously transformed through lower body suspension surgery. This surgery, whereby you pretty much lift up and tighten everything from the lower thigh to the waist, certainly provides an impressive change in the body's contours. Although I found the "after" pictures a bit horrifying because of the scars, I also recognized that the women would look markedly different in everything from bathing suits to blue jeans. In fact, the scars are especially tailored to be hidden by a bathing suit or bikini underwear. The scars, then, are simply the residue of the "real, old" body dis-

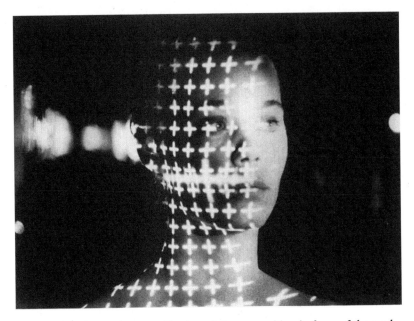

Figures 10 and 11.   A scanned body and the scanned head of one of the models, played by Susan Dey, in *Looker*. Courtesy of Photofest.

guised and improved by surgery. For surgeons to minimize the scars is to minimize the very body to which they point; oh yes, sure, there are scars, but that's only a concern when you're naked. The displayed body, the body-in-the-world, the two-dimensional transformational body, is what counts.

The 1981 film *Looker* suggests that a culture driven by the perfectibility of the image may find even surgically corrected bodies insufficient—in the end flawed by their intransigent materiality. In this film, the most recent incarnation of the mad scientist, the advertising mogul, has created a method for computer-generating perfect bodies. As his partner explains to the protagonist, himself a plastic surgeon who has been unwittingly servicing this company:[36] "We intended to create a group of actors with the exact specifications for visual impact. This is Lisa before surgery, scoring 92.7. After surgery, she scores 99.4, which is the video score registration limit. So she's perfect. But when she starts to move, her score drops back to 92.9. That was our problem. The girls couldn't maintain their scores. They looked perfect, but they weren't really perfect." Like Frankenstein's creature, once they are alive, they fall short of the perfection that resides in the image. It is not simply two-dimensionality, then, that is the mode of perfection—it is a static two-dimensionality. The company murders the models after they have been scanned into the computer.[37] There can be no competition between the body and its image.

The scanning process in *Looker*, where the "real" body is read into the computer, its measurements captured for all time, is very similar to a "facial analysis" machine that also creates three-dimensional grids (see figs. 10 and 11). "With the development of relatively inexpensive three-dimensional digitalizers, a new approach to facial analysis is possible. We are using a digitalizer and microcomputer to make both standard cephalometric measurements and create a graphic representation of the facial structure" (Larrabee et al. 1274). Such imaging can be used for the purposes of imposing on the photographed face a precise grid of the "correct," (universally) "most harmonious" facial proportions. This allows the surgeon to assess, in relation to the superimposed coordinates of perfection, just how out of line our faces are. "The system proposed herein provides a more rapid evaluation of selected criteria and allows for immediate feedback on proposed facial changes" (Papel and Park 1456). In case you don't already know, the video machine will reveal your inharmonious "lateral view," the oversized "alar region," all your rough angles. But what happens to our real bodies once we've been scanned?

In *Looker*, looking is as passive as being looked at. This is precisely the paradox Lacan indicates in the mirror phase. The infant's seduction by its mirror image leads to a lifetime of subjection to the image, its lure, its *attraction*. The term "looker" itself underscores the paradox. The "looker" is the beautiful woman—not the real looker, the one who looks at her. This paradox suggests that the look comes from all sides. You who look in the mirror are looked back at—from the place of identification. "You never look at me from the place from which I see you," writes Lacan as he considers the inevitably unsatisfactory nature of love (*Four Fundamental Concepts* 103). He is talking about the failure of the primary caregiver's gaze to merge with the child's own self-image. In psychoanalytic terms, once the child can see the mother, she is lost—and so is the child. This is the dawning of separation, isolation, the fall into a body—mortality. The look happens only when there is an object to be looked at as well as a subject who is seen; their looks span and insist upon the distance between the two. Everyone will be a "looker"—thereby marking (just as we try to eliminate) the insuperable separation. Moreover, the very beauty of highly artificial and impossible images experienced as two-dimensional lures may indeed represent *how essentially captivating the image itself is.* In identifying with two-dimensional bodies (which is the invitation implicit in celebrity culture), we simultaneously experience seeing and being seen. We are subject and object of the gaze, which is the ultimate achievement of the narcissistic subject.[38]

The image may hold up to you your defects, but at the same time it restores what you lost. It completes you. It may tear you apart, but then it promises to put you back together. The transformations of the image make it seem as though it is always heading toward increasing perfection, and it sweeps you along, to the degree that you identify with this image, closer than ever before to that prelapsarian state. It will heal the rupture. You will be cut to be made whole. You will change to go back. Your measurements, even when you move, will be perfect—no shattering of the form in the field of visual desire. The camera itself becomes the place of coherence—it pieces us back together, edits us, makes us beautiful, reshapes us, defends against all loss, allows us to look at ourselves from the place from which we see the other, collapses the distance between lookers.

SIX

The Monster
and the Movie Star

"Can I drop off my face with you and pick it up later?"
A woman to her plastic surgeon (interview)

BEFORE AND AFTER—HOLLYWOOD STYLE

By way of celebrating Oscar's seventieth birthday in 1998, we were
treated to "Oscar's family album." This was a collection of former Academy Award winners packed on stage to have their Oscar turns recited.
Never before had I beheld such a density of surgically altered faces in a
single place. As the names of actresses such as Lee Grant, Ellen Burstyn,
Shirley Temple, and Cloris Leachman were announced, I was unsettled
by the radical difference between their current incarnations and clips
from their award-winning appearances that hovered around them like
ghosts from someone else's life. Of course, it was not the aging process
that had so dramatically reconfigured facial contours, had widened
cheekbones and emboldened chins. It was not time that had cast a shell-
like gloss to their skin.

So why was I unsettled, especially when Hollywood face-lifts are
hardly rare, and the Academy Awards ceremony is typically where I see

188

a lot of them crowded into one auditorium? Perhaps it was because there was such an enormous difference between what they looked like now and how I remembered them, a difference heavily underscored by the film clips—and perhaps because of the sheer number of surgically altered faces that year along with the difficulty I had in sorting out who was who—that made me feel there was something almost allegorical about the superabundance of these Hollywood-style overdone surgeries of aging celebrities.

Why is it, I wondered, that Hollywood tolerates no natural course of "after" for its story of woman's youth and beauty? No, for Hollywood, "after" always has to be more beautiful and glamorous, not less. For a celebrity, aging seems like some tragic illness instead of the most predictable after of all. Given their iconic status as young and beautiful, it's no surprise that celebrities become slaves to camera angles, good lighting, cosmetic surgery. But what about the rest of us who must watch them restage the story of compulsive beauty?

The before and after pattern of the ugly duckling transformed into the gorgeous center of attention is a favorite Hollywood story that saturates female culture; in part, it teaches us that beauty is the inevitable "right end." Barbra Streisand's 1996 film, *The Mirror Has Two Faces*, crystallizes the contradictory impulses that shape Hollywood's style of before and after beauty. Here's the film in brief: Smart, funny, likable, but dowdy Columbia University English professor Rose lives with her once-gorgeous mother, who continues to nag her about her looks as she stokes her own fading beauty. Handsome Columbia University math professor Gregory, who too easily succumbs to the wiles of pretty women, decides to find a mate to whom he is *not* physically attracted. On the basis of his physical indifference and their personal compatibility, he and Rose marry and live platonically until it's all too much for Rose to be rejected physically. Just as he is beginning to fall in love with her "inner self," he goes off for a European lecture tour while Rose spends the summer losing weight, getting her hair dyed blonde, and (I think) having pedicures. Her newfound great looks turn not only the head of her own husband but her sister's husband as well. To make Streisand's level of self-adoration as clear as possible, let me describe one post-transformation scene. She goes to teach her literature class dressed in a form-fitting black power-vixen suit with plunging neckline, along with black high heels and black stockings. Her male students are visibly overwhelmed and stare glassy-eyed and entranced. One licks his lips. "What? *What?*" she asks them. "Yes," she registers rapidly, "I have breasts." Suffice it to say that the film's goal is for everyone in sight to recognize Barbra for the sex goddess she is.[1] Her overweight former friend-in-dowdiness, played by Brenda Vacarro, feels betrayed by Rose's astonishing transformation.

As well she might. And not just by the false and ultimately overturned dichotomy between internal and external value. It is not the act of surgery that is disturbing or the desperation to continually display something beautiful of their "reality" to the public. It is the large-scale reversal of calling real what is retouched and recasting as fiction what is plain or homely or downright ugly. When Meryl Streep plays Karen Silkwood, certainly not a Hollywood-attractive person, that is fiction. When Meryl Streep accepts the award for that performance, that is the real and beautiful Meryl Streep triumphing over the representation of dismal real life. These are the "after" stories endemic to Hollywood itself.

Somehow, Rose's willingness to be plainly, naturally brunette is read as suppressing her true beauty, which can emerge only with a hairdresser's application of peroxide. Her unmade-up self is read as the concealment of her authentic *surface* beauty that nevertheless has to be *applied* to the surface—as though there is more than one surface to Rose. So, is the "real" Barbra the retiring, modest university professor, or is she the exhibitionistic cynosure of every handsome man? (See fig. 12.) And if the retiring modest version gets to have her vanity and choke on it at the same time—how might that double-edged and two-faced agenda play out in the self-images of the women in the audience, who learn that in order to be our true selves we need a makeover? Interestingly, the

Figure 12.   Two-faced Rose (played by Barbra Streisand), before and after, in *The Mirror Has Two Faces.* Courtesy of Photofest.

mother character assumes the burden of Barbra's shamelessly disavowed vanity. By having Lauren Bacall rhapsodize at length on the joys of being pretty, we are urged to ignore the objective of the entire film—to find Barbra herself heart-throbbingly stunning. And who is her performance for? Women? If so, what are we supposed to learn from her story? Surely not that we can find happiness through weight loss and a bottle of peroxide. Or can we?

According to the makeover story of modern female culture, the after is always construed as the real you that was just itching to assert her identity, to reveal her real face. After enough of these stories, however, not only is there no difference between character and appearance; the story of inner value collapses into yet another story of the surface. This before and after Hollywood effect plays out in countless ways. Think of pretty actresses praised for gaining weight for a part (Minnie Driver for *Circle of Friends*, Toni Collette for *Muriel's Wedding*) or even for losing weight (Julianne Moore for *Safe*), or real-life beauties who play homely women (Ellen Barkin in *Diner*). If they aren't well known to begin with, the public display of their "real" beauty makes one feel all too painfully that plainness is a state that should only be performed, never lived. Conversely, in viewing actresses who are playing "average" but are known to be great beauties, we cannot forget that it is Farrah Fawcett as the desperate housewife in *The Burning Bed* or Sharon Stone who is eager to be filmed without makeup in *Last Dance* if only to prove that she can *do* plain in between her star turns at gala events swathed in Armani. Regardless, the great beauty's beautiful image poignantly haunts her representation of ordinary-looking.

In a movie that repeatedly informed me that media images torture us with false images of love and passion and beauty, I eventually learned that those images are fine as long as they're the "real" thing. In response to her brother-in-law's claims that he must have loved her all along, sharp-witted Rose retorts: "So now you want who I am because I'm not who I was anymore?" We are supposed to understand her as chastising him for mistaking his infatuation with the "outside" for the "inside." But in fact, the whole movie teaches us, the audience, that the route to love and happiness is through becoming someone else—if only your own after picture.

And how are we to respond to the fact that it was a fifty-something-year-old Streisand playing fortyish Rose? Where do we locate "before," and what comes "after" in movies where chronological age is invisible and actresses wind up looking ten years younger than they did in movies they made ten years earlier? When the look of youth is preferable to age, then after must always of necessity look like it's before, and before is always the body's failure to achieve the perfection of after—whether through a director's stockpile of angles and lighting or a good surgeon.

When Barbra Streisand, Hollywood's ultimate makeover story in the flesh, reinforces the requirement of an after-life of good looks for women, she is telling us that the only acceptable mode for homely is to make sure it comes before. To cast plain or average as an early version of the self-in-progress is to cast imperfect bodies as so many underachievers.

Why can't we all transform in similar ways? Given so many fictional episodes of beauty risen from the ashes of homeliness, we might start thinking that it's our duty to our own identity to confirm it through some bold ritual—say, cosmetic surgery. These cosmetic surgery rites performed by almost every actress we see (later if not sooner) confirms the larger cultural investment in an after-life, which Hollywood both reflects and exacerbates.

The story of beauty after plainness is the Hollywood story par excellence, the story of the image transcending the body's frail lapses into weight or age or ugliness or just being caught in bad lighting. The resistance to an unretouched "after" is exactly what I glimpsed on the poly-surgical faces of Oscar's family album.

I see them again, spread out before me, as their names are announced, one after another, some with jawlines strangely lopsided, some with silastic implants to replump facial contours that had lost the roundness of youth, others with distended lips or staring eyes. So much bad, over-done surgery, as though they had urged their surgeons to efface the slightest droop or line, desperate to restore the face utterly to its original pristine screen condition. This is what is so frightening about them—the parody of the camera's generosity, beauty's "after" hardening onto their faces for all time.

BEFORE AND AFTER PICTURES—
METAMORPHOSIS

Oscar night is the palpitating, career-making or -trashing unveiling of Hollywood surgeons' most treasured after shots. "When the biggest stars on the planet gathered recently for that annual rite of teary acceptance speeches and over-the-top gowns known as the Oscars, the rapt TV audience included every plastic surgeon worth his scalpel from Manhattan to Beverly Hills" (Davis and Davis).

And why not? With their carefully crafted handiwork dazzling more than a billion people worldwide, the doctors consider the Academy Awards their big night too. Actors flutter out in their Vera Wang gowns and their Zarem or Kamer or Markowitz faces. The next day, Los Angeles is abuzz with who's done what to whom. But sometimes the stars, well, they are precipitous—they reveal themselves too soon—and are blasted by the press.

So often, in their efforts to stay the same or look better, they stop looking like "themselves," for lack of any other term. Yet, as celebrities increasingly sue for the misuse of their images, they seem to be relying on an identification between their flesh-and-blood bodies and their images. Tracing the relationship between the body and the soul in photography, Marina Warner writes: "The establishment of the photograph as a relic, a material trace of the body in the image, this new twist to the old myth that the camera steals the soul, has inspired various legal moves, on the part of the subjects, to control the terms on which a photograph may be taken. Some people are beginning to charge for their image, so that they are in a greater position of power in the transaction" (57).[2] Postsurgery, which image is theirs? How can we tell? When they intentionally distance themselves from their own trademark looks, do they now own new body images?

The metamorphosis of the movie star is a story that stars tell both in their films and on their bodies. Suggestively, *The Mirror Has Two Faces* was originally intended to have plastic surgery (not diet and hair dye) transform dowdy Rose into a glamour-puss. Barbra, however, insisted that her real body wouldn't go under the knife; rather, she would be digitally altered (Kron, *Lift*). Even though the plastic surgery was scuttled as too far-fetched (and too much like the novel *The Life and Loves of a She-Devil*, perhaps?), surgery is nevertheless implicit in Rose's story of beauty reborn.

The earliest film narratives tell very similar metamorphic stories, specifically of "plain" unloved wives who miraculously recover spousal love
through beautification. Cecil B. De Mille frequently drew on this plot
for his silent films. Stuart and Elizabeth Ewen write, "In the De Mille
formula, the key to modern marriage lay in the ability of women to
maintain a sexually attractive appearance" (68).[3] Plots routinely focus on
the wife's needing to transform herself (through numerous purchases,
of course) into a desirable object in order to save her marriage. As the
Ewens assert, this kind of film "emphasized that the metamorphosis of
the female self was the new condition for securing the means of survival
in modern society—getting and keeping a husband" (70). In his 1920
film *Why Change Your Wife?* the upper-class, uptight, and dowdy wife
(she overhears a woman claim she dresses more like her husband's "aunt"
than his wife) is exchanged for a seductive playmate-style model, whom
the husband meets, tellingly, while shopping for a negligee for his wife.
Later, the wife transforms herself during a shopping trip makeover—in
the same store where her husband met the model. Appraising herself in
the mirror, the wife becomes a "model" in order to supplant the model
who supplanted her—a veritable *mise en abyme* of imitation and transformation.[4] Since transformation was already central to a culture for
which upward mobility was the crowning achievement, it was inevitable that what career and financial opportunity were for men appearance became for women, whose "marketplace" was connubial. Cosmetic
and diet makeovers are one thing, however; surgery is on an entirely
different plane. I will suggest that it's through turning the success story
into an "after picture" that cosmetic surgery lays claim to the social
imaginary.

People are always astonished to find out how many women with relatively low incomes have plastic surgery. Often they are women in lower
white-collar administrative positions or pink-collar workers or newly divorced and hoping to find jobs. Because many surgeries are performed
by nonspecialists, such as gynecologists, who may have taken a weekend
seminar on liposuction or breast augmentation or tummy tucks, there

are surgical prices to meet a range of incomes.[5] In the world of the health management organization, cosmetic surgery remains the one arena where patients pay out of pocket. Many pay by a major credit card or by credit cards offered by the surgical facility for the express purpose of funding these surgeries. The story of upward mobility through bodily transformation has a purchase on many people who aren't members of the privileged classes. Similarly, studies on plastic surgery among racial and ethnic minorities indicate that people who don't look "mainstream" white in a white supremacist culture seize on facial transformation as a route toward the culture's multiple options. These are the cultural after pictures necessary for success—and increasingly we are encouraged to work from the outside in.

Transformative surgery can make us feel as though our bodies have become after pictures that we want to pass around like pictures from a summer's holiday. A thirty-four-year-old patient finally had her congenital lip deformity corrected. The surgery made a significant difference in her appearance. "A few weeks after her operation, Mrs. Benchley went back to her home town to show the results of her operation to her family and neighbors" (MacGregor et al. 36). People who had once been cruel and shunned her now invited her into their homes, but she proudly refused. She thought they should have recognized her internal value all along. Nevertheless her trip home was expressly for the purpose of showing off this new and improved self. "Mrs. Benchley seemed very satisfied . . . with her trip back to her home town, where she had been able to exhibit herself and walk along the streets 'no longer handicapped but normal like other people'" (36).

The patients of surgeon Daniel Man are thrilled to be featured in his book, where they display their before and after bodies alongside their stories of miraculous improvement. One seventy-two-year-old face-lift patient reports how she and her husband of fifty-three years first fell in love while dancing in a shoe store. "We've been dancing ever since. . . . Dancing keeps us young. . . . I stayed active and felt young. What I felt inside didn't match the outside. So I had the facelift" (Man and Shelkofsky 51). Sylvia smiles delightedly at us, as though to signify her pleasure over her success story. There is something so captivating about seventy-two-year-olds telling the story of becoming "better" despite what seemed like inevitable old age and decline. A forty-eight-year-old patient of Man's is so thrilled with her new look that she assures us, "I plan on maintaining my face and body so I can keep getting better and better" (55). But she won't get better and better. She will just keep making interventions in what is getting, from the surgical standpoint, worse. Margaret Morganroth Gullette characterizes the way in which the ideal of progress intersects with conventional developmental narratives: "We have all been taught from childhood on through everyday practices and celebratory occasions that we relinquish a past self only to come into a same-but-better one" (50). What a shock for us, then, points out Gullette, when we encounter the reverse cultural story of middle age as decline. Plastic surgery is a way of reconciling these two counternarratives of a future that is either "better" or "worse." Indeed, transformational bodily practices have the magical ability to reassure us of the infallible superiority of after. Before and after photography tricks us into believing in the ever-looming horizon of this "better," because no matter what we were *before* "before," the surgical narrative is always optimistic.

AFTER PICTURES

The after picture is a vexed issue among plastic surgeons, who argue over discrepancies in lighting and angles between the before and after shots. Typically, freshly made-up glowing faces after surgery replace sullen preoperative faces that could easily pass for police mug shots. Moreover, as everyone knows, most surgeons select only their best work to publish or show to prospective patients. The lack of rigor around these photographs, complained one surgeon who serves as a referee for a major journal, can render them useless as informational resources. "A big laugh goes up if they've got a dark before picture, and all the other pictures are all lit up, and she's got makeup on, and she looks good." Furthermore, to show your best after pictures to the prospective patient is to risk an unhappy patient in the end. One surgeon said he likes to show a range. Many surgeons have told me they no longer show photographs at all, because they think it's misleading; everyone is different, and we bring different raw material to the table. Meanwhile, patients carry in photographs of actresses and models and point to the desired features, which are themselves often surgically produced. These have become the after pictures for the culture. There is a history to our investment in the photograph of the surgical makeover.

Photography, with its claims to reality, became over the course of the nineteenth century the preeminent form of evidence for criminals, the mentally deranged, and ethnic and racial "types." It was supposed to reveal what one really looked like, without benefit of the imaginative flourishes of the paintbrush. The development of photographic portraiture little by little transformed the body into a potential after picture of itself. Alan Trachtenberg describes the initial difficulties of training bodies to pose to their aesthetic advantage: "The look was all-important, and what to do with the eyes, the key problem. To avoid the blankness of expression, or the pained scowl of a direct, frontal look into the camera, the Frenchman Lerebours advised photographers to have their sitters gaze '*vaguely* at a distant object'" (26).[6] Because photographic portraiture was initially very expensive, having oneself photographed represented one's socioeconomic arrival, and then the elements of the photograph were arranged to display one's class achievements. "What they wanted was a portrait which would display all their newly acquired refinement and dignity and also the status they occupied in the social hierarchy" (Starl 42). The early photographic portrait, then, in contrast to portrait painting, was instantly adopted as a sort of "after" picture of class accomplishment, intended to represent how far one had progressed from one's roots.[7] As photographic portraiture rapidly became accessible to newly ascendant middle classes (portrait painting had for centuries been the preserve of the aristocracy), one could argue for a democratization of the image, what John Tagg has termed a felt "democratic right" of those who wanted to possess and circulate their own images (37).

By the 1890s, photography was becoming the ideal means for plastic surgeons to display their results. In 1891, John Orlando Roe used before and after photographs to illustrate the removal of the dorsal hump from a nose (Wallace 26). In the late nineteenth century, Joseph L. Goodale also extensively used photographs of his rhinoplasties to keep a visual record (Wallace 27). Both scientific and aesthetic, the after photograph would provide evidence of what the consequences might be of any given technique at the same time that it would ultimately become an advertising tool. Henry J. Schireson described his use of photography to measure the amount of correction needed on the preoperative face:

> The method of measuring a face begins with the taking of a photograph. . . . This photograph is then overlaid with squared transparent paper.
>
> The lengths of forehead, nose, mouth and chin are measured and noted in the square. A photograph of a face with the ideal profile is then taken as the standard on the same ruled and squared paper. If the ideal length of the nose is twelve squares and that of the patient is fifteen, the first indication is that the nose should be reduced by three. (79)

This preoperative face is hence surgically launched toward the "perfect" photograph from which it currently deviates.

The after photograph has a powerful effect on us. I have shown people even mediocre surgical results, over which they marvel. Sometimes, it seems as though all they admire is transformation itself, signified portentously by the "after" as such. Or perhaps the after picture automatically fuses with the triumph-over-adversity mainstream story, which underlies all our fantasies around plastic surgery. The after photograph proves that something at least has happened, something has changed.

Photography is a pivotal technological innovation en route to what has become a widespread practice of assessing bodies through the lens of surgical possibilities. As a result of the secularization of the body, which no longer was seen as merely the dwelling for the immortal soul, and of the mobilization of the body (both spatial and socioeconomic), the body's surface, specifically what is visible, became the place where human achievement was located and exhibited. If you are materially successful, you will reveal as much through the quality of your clothing. At the same time, the visible body is always on the brink of revealing one's decline—you fall into illness, decrepitude.

The photograph can render permanent the image of one's impermanent flesh—see what I looked like at twenty, you tell your children. You hold yourself still for all times, youthful and blooming. But the hand that touches the pictured face is, maybe, thirty years older, and so the photograph can come to feel disturbingly like a harbinger of death. Your permanently youthful smile brightly looking back at you, at your children, who want to see "what Mommy and Daddy looked like," ironically intensifies the experience of your impermanence.

Roland Barthes names that "terrible thing which is there in every photograph: the return of the dead" (9). Even in the moment of being taken, photographs capture a time lost. Thus, they not only defend against death, they are on death's trail, so to speak. Death erupts in the immediately opening chasm between the mortal body and the photograph. The only defense is to reconcile the body with the image; you must yourself become an after picture, identical to the photograph. Through plastic surgery we transcend the divide and become the frozen image captured by the photograph as a picture of our desire—literally written in light.

PHOTOGRAPHIC MEMORIES

Without the camera, there could be no cosmetic surgery. Because our mirror image can seem like a photograph, we might feel driven to make ourselves photographically beautiful. "So successful has been the camera's role in beautifying the world," writes Susan Sontag, "that photographs, rather than the world, have become the standard of the beautiful. . . . We learn to see ourselves photographically: to regard oneself as attractive is, precisely, to judge that one would look good in a photograph" (85). Leo Braudy suggests that photographs are a means for controlling the body's presentation. Increasingly, there "is a self-conscious awareness of the inadequacies of the body and a blithe belief that, no matter how extreme, they can be easily corrected into a 'more photographic' and thereby more real image" (*Frenzy* 569–70). Here he is alluding to the epistemological history of photography, which was its putatively indisputable depiction of reality in contrast with, say, a painting or a prose account. Thus to appear beautiful in this imagined place of "truth" can begin to feel more important than how one appears in "real" life. Even my face in the mirror doesn't belong to me. It haunts me, a specter from a dark room developing into the frame to reveal the relative success or failure of the shot. What if I change the lighting in the bathroom? Pink lights—which soften the harsh shadows. What to make of those true-to-light mirrors that show you your face in different lighting? I'm going to the office today. Under fluorescent lights I will wear mauve on my cheeks and do without foundation.

With the advent of photography, the image can be entirely dissevered from the body, which Tom Gunning calls its "detachable nature" ("Tracing the Individual Body" 20). Circulated in our place, after our death, it has a life of its own that exceeds the material body. We no longer need be physically present for our image to have a powerful presence. The investment in the difference between the original and the copy came to fruition in the 1839 technology of the daguerreotype, which could capture for all time the evanescent image, now more permanent than the body. As Jonathan Crary emphasizes in his account of modern visual apparatuses, *Techniques of the Observer*, this efflorescence in the discovery and creation of new visual technologies was intimately linked to changes in the relationship between observing subjects and their objects. First, the "discovery" of the retinal afterimage proved that there is always a difference between the eye's perception and the perceived object. This knowledge is precisely what led to the notion of linking together sequential images to give the effect of movement—as in the diorama. Only a culture very concerned with vision as a way of processing reality, however, would be in the business of speculating on how eyes work; moreover, only a culture ready to concede (and anxious about) the discrepancy between material phenomena and human perceptual organs would be prepared to find the eyes a slightly inaccurate measure of what they see.

This increasingly vision-oriented culture ensuing from Enlightenment empiricism—where the field of observation is at once more venerated and more suspect—leads to perplexed relationships between copy and original. The idea of a photograph is supposed to preempt the worry about copying. It isn't a copy, because it's the real thing—down there in black and white. Photographs cleave through reality while words languish to the side in the diffuseness of their subjectivity. Photographs tell an objective, hard truth. Words are "soft," poetic, free associative, transformative. Photographs are evidence. Nevertheless, as Sontag points out, within ten years of the invention of photography, the possibility of altering the photograph arose.[8] Sontag is especially concerned with what happens to conceptions of reality in a culture where our most treasured evidence is also the most technologically mutable. Yet in the current panic over digitally manipulated images the photograph once again seems umbilically linked to the real.[9] It's as though these new imaging technologies have taken over the peripheral anxiety previously associated with photography.[10]

EVIDENCE

In his landmark essay "The Work of Art in the Age of Mechanical Reproduction," Walter Benjamin worried that the reproducibility of the art object, through prints and mass circulation, would destroy what he termed its "aura," associated with its singularity—not only of substance but also of place.[11] In other words, the existence and circulation of copies compromise the authenticity of the original. Although the original work is untouched, "the quality of its presence is always depreciated" (221). "The authenticity of a thing is the essence of all that is transmissible from its beginning, ranging from its substantive duration to its testimony to the history which it has experienced. Since the historical testimony rests on the authenticity, the former, too, is jeopardized by reproduction when substantive duration ceases to matter" (221). History itself is unhinged.

It is ironic that photography, the perfect evidentiary tool that exactly records the changes between the preoperative and the postoperative body, also has the capacity to make the after picture exceed the authenticity of the body in two ways. First, the prior body itself is vanquished in a sense; the before photograph proves that it was there but at the same time is a record of what is gone. I think of countless before and after photos of rhinoplasties; first you see the dorsal hump, and then you don't. Adjacent to the after picture, the before picture is elegiac in content; it's about its own effacement. Second, the after picture represents what the body grew toward—something more beautiful, an after, which results in the picture assuming more importance than the body it represents.

Susan Sontag reminds us that one of the initial purposes of photography was as evidence—specifically the mug shot.[12] You can show photographs to witnesses, and they can identify the perpetrator. After all, the camera eye is neutral, we think, an unbiased third term. Although from the beginning "photography was seen as a future source of authentic historical record," it can play tricks with history, just as the body as a historical record of the human being can also mislead (Frizot, "Body of Evidence" 259). It is a concern with the body being an authentic recorder of its own history, through wrinkles, sags, lines, and so forth that leads some to disapprove of cosmetic surgery. Instead of accurately recording our age and experience, the body of surgery is like an altered photograph—the radical undermining of what we take to be the most reliable evidence.[13]

Aging leaves evidence on the surface of the body. Those lines around my mouth are evidence that I used to smoke as well as evidence that I am no longer in my thirties. I am considering a chemical peel. Interventions in aging are meant to conceal the evidence. Those of us who claim (myself among them) that we don't care if we are taken for younger than we are as long as we look good are not being altogether honest about the relationship between aesthetics and age, or about the impact of evidence on the senses—the way in which the lineless face of a forty-five-year-old is "read" as a younger face. When she reveals her true age, there is a hesitation on the part of others. They missed the evidence. Was it in her hands? I know some who search people for the evidence of aging when they superficially appear youthful (the hands, for example). I know others who hunt down the evidence of a face-lift. Is there a disruption between the neck and the face? Or erratic little tugs of flesh that seem to pull in the wrong direction? The body is a place where surgery's effects are supposed to be visible at the same time that the process itself is hidden.

BODIES OF EVIDENCE:
MOVIE-STAR SURGERIES

Media images historically occupy the place of utter truth and blatant falsehood. Just as we are misled by camera filters and digital pyrotechnics, we are given the most irrefutable evidence of celebrity surgery—by comparing movies. The metamorphic vehicle of film is also the intractable ethical record of the star body's history. Frequently, in Internet discussions about celebrity surgery, people turn to films and photographs to prove their point. It's so easy to trace. Yet, when you consider that the reason movie stars have so much surgery is to look as flawless as we expect them to be, it is ironic that their films ultimately give them away as just another collection of after pictures. When I read Internet discussion lists tracing Michelle Pfeiffer's cheek implants or Sharon Stone's nose, I see how eager people are to uncover the history of the star's fraudulent body, the very body whose photograph we bear to the surgeon, asking for those cheekbones, that nose. This double position of stars' filmic images as at once a celebration of their beauty and evidence of their surgical changes matches perfectly the original double use of the photograph as personal portraiture and police mug shot—idealization or exposure.[14]

According to film historian Richard de Cordova, the star system was from the beginning based on the audience's increasing need to know about them; specifically, we want to know their sexual secrets. Not only do we want their "real lives" and film roles to match up, but we also long to know the difference between those two dimensions, the erotic underside that eludes, de Cordova argues, any kind of knowledge we gain through the visual. He compares fan obsession with the sexual secrets of stars to the psychoanalytic conviction that the secret origin of the patient's pathology is always sexual.

Writes de Cordova: "The star system, of course, depends heavily on scenes of confession in which the stars, in interviews or in first-person accounts, bare their souls and confess the secrets of their true feelings and their private lives" (142). The "fanaticism of the fan" to know everything about the star largely derives from our sexual attraction to the stars (143). Yet, part of what makes stars sexually attractive, he theorizes, is their embeddedness in a particular system of concealment and disclosure. The production and control of knowledge through the defiles of the studio system, journals, and talk shows involve a strategy that is deeply linked to the production of the sexual as such in our culture.

At the turn of the century, when film technology was in its infancy, the paranoid fantasy of being filmed (hence caught) in the private act of lovemaking was a popular story, suggesting that from its inception the motion picture camera was associated with witnessing scandal, proving it happened (just as the photograph provided "evidence") and at the same time revealing what it looked like.[15] While the voyeuristic nature of film viewing is a common theme among film theorists, what is interesting to consider from the perspective of celebrity culture is the way in which the film actor's body is itself always potentially scandalous. If part of our visual pleasure arises from the fantasy (built into the very nature of film) of watching our favorite stars behave scandalously, if the closeness with which we can interrogate them stands in for the scandalous behavior we really want to witness, then the fixation on the movie star is related to the feeling that the body's deepest secrets are legible in its surface phenomena.[16]

For those of us who scan the tabloids in supermarket checkout lines, it becomes clear that these days exposés of the stars' plastic surgeries are every bit as interesting (if not more so) than their predictably chaotic sex lives. Not only are stars hunted down in the private office entryways of well-known surgeons, the tabloids invite their "expert" surgeons to testify. Although James Caan "denies he's had any cosmetic surgery," the *Globe*'s expert cosmetic surgeon insists "he's had his eyes lifted and quite possibly his jawline, too" ("Stars' Plastic Surgeries" 24). It's all in the pictures, or so we're led to believe. Just like the horrified sexual couple trapped on the wrong end of a telephoto lens, pictures prove the otherwise hidden story. I compare the then and now photos of Caan and see only that he has lost a bit of weight. One eyebrow is hiked up in a question, but the other droops agedly over his eye. In this picture at least, Caan's eyes appear scalpel-free. But it doesn't matter. His photos are trapped within a surgery article; whether he likes it or not, as far as his audience is concerned, Caan is surgical. Rene Russo also "denied any cosmetic surgery." But the tabloid expert knows better. She "appears to have enhanced her jawline either through surgery or laser liposuction" (25).

Just what are we looking for when we pursue their surgical secrets? I did a search through Dejanews on the Internet for some insight into our ongoing and evidently insatiable desire for more information. On discussion lists alt.gossip.celebrity and alt.showbiz.gossip, contributors endlessly speculate on who's had which surgeries. When some were wondering why Nicholas Cage looks better these days, one person had this to contribute: "The secret is plastic surgery. Cage had no chin in his first few films, now he's got a prominent jawline, all thanks to the surgeon's knife and an implant. Speaking of celebrity plastic surgery . . . I just saw Grease 2 . . . what has Michelle Pfeiffer had done? Something, but not sure what."

Theories, of course, abounded.

Yah, Calista Flockhart's new nose this year for example. It looks real good.

This comment is certainly ironic in juxtaposition with an April 2000 episode of *Ally McBeal* in which she prosecutes a husband trying to annul his marriage to a woman who concealed her plastic surgeries. As Ally cross-examines the husband, he observes that she obviously has had her nose operated on. Ally is outraged. Of course she hasn't had surgery, she insists—even though her (possibly) "real life" surgery was by that time widely discussed. The allusion to her real surgery cannot help but feel gratifying within the system of star culture; we (the audience) know the true truth.

These ongoing discussions about star bodies take place within a requisite system of secrecy and disclosure structuring movie-star surgeries. Given the career benefits, we can understand why screen actors especially continue to be the most eager and chronic visitors to the plastic surgeon. Aside from the trade logic, however, there is a profound effect on the culture of linking cosmetic surgery to the faces and bodies of actors. This is their depth and their surface—what's hidden (secret) and at the same time enormously visible. When hidden surgery becomes the visible truth of the outwardly beautiful movie stars, we hungrily chase their beauty to its origins. In the realm of the visible, we want to see and know everything about them. They confide their beauty secrets. "Yoga," soberly explains one movie-star surgery addict; "soy," intones another. "They lie like dogs," writes Helen Bransford, who describes her own face-lift experience in *Welcome to Your Facelift*. But we know that—

it's all part of the game, a swing between concealment and outing that has fans utterly gleeful in the face of habitually and professionally lying celebrities (30). This is indeed the same dynamic identified by de Cordova regarding the sexual secrets of the movie stars—the same play of surface and depth. It is what Freud would call the primal scene, which refers to the child's witnessing the parental sex act. What is most important about the primal scene fantasy is the way it offers the solution to the riddle of origins.[17] It is the answer not only to "where do babies come from?" but also to the more worrisome question of "where do *I* come from?" To turn star surgery stories into primal scene events ("who made you—parents or the surgery-machine?" is the central question) makes sense given the deeply identificatory structure of movie star culture.[18] We feel as though we are following the history of just how one becomes a celebrity.[19]

ACTRESSES AND COSMETIC SURGERY: A SHARED HISTORY

Susan Sontag writes: "In the mansions of pre-democratic culture, someone who gets photographed is a celebrity. In the open fields of American experience, as catalogued with passion by Whitman and as sized up with a shrug by Warhol, everybody is a celebrity" (28). Photography was invented to turn us all into would-be celebrities, its very reproducibility guaranteeing that we could all be memorialized on the two-dimensional landscape. The after picture, thus, is the picture itself, any picture, which is always the longed-for "after" of identity. Screen actors epitomize the cultural desire for an after-life as a beautiful picture.

From the late nineteenth century, cosmetic surgery was associated with actresses—originally stage actresses. Subcutaneous injections of paraffin wax into tissue defects, sags, hollows, and wrinkles were performed by dermatologists and "irregular physicians," as Lois Banner puts it (213). Face peeling was developed in 1886. "Face peeling, or skinning, involved the application of acid and electricity to remove the upper layers of skin in order to eliminate scarring or simply to give a youthful appearance" (213–14). Banner notes that face skinning was especially popular among actresses reaching middle age. It makes perfect sense that the first people to rush into cosmetic operations would have been actresses, whose careers always have depended on the longevity of their good looks.

Cosmetic surgery as a celebrity practice was fixed in the public imagination in 1923, when the famous *Ziegfeld Follies* star Fanny Brice had her nose fixed by the notorious surgeon Henry J. Schireson.[20] Biographer Barbara W. Grossman comments that Brice treated her surgery as "another publicity stunt" (147). The surgery was widely publicized not only by *Variety* but also by mainstream papers like the *New York Times*. Brice, claims her biographer, wanted both to efface her ethnicity and play dramatic roles (like Nora in Ibsen's *A Doll's House*) with a more serious, conventionally attractive, and hence less comic, countenance (146–51). These two agendas, assimilation and "new roles," are hardly mutually exclusive. What was comic about Brice's appearance for a Protestant-aesthetic audience was precisely her outstanding Jewish features. Just as MacGregor's Jewish patient didn't want to be "stereotyped" as Jewish, Brice didn't want to be typecast either. Her surgeon wrote that, after the surgery, "people speak of her beauty—instead of her funny nose" (Schireson 88). The acting role is a social role and vice versa. As important, Brice's surgery highlights the relationship between the metamorphic quality of the actor and the metamorphic potential of plastic surgery.

The surgeon Schireson, in his transparent efforts at self-promotion, altered Brice's before and after pictures to make the before nose much larger and the after nose considerably smaller than either really was. At least the pictures measured up to public fantasy, if not to Brice's real face. From what the unretouched pictures show, the change was minimal; I can hardly tell the difference. The surgical nose seems maybe a shade smaller. Yet, biographer Grossman makes the following comment: "Legitimate photographs indicated that the new nose was not only less shapely than she might have hoped it would be, but also managed to rob her face of its distinctive character" (150). "Distinctive character" is a code for ethnic difference—and this is a standard remark made in response to ethnic changes. I've heard it countless times: "Yes, she's pretty now, but *before* she was so striking looking." Or, someone clucks, "It's too bad, now she just looks like everyone else." Just like the overly enthusiastic responses to uneventful after pictures, Grossman is overreacting to the very idea of transformation, in this instance registered as the pitiable effacement of ethnic heritage.

A few years after Brice's surgery, as Elizabeth Haiken reports, the plastic surgeon J. Howard Crum "provided the highlight of the 1931 International Beauty Shop Owners' Convention when he performed 'the first public face-lifting operation on record' in the Grand Ballroom of New York City's Pennsylvania Hotel. Mrs. Martha Petelle, a sixty-year-old character actress, submitted to the operation 'voluntarily and with much apparent joy,' explaining that her employment opportunities would be enhanced if some of her wrinkles were removed" (76).[21] Not only had cosmetic surgery gone public; its featured player was an actress who, in an extraordinary *mise en abyme*, was taking part in this surgical flesh-and-blood performance in order to be allowed to keep performing in the make-believe realm. Inscribed on actors' bodies is their "essential" quality of looking good enough to do their job. You might say that Petelle was becoming herself—an after picture good enough to film.

Actors frequently have surgery in order to photograph better. Joan Kron writes: "On their way *up*, stars like Hedy Lamarr (touted as the most beautiful woman in the world) and Merle Oberon had surgery to photograph *better*. And on their way *down*, Joan Crawford, Lana Turner, Burt Lancaster, Robert Mitchum, John Wayne—and Hedy Lamarr— had work done so they would photograph *younger*" (*Lift* 41). Of course "*younger*" *is* "*better*," and beauty has become equated with (indeed, has modeled itself on) photogenicity. All we need do is notice the remarkable change in facial aesthetics over the course of the twentieth century.

Lakoff and Scherr maintain that the advent of camera-created beauty dramatically changed the standards:

> Suddenly, beauty begins to be judged on new terms. This means that the figures and faces that had been considered beautiful until the turn of the century were to become a thing of the past. The camera desires motion. . . . Ideally the face should be as mobile as the body. High cheekbones and hollow cheeks, irregular features lend a note of drama to the face with their interplay of shadow and light. (74)

Despite the enormous gap between these emergent camera images and what were the current standards for feminine beauty, as the image supervened, whatever the camera looked at, the consumer would learn to love—and would also long to become. Of course, as Lakoff and Scherr make clear, camera-friendly subjects react to lighting in predictable ways. Actors turned to surgery in order to transform themselves into camera-ready images, which yoked the history of cosmetic surgery to the history of acting.

The cosmetic surgery of movie stars is meant to make them superior to the natural forces of aging or slight defects that show up all too clearly on the big screen. But the big screen is also the place where the film actor acquires godlike proportions, like Frankenstein's creature, bigger than the rest of us—they would terrify us if they weren't so beautiful. Logically, if your face extends across a film screen, you want to disguise that odd tilt to your nose. You can insist upon being shot from a different angle (many do) as a form of image control, or you can visit the plastic surgeon for a permanent correction of all possible angles. "'You can imagine,'" a Los Angeles surgeon is quoted as saying, "'what a face wrinkle or a baggy eye looks like multiplied 100 times and shown on a movie screen 60 feet high'" (Davis and Davis). Joan Kron calls the filmic close-up a "defining event" for cosmetic surgery, because actors feel compelled to correct features whose flaws are otherwise indiscernible (*Lift*

43). Just as photographs can reveal details invisible to the naked eye, the blowup of the human face invites us to hunt for evidence of its imperfection as we look virtually straight down its pores.

The early cinema put extreme pressure on the actor's appearance. Alexander Walker explains that performers needed to be very young, because "the crude lighting and make-up . . . could do little to shield the wrinkles of an ageing 21-year-old against the sharpness of the excellent, custom-made camera lenses then in use" (*Stardom* 24). Such youth and beauty had never been required for stage acting. Moreover, it was "demeaning," Walker writes, for stage actors to take film roles for which acting talent counted little next to their looks (28). Intensifying the looks-centeredness of the film performer was the namelessness of the earliest performers: "Lacking names to put to the players, they [nickelodeon exhibitors] did what their filmgoers did and referred to them as 'the girl with the curls,' or 'the sad-eyed man,' or 'the fat guy'" (29)—in other words, identifying them mainly by their physical characteristics. Thus, from the beginning, the new medium's technology (the hypercandor of the camera lens in other words) informed its content. More than that, it created a new aesthetic landscape where the facial lines of a twenty-one-year-old would be "too" visible. Later on, as the technology was refined, the opposite became true, and the camera lens with its assorted filters was better than a laser peel. Nevertheless, what remained constant in either circumstance, in front of the cruel or the kind camera lens, was the screen image of flawlessly youthful faces. A trend that originated as a consequence of technical limitations became part and parcel of the medium itself.

It is perhaps as a consequence of this utter identification with the celluloid image that actors so frequently submit to hideous surgical makeovers. I ask the surgeons what goes wrong, why movie stars who presumably have access to the best surgeons in the world, often end up so . . . well . . . monstrous. Like the gap between Frankenstein's plan of a super-race and the hideous outcome, movie star face-lifts are often the most startling of failures. The surgeons shrug. Some say that the stars aren't going to the "right" surgeons. Or that the best surgeons aren't in Southern California (despite what the public might think). Others blame celebrity expectation. They want too much. They tell the surgeon they want no sign of a wrinkle or sag after surgery; they want everything as taut as possible—mistaking taut for youth. Plumped-up lips make them look younger, so why not make them twice as plump? They demand surgical transformations that they expect to look as miraculous as the tricks of the camera.

"They look like aliens"—pronounced one surgeon.

That many surgical actors are best suited to the screen world seems logical. An *Elle Magazine* article on facial augmentation surgery (implants that change facial contour) underscores the degree to which celebrity appearance only matters in its two-dimensional versions: "What can look fake in person can look fantastic on film. For a celebrity, the millions of people who see you looking wonderful on camera outweigh the relatively few people who see you looking weird in real life" (Serrano 312). Nevertheless, this difference, which is a reasonable professional decision for those whose livelihood depends on their screen appeal, has metaphoric power for their audience.[22]

SURGICAL SECRETS/CULTURAL LIES:
WHY WE LIKE MAKEOVER STORIES

We not only like makeover stories; we also believe them. Read about the latest in laser resurfacing or ultrasonic liposuction. When journalists stop writing celebratory accounts of these miracle treatments, no one bothers to tell you that it's because they aren't all they were cracked up to be. Instead, these miracle cures are supplanted by newer, even more miraculous cures. The point is not to disclose real innovations but rather to keep us believing that one day in the not-too-distant future a cure for ugliness and old age will be found. Not only does it seem fair, it seems inevitable—just around the corner of genetic testing and endoscopy.

We hold fast to our illusions in the face of evidence to the contrary; for example, to date sufferers from burn injuries remain permanently scarred, and severe congenital anomalies never approach "normal." Why, knowing so much, do we continue to picture ourselves made forever young and beautiful through plastic surgery?

One lie is that, if you have the money and the right surgeon, you too can go under the knife and come out looking like Elizabeth Taylor. Yet, surgery simply doesn't work that way. It is not miraculous. It's okay. We need to ask ourselves why it is that we will get face-lifts and tummy tucks and so forth when they are always only approximations of the thing we really want—to be younger, to be better looking. Save those rare exceptions, even major face-changing, craniofacial surgeries have their limits. There are always trade-offs. The most radical surgeries leave in their wake radical scars, thereby belying the sense of magical transformation. The performance artist Orlan's project of having the features of six famous paintings surgically reproduced on her face is a parody of our fantasies regarding surgical transformation. Our shopping mall version of surgery yoked to our enormous confidence in technology encourages us to take all too literally the idea of other women's features supplanting our own. Orlan has needed to explain to her audience the surgical realities. Unless you start with a lot of facial features in common, you cannot order a particular movie star's face. If the measurements of our faces diverge from the current standard, we can play with them—within limits. If you like, for example, you can shorten the distance between the upper lip and the nose but you will be left with a visible scar, a shiny path curving around the nostrils to memorialize the cut. You can pull back tissue and muscle behind your ears, but you will have imperturbable lines in your skin and you will be left with the telltale stretches and incongruities of a face-lift. You can inject fat into your hands to replump them—but the fat will resorb unevenly, leaving behind an assemblage of mounds in place of the network of veins.

As though in anticipation of the plastic surgery stories in which her own "real" body would one day star, the forty-one-year-old Elizabeth

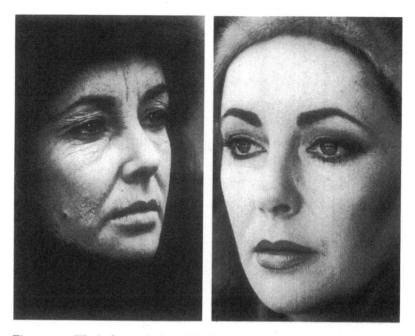

Figure 13.   The before and after of Barbara, played by Elizabeth Taylor, in *Ash Wednesday*. Courtesy of Photofest.

Taylor played a woman having a face-lift in the 1973 film *Ash Wednesday*. Elizabeth Taylor plays a fifty-something wife, Barbara, who has herself surgically rejuvenated from top to bottom in a last-ditch effort to hold on to her unfaithful husband. At the hands of a Swiss (of course) plastic surgeon, the makeup-aged Taylor is reborn as the forty-one-year-old Taylor. She truly looks like a young woman because—here's the catch— she *is* (fig. 13).

This fantasy purveyed by the film industry in which the privileged can go into a hospital and come out looking fifteen years younger is ideologically affixed to the very idea of the movie star whose interminable good looks seem glued to her or him through a combination of lighting, makeup, surgery, and camera angles. Surgeons complain about how film accounts of surgical-makeover stories mislead the public, but since plastic surgery and the film industry are blood relatives in so many different ways, we have to consider that such filmic fantasies are the realization of the cultural fantasy that gave rise to plastic surgery in the first place.[23] The impossibility of the surgery the film represents is irrelevant, because in the end the film is about the restoration of the image itself. The star becomes herself—she strays momentarily into old age only to be recuperated into her own rightful enduringly youthful image. Lit up along the walls of the operating room are blow-ups of the young and beautiful woman the plastic surgery team is working to restore. To return her to her own ideal image is their business—as well as the business of the movie, which leaves its audience with the simultaneously soothing and unsettling sense that the surgery is just another kind of film technology.

Although Barbara's husband has left her for a woman the age of their daughter, he insists that his changed feelings are unrelated to her appearance. Her restored youth and beauty cannot win him back, because he has fallen out of love with her, not with her appearance. "Yes," he tells her, after she's been rejuvenated, "you look exactly like the woman I married. But then you always did. And you always will. No amount of surgery is going to change the way I see you." Apparently, Barbara has gotten it all wrong. At the same time, however, in naively ironic contrast to the numbing platitudes about the relationship between looks and self-worth, we learn that through this tremendous act of self-determination, Barbara has proved her independence from her husband. With her new/old "self," a whole new world of sexual possibilities is opened up to her. Younger men pursue her. She is the center of attention when she enters a room. Certainly this cannot *be* the same person who otherwise ages quietly to the side, ignored, unappreciated, and untouched.

This is Kathy Davis's point when she describes the decision to have surgery as a form of agency for women in an obdurately appearance-centered culture. Saying appearances don't matter is simply untrue—just as untrue as Barbara's husband's insistence that her aging appearance had nothing to do with his falling for a much younger woman. Telling aging women that they should grin and bear it is puritanical at best. At the same time, as Susan Bordo points out, a general insistence on a perfectly toned, ageless, surgically fine-tuned body is puritanical in its own way. That both perspectives seem controlling is suggestive. Because the deployment of the body is currently so pivotal in how we view the relationship between social forces and individual agency, all body-related practices can wind up feeling oppressive.

Another lie (circulated by both surgeons and the culture at large) is that surgery cannot change the "inner you." Of course it can. If your nose turns up, if your thighs are thinner, if you look younger—you *can* have a better life. You will in turn feel better. The inner you—however you describe that being—will be transformed. When Barbara learns that all the plastic surgery that rewound her body from fifty-something to forty has nevertheless failed to keep her husband from skipping off with his daughter-aged younger woman, she is confounded. "Look at these!" she exclaims, gripping together her restored breasts. "Look at this!" pointing to her face. Why doesn't he want her—now that she looks closer to what he fell in love with? He tells her that it has nothing to do with appearance. He just fell out of love with *her*—the inner her. Somehow, this moral apotheosis of *Ash Wednesday* is supposed to comfort us with its homely insight. People are more than skin deep, and husbands don't leave wives just because they want prettier, younger women on their arms. After all, love is directed toward the inside, not the outside. The film artfully tries to feed us this morally improving insight alongside the cultural reality of the significance of physical appearance. In the end, *Ash Wednesday* is the quintessential "after" story, whereby the rejected fifty-something wife is given a fresh start with her rejuvenated physical equipment. So what if she can't win back the wayward husband; she has what it takes, as her daughter advises her, to attract another mate. Plastic surgery saves the day, restores lost opportunity.

In 1997 Elizabeth Taylor starred in another after story—this time her own. The *National Enquirer* ran a cover story about how she found love and recovered her lost youth all within a swift forty-eight hours. The day after her first date with what was described as the new man in

Figure 14. Liz's new body.

her life, she had arms, hips, sides, and abdomen liposuctioned. The *Enquirer* reports that "the dashing bachelor provided just the right prescription for Liz' woes" ("Liz Plastic Surgery Miracle"). Like the medical procedure temporally proximate to the first date, the liposuction will provide a "cure" for postdivorce heart sickness. For the inquisitive, there is a diagram indicating "where she had fat sucked out to give herself a new shape" (see fig. 14). But the putative new shape, we learn quickly enough, is not so new at all, for Liz is quoted as saying, "I want to look like I did 20 years ago." We also learn that the new man is a former doctor and a pal—something rediscovered as it were, like the body we are told will be like her former body. This is a before and after story in all respects. Before, the bad fat old body was the good thin young body. The lost body is recuperated through a cosmetic procedure that literally inhales off the years. Her svelte figure, all along asleep but available under the "false" fat, is once again revealed (unveiled) in its true form. In order for Liz to have/keep the man, she must resurrect the prior body that she in some way still has—viable but dormant. These parallel plots, romance and surgery, converge in the happily-ever-after of woman's romantic success through physical appearance.[24]

The article pictures Liz in a film role from twenty years earlier, and we take for granted the equivalence of this before picture to her projected after picture. This is exactly the story offered by *Ash Wednesday*. For movie stars, the metamorphosis is always from the fake dowdy or overweight or old to the thrilling unfolding of their real and shining beauty. Better yet if the stars are themselves an after picture of an earlier and plainer version. Their bodies are just part of the ever-unfolding twentieth-century story of changing your life.

SEVEN

Being and Having
Celebrity Culture
and the Wages of Love

I had admired the perfect forms of my cottagers—their grace, beauty, and delicate complexions; but how was I terrified, when I viewed my-self in a transparent pool! At first I started back, unable to believe that it was indeed I who was reflected in the mirror; and when I be-came fully convinced that I was in reality the monster that I am, I was filled with the bitterest sensations of despondence and mortification.

                                    The creature *in* Frankenstein

In *Frankenstein*, the creature's horrifying encounter with his own reflec-tion is a direct reversal of the Greek myth of Narcissus, who falls in love with his own beautiful reflection. Instead, the creature plummets into intense self-hatred. While the ancient Greek myth worries about the dangerously intoxicating potential of one's own mirror image, this early-nineteenth-century novel suggests that the primary narcissistic en-counter with the perfect counterpart is one of abjection. "I was in real-ity [in the reflection] the monster that I am" (Shelley 90). Looking at the reflection has become a metaphor for the inadequacy of the viewing subject to ideal images.

With the move away from traditional societies, in which one's iden-tity was both restricted and known, image becomes supervening. "What we are faced with," writes Lacan, ". . . is the increasing absence of all those saturations of the superego and ego ideal that are realized in all kinds of organic forms in traditional societies" ("Aggressivity" 26). Traditional societies offer both stable social roles and cultural ideals that allow one's self-image to come to rest at the door of an identity experienced as immutable, shored up as it is by the invariability of the social order itself. The continuousness of a community leads to a felt stability of psychical organization in contrast to a society invested in transformation and change.

Instead, we seem to be stranded in a narcissistic hell of unresolved rivalry with ideal counterparts. The mirror stage never ends—almost every day we are called on to reproduce the primordially narcissistic event of becoming human. That the creature in *Frankenstein* is a "child" who happens to be full grown suggests exactly the ongoing effects of the interminable narcissistic encounter—in relation to the ideal image, one is always a child and always in danger. As a culture we have found a way to represent this interminable and dangerous encounter with ideal images that render our own image insufficient: the movie star.

BEAUTY BASHING

"Sick Computer Game Lets You 'Kill' Stars," claims the story headline from an issue of *Star* (see fig. 15). It seems there are various web sites where you personally can experience the thrill of cyber killing or otherwise maiming and abusing celebrities. *Star* reports: "Outraged experts warn that the games could encourage real crimes of violence against celebrities—especially by young people." According to a recent law journal article, 49 percent of stalkings involve someone in the entertainment field.[1] Two famous celebrity murderers, Richard Bardo, who killed Rebecca Schaeffer, and John Lennon's killer, Mark David Chapman, have said that this was a way for them to become famous themselves.[2] Prosecuting attorney Marcia Clark reported that Bardo's motivation for killing Rebecca Schaeffer was "'to be famous'" (qtd. in Tharpe).

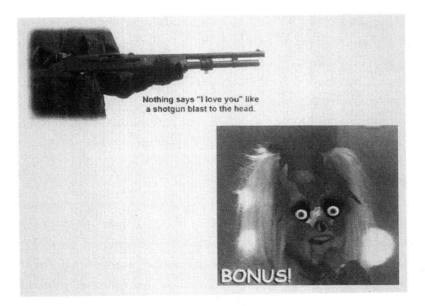

Figure 15. A computer game lets you "kill" stars.

Their identification with the celebrity is twofold: first, they literally "become famous" when they hit the national news; second, they identify with the fantasy-trajectory of celebrity itself. It can happen to anyone, you and me; all it takes are the right circumstances, the right timing. Instantly, these stalkers ascend from nobody to somebody. Nobody, according to the received wisdom of celebrity culture, means noncelebrity. Somebody is celebrity. Moreover, celebrity murder seems inevitable when we consider the aggressive structure of celebrity in contemporary culture.

This inevitability occurs because star culture invites ongoing intense and unresolved identifications that are simultaneously adoring and hostile. "Identification," Freud writes in "Group Psychology and the Analysis of the Ego," "is ambivalent from the very first; it can turn into an expression of tenderness as easily as into a wish for someone's removal" (105). In a culture that induces strong identifications with celebrities (their images and their lifestyles), every now and then such identifications will turn deadly. More typically, the aggressivity experienced toward the celebrity image turns inward and claims our own bodies.

We identify with beings whose very job in life is to be the object of the gaze. Being the object of the gaze can pull you together and make you feel whole, says Lacan. Movie stars' role as objects of the *cultural* gaze can feel satisfying when you identify with them and frustrating when you perceive them as having an experience forever lost to you.

There are times when we look at another who seems to be complete—whose satisfaction seems blissfully equal to their desire; in these instances, we experience aggressive envy. Lacan refers to St. Augustine's description of his childish envy upon watching his infant brother nurse. He gave him "a bitter look, which seems to tear him to pieces and has on himself the effect of a poison" (*Four Fundamental Concepts* 116). What the infant has, explains Lacan, is exactly what can no longer satisfy his older brother.

> Everyone knows that envy is usually aroused by the possession of goods which would be of no use to the person who is envious of them, and about the true nature of which he does not have the least idea.
>
> Such is true envy—the envy that makes the subject pale before the image of a completeness closed upon itself. . . . (116)

This envious look threatens to tear apart not only the object of envy, by destroying its self-sufficiency, the "completeness closed upon itself," but the envier as well. It is not the milk per se that would satisfy the onlooking brother. Instead, it is the knowledge that he can never again experience what the infant appears to have. Thus, the envious look has a disintegrating effect on the self exiled from the experience of "completeness closed upon itself."

Celebrities, movie stars in particular, seem to have been created for the express purpose of occupying the imaginary love- and envy-inspiring place of "completeness closed upon itself." When we identify with the celebrity, our looks momentarily converge and Lacan's formula is sub-

verted. We enter the sphere of the celebrity we admire. It is the fantasmatic undoing of *"You never look at me from the place from which I see you."*
When we identify with the celebrity, we imagine that the celebrity looks
back at us—from the same place—a perfect match. Anne Friedberg
I believes that the objective of identification "is that which conceals and
defers the recognition of dissimilitude" (40). The gap between momentarily seals shut. But then we wake up into a "difference" experienced
as inadequate bodies. Like the child who shared its mother's powerful
skin, we feel as though we lose *both* precious skins, the mother's and
our own. The process of identification and disidentification may happen in a later developmental stage than the primary assumption of the
skin ego, but it is nevertheless structurally equivalent. The structure
of melancholia as well is echoed here in our bond with and subsequent
falling away from the idealized object. We have lost both the object
of identification and the identifying self that was elevated *through* the
identification.

YOU OUGHT TO BE IN PICTURES

Richard Dyer argues that those who become stars are those who best
reconcile the ideological contradictions of a culture; that these apparent
contradictions can inhabit a single body suggests that they aren't contradictions at all *(Stars; Heavenly Bodies)*. In other words, in all respects
they perform coherent subjectivity. Is this why we want to tear them
apart through assessing their bad surgeries or their taste in clothes or
something as banal as their beauty secrets? Why would we go so far as
to punch them out in cyberspace? or kill them? The body of the celebrity is the very place where being converges with image. By "image,"
here, I mean both the two-dimensional surface of their visual appearance and the projection of a certain style of self. Leo Braudy calls actors
"forerunners in self-consciousness" who became the model for a society

increasingly concerned with "self-presentation" (*Frenzy of Renown* 568). "It was inevitable," he writes, "that the etiquette of being should be learned from those whose actual business was performance" (568).[3] If this is the ideal body of the modern subject, for whom all being has become the performance of an image-on-command, then it seems obvious that we would want to tear this body/being apart at the seams to see what it's made of—whether by relentlessly invading their private lives through interviews or telephoto lenses, by asking for the physical proof of connection by way of an autograph on a piece of paper, by stalking them, by killing them.

When you visit the *Smack Pamela Anderson* web site, you are enthusiastically informed that "you, the reader, have a chance to rearrange Pamela Anderson's face without the aid of silicone & scalpel. Looks like you'll just have to use your fist." Then we read, "Click here." Here in the *Smack Pamela Anderson* web site we find a distillation of all the ingredients that go into packaging that aggressive, erotic, identificatory mixture that forges the culture's relationship with celebrity bodies.

This web site invites "real" assaults on her body—punches instead of silicone. At each level of punching, she is ridiculed for being plastic. The punches somehow are intended to punish her into becoming real flesh and blood.

Click here

Then attempt to do real damage to the "plastic wench." Yet, the confusion between the cursor and the fist unnervingly reiterates the implacable two-dimensionality of the celebrity body. You can't do real damage. They aren't real. This is what you love and hate about them. The refusal of the celebrity body to succumb to your demand unleashes your aggressivity even further. I click, then a long pause, then slowly as the image takes shape on my screen, a bruise emerges. I can click again and do further damage, only with another long pause that asserts the gap between my click and the screen body that is the target of my aggression. This isn't just any old screen body—it is Pamela Anderson, who epitomizes the conversion of flesh into silicone and celluloid; she seems like the allegorical figure of the screen image.

Pamela Anderson stands not only for cosmetic surgery with her breasts and mouth, which are purely a surgical aesthetic, but, it is important to note, she also literally embodies the ways in which cosmetic surgery and movie star culture are related phenomena. When patients request Pamela Anderson breasts (which they do), they are asking for a body with a well-known signature of surgery.[4] They thus not only model themselves on a television star through visual identification, they also implicitly imitate what amounts to an imitation of an imitation. For surely Anderson herself is imitation Jayne Mansfield, who is imitation Marilyn Monroe, and so on down the corridor of celebrity bodies with their requirement to be both extraordinary individuals and reiterable types.

Another web site, *Mr. Showbiz* (http://mrshowbiz.go.com/games/index.html), allows you to "slice and dice" celebrities. Recent celebrity surgery candidates were various cast members from the *Star Wars* movies: "The good doctors of the *Mr. Showbiz* Plastic Surgery Lab invite you to pick up a scalpel (or lightsaber if you're so inclined) and do a little work on the familiar . . . faces of *Star Wars*: Ewan McGregor, Carrie Fisher, Harrison Ford, and Natalie Portman." Here we have the opportunity to mix and match star features and create a face with, say, the nose of McGregor, the eyes of Ford, the mouth of Fisher, and the facial shape of Portman. We can be pretend plastic surgeons, just as watching the stars can induce in us the desire to be operated on. Boundaries—between us and them, image and flesh—disappear. And the aggression cuts both ways.[5]

STEAL THIS LOOK

When Pantene model Kelly LeBrock winsomely urges us, "Don't hate me because I'm beautiful," she is condensing the impasses between real

Figure 16.   Steal this look. *In Style*, on Andie MacDowell.

bodies and the celebrity images to which we submit (including the celebrities themselves). We shouldn't hate her because she's beautiful, because the beauty she has is transitory, not hers at all. Indeed, the model herself may wake up the following morning in the throes of a "bad hair day" no amount of Pantene hair products could dispel. At the same time, as the advertising executives well know, the only way to resolve our rivalry is to become her.

After the decades worth of magazine articles revealing Betty Grable's beauty secrets or how Sophia Loren keeps her skin so young-looking, we now have an entire magazine devoted to telling ordinary people how to dress or what makeup to wear in order to achieve the look of a favorite star. "Steal this look" urges a regular feature in *In Style* (see fig. 16).

"The look" is something you can have for the purchase—the makeup, the magazine itself—and it's something you can be, in other words, be looked at in the way she is looked at. You can be the actress as the object of the look. Yet this desire to be the star is portrayed as aggressive: you have to *steal* the look (what she looks like and the gaze that distinguishes her from you—the beautiful actress/model who's "worth" looking at). Steal the look meant for *her*. Steal her looks so no one looks at her. You supplant her. These are all aggressive identifications.

Part of what we like about actors, claims Richard Dyer, is the way in which they "are always 'themselves'": "People often say that they do not rate such and such a star because he or she is always the same. In this view, the trouble with, say, Gary Cooper or Doris Day, is that they are always Gary Cooper and Doris Day. But if you like Cooper or Day, then precisely what you value about them is that they are always 'themselves'—no matter how different their roles, they bear witness to the continuousness of their own selves. This coherent continuousness within becomes what the star 'really is'" (*Heavenly Bodies* 11).

For the rest of us, then, what is so transporting about the experience of watching a star or following his or her career is the sense of being able to articulate continuousness within discontinuousness. From one role to another, one marriage to another, throughout even a variety of "looks," what remains the same is their essential star-ness that transcends the changes and, most important, stands for putting together a single self out of an array of differences. The visible aging of stars, moreover, is disturbing not just for the stars themselves, but for their audience, who brings to their image a certain set of expectations regarding what constitutes star qualities. We want them to stay in place. We are caught in a double bind. We depend upon them to hold together the images (with which we identify), intact and complete, their perfect images, the iconic objects of our simultaneous love and rivalry, which threaten to make our own images fall apart.

Moreover, such "continuousness within discontinousness" is always on the edge of betraying its own sustaining paradox. Similarly, plastic surgery pretends to unify the self rather than blast it to pieces. Indeed, plastic surgery offers a sustaining fiction of the self. The foes to the self's continuity are ugliness and aging; it is these twin demons who threaten to disengage how we "feel" from what we "look like." How is it that the forces most structurally threatening to a unified self seem nevertheless to participate in the conventions they undermine? The star who floats from role to role pulls together these roles with the combination of his or her flesh-and-bloodness and star quality, just as the cosmetic-surgery patient claims a match between inner spirit and outer appearance. It is possible that locating the felt continuity in the culture's most fragmenting practices is part of the point after all. As Dyer observes: "Stars . . . [shore] up the notion of the individual but also at times [register] the doubts and anxieties attendant upon it" (*Heavenly Bodies* 10). Perhaps star culture and plastic surgery are themselves transitional practices that mark as they obfuscate the radical cultural shifts around the experience of the self; they prompt us to experience fragmentation *as though* it is continuousness. That our bodies must bear the weight of these uninterrogated paradoxes leads to aggressivity—directed either outward or inward.

The more that celebrity bodies become the site of identification, desire, and imitation, the more ordinary people will turn to surgery, and the more aggressive we will become in our relationships to our own mirror images. Those who are in the thorough grip of the aggressive passion toward the image may act out against the paradigmatic image itself. Said the slayer of Rebecca Schaeffer: "'I saw a commercial for her TV show . . . her personality came out . . . an open personality . . . it interested me in the show . . . I felt like I knew her'" (qtd. in Mulgannon). Celebrity personalities are meant to be open to us in an almost literal way—so we can step right in, try them on for size, like a skin.

A remarkable example of the kinds of aggressivity tapped by the pervasive imposition of screen images as models is Georges Franju's 1959 film, *Les Yeux sans visage* (Eyes without a face).[6] In the aftermath of a devastating car accident in which his beautiful daughter's face was de-

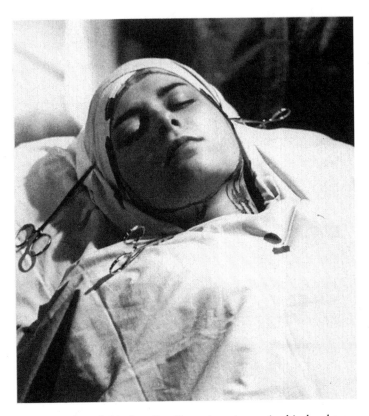

Figure 17. Steal this face. Dr. Genessier tries to give his daughter another woman's face in *Les Yeux sans visage*. Courtesy of Photofest.

stroyed, plastic surgeon Dr. Genessier repeatedly tries to harvest the faces of young women to transplant onto his daughter Christianne's face (see fig. 17). The surgeries are always unsuccessful, as though to illustrate the impossibility of such transformations.[7] Of course, the kidnapped donors of the faces always die, pointing to the implicit violence in stealing another's image. Although Franju's film renders the experiments failures to prove didactically that one cannot borrow or transplant this central locus of the self, the face, during the surgeries the face ironically is depicted as no more than a fragile two-dimensional surface.[8] Nevertheless, Genessier's daughter cannot live as a subject in the world without this image appended to her, because the face is precisely where image is wedded to identity.

The eventual disintegration of Christianne's image (the chilling daily record of her necrosis) is a familiar motif. In the 1973 film *Frankenstein: The True Story*, the monster is played by strikingly handsome Michael Sarrazin, whose perfect face soon begins to decay. Indeed, it is the loss of this beauty—his falling away from the ideal image that he *was*—that enrages him and leads to violence. Similarly, in Terry Gilliam's 1985 film, *Brazil*, Sam Lowry's mother, in her bid to become even younger-looking than her son through a series of plastic surgeries, is "punished" by ultimately losing her bodily substance and dissolving into jelly. In D'Amato's novel *Beauty*, Jamie Angelo's Virtual Skin creations shrink, turning these perfect faces into grotesque masks. His girlfriend, whom he has entirely remade, develops cancer. These morality plays around aesthetic hubris seem to be directed against movie-star two-dimensional images in particular. Ironically, like the supramortals I discuss in chapter 5, the images wind up tormented by the very vulnerabilities we enviously imagine they've overcome.

DEATH AND CELEBRITY

J. G. Ballard's 1973 novel, *Crash*, caught the aggressivity of star identifications in the midst of their increasing effect on the identity formation of the culture. By creating a sense of intimate relationships with the products of modern technology (film and television images), Ballard emphasizes star culture's important affiliation with technoculture. His central character, Vaughn, erotically addicted to car crashes, spends his days planning for his most cherished fantasy, to die in a car crash with Elizabeth Taylor: "The automobile crash had made possible the final and longed-for union of the actress and the members of her audience" (189–90). It is suggestive that Vaughn chooses Elizabeth Taylor, that icon of seductive Hollywood beauty, whose extraordinary career in many ways represents the ascendance of beauty over talent in the film industry and whose body to this day remains fetishized by the tabloids. The very same year that Ballard published *Crash*, Elizabeth Taylor starred in *Ash Wednesday*.

What is so beguiling about Elizabeth Taylor is her cinematic-quality beauty, literally a spectacular beauty, linked to a "material" body that has from the beginning of her career experienced a succession of catastrophic illnesses, along with her tabloid-news-making fluctuations in weight. Wayne Koestenbaum discusses the public fixation on Elizabeth Taylor's weight:

> She was called plump long before she was actually plump. Fluids and solids that pass through Elizabeth Taylor's body, or that stay in her body, are part of the public record. . . . In 1946, at fourteen, in *Nibbles and Me*, before she developed the body whose bosom and salary and appetite became fable, Elizabeth Taylor sketched the matrix of eating and being eaten, of mouth and breast, of cannibalism and nourishment, which would define her body in the public imagination. (110–11)

After Taylor's widely publicized weight gain, Joan Rivers joked that she "'used to be the one woman in America every other woman wanted to look like, now we all do'" (qtd. in Heymann 10).

It is perhaps because she is the most iconically and verbally embodied of celebrities that Elizabeth Taylor represents the insurmountable impasse between the two arenas—material and celluloid. No doubt it is this impossibility that drives Vaughn's passion. She is both all body (as vulnerable as bodies get) and thoroughly celluloid. Thus, structurally having the effect of a fetish, which both denies and asseverates the thing it stands in place of, Elizabeth Taylor herself "embodies" the intrinsic paradoxes of celebrity culture.

The original of the telephotographed celebrity, Elizabeth Taylor was scandalously and famously "caught" in an amorous moment on a yacht with her then-married *Cleopatra* costar, Richard Burton. She is also a star who gives rise to a number of plastic surgery stories—whether or not they are real. Taylor's hyperembodiment may well lie in her having been in the "business" since she was very young. With *National Velvet* she became a child star and subsequently seemed to grow up on the screen itself.

Flipping through the photographs in her various biographies, one is struck by how many of the pictures are from scenes in films or publicity shots—in place of family photographs. She has explained that their painful history as child stars is part of the emotional bond between her and good friend Michael Jackson (Theroux 169). Perhaps Jackson as well is the fallout of a childhood spent as image. Paul Theroux describes the metamorphic history of both stars:

> Michael, who indulges in iconography, had for years collected images of Elizabeth Taylor, as he had of Diana Ross—and, for that matter, of Mickey Mouse and Peter Pan—most of whom, over the years in what is less a life than a metamorphosis, he has come at some point to resemble physically. Elizabeth, in the almost 60 years of her stardom, has similarly altered: The winsome child has morphed from Velvet Brown to Pearl Slaghoope (and most recently God's girlfriend Sarah in a new NBC cartoon series) via Cleopatra and Maggie the Cat. Each movie . . . has produced a different face and figure, a new image. . . . (168)

Growing up in front of cameras would influence the public's reaction to these stars as much as it shaped their experience of their own identities. Anne Hollander puts it this way: "Taylor was trained early to glow for the camera, to sustain herself as a perfect image rather than as a particular character." The transformational acts of those raised by the camera (Michael's surgeries, Liz's weight changes) could be read as a kind of self-impaling, an ongoing conversion of flesh into image, and reversion of image into flesh.

In his collection of essays entitled *The Atrocity Exhibition*, Ballard considers the paradox of the celebrity's remoteness (he says they "move across an electric terrain of limousines and bodyguards, private helicopters and state functions" 111) in combination with our imagined access to their most private moments and thoughts through zoom lenses and interviews. "The most intimate details of their lives seem to lie beyond an already open bathroom door that our imaginations can easily push aside. Caught in the glare of our relentless fascination, they can do nothing to stop us exploring every blocked pore and hesitant glance, imagining ourselves their lovers and confidantes" (111). While the star's body is visually available to our most scrutinizing inquiry—as they play their cinematic roles, their bodies (and bodily practices) seem so much more vivid than those of even our closest friends and family—beyond it all we recognize that this hyperembodiment of the film star is a fraud that occurs on multiple levels.[9] Not only are film stars usually close-up bodies that are all the while materially remote, but they are also idealized bodies that are equally inaccessible to their viewers (even to themselves, as I've said).

Ballard relates what he calls our "anatomizing fascination" with celebrities to the scientific text of the plastic surgery procedure. Through substituting the names of three famous people, Princess Margaret, Mae West, and Queen Elizabeth, for unnamed patients undergoing, respectively, face-lift, reduction mammoplasty, and rhinoplasty, Ballard suggests the pornographic possibilities inherent in juxtaposing our "anatomizing fascination" with the "magic of fame."[10]

> The reduction in size of Mae West's breasts presented a surgical challenge of some magnitude, considerably complicated by the patient's demand that her nipples be retained as oral mounts during sexual intercourse. There were many other factors to be taken into account: Miss West's age, the type of enlargement, whether the condition was one of pure hypertrophy, the degree of ptosis present, the actual scale of enlargement and, finally, the presence of any pathology in the breast tissue itself. (*The Atrocity Exhibition* 114)

Of course, as a screen idol, Mae West's breasts are anything but too large. They are part of the set decoration, what makes West's body assume legendary screen-sized proportions. As Ballard comments, "Beyond our physical touch, the breasts of these screen actresses incite our imaginations to explore and reshape them" (114). Placing West's celluloid breasts in the surgical field, however, converts the bombshell into a hypertrophic freak. Her star qualities slump into grotesqueness. She is worse than a mere mortal. This is why stars need to keep their surgeries secret, to preserve their specialness. It is also why we long to keep unraveling the fabric of their hypermortal bodies to discover what they are made of. We need to strip them bare (and mortal) in order to ward off the very visual menace with which we endow them.

RIPPING THEM TO SHREDS

As Lary May points out, what is so appealing about the movie star is how close they are to you and me—ordinary people who somehow "made it." Yet at the same time, they show us how to transcend ordinariness—how to elevate the body into the image. The theater critic Addison De-Witt in *All about Eve* explains the implicit contradiction in star culture: "Every now and then some elder statesman of the theater or cinema assures the public that actors and actresses are just plain folks, ignoring the fact that their greatest attraction for the public is their complete lack of resemblance to normal human beings."

There is an ongoing representational distinction in star culture between stars as exotic beings who inhabit worlds of privilege and glamour, dwelling in homes the size of Disneyland while they have access to geographic and psychical regions the rest of us can only dream about, and the I'm-just-a-regular-person mode of stardom, where we see stars preoccupied with everyday concerns like carpooling the kids and trying to find quality time with their spouses. "A new fiction of ordinariness" writes Richard Schickel, "prevailed from the early thirties to the mid-fifties. It was a fiction in which extraordinary people—if not always in talent, then assuredly in looks and income level—were supposed to be seen as entirely like their audience in basic values and desires" (*Intimate*

Strangers 74). They were shown in suburban-ish looking circumstances and came off as tamely middle-class. Uncannily, Schickel points out, it began to seem as though "the conventional relationship between media figures and their auditors was here reversed, that the movie stars were imitating us" (76). But all along, as others have documented, the notion of the ordinariness of the star has been central to their reception—especially in a democratic culture that disdains the cavortings of the hereditarily elite.[11] Ordinariness, which is really no more than the remnant of flesh-and-bloodness of the image, is the bridge concept for our identification with the star's image.

While movie stars are often presented as having been "discovered" in the most ordinary of settings, say, a soda shop, they are also imagined as somehow having transcended the mundane and decidedly mortal circumstances of the rest of us. Lana Turner is a case in point. Widely known for being "discovered" in Schwab's Drug Store, this actress, whom Richard Dyer calls "sexy-ordinary," had no such fantasy beginning. Nevertheless, the iconic cultural story of the everyday woman being lifted miraculously from her obscurity and vaulted to the height of celebrity and wealth could make the rest of us wonder, Why not me? What makes this otherwise ordinary person so special? Moreover, the visual element of the exemplary story is crucial to the fantasy of specialness that is somehow concealed but identifiable by the right (talent-trained) set of eyes. This tension between being "like you and me" and "special" can lead to aggressive identifications. The well-known plastic surgeries of the stars intensify this felt contradiction between ordinariness and specialness. If they were born beautiful, why do they need surgical interventions? If they can be "made" to look like that, so can I. Star beauty induces in the culture a desire to emulate (through diets, exercise, beauty products, surgery, and, most intangible of all, lifestyle) the very process of "becoming-celebrity." Moreover, in the midst of the desire to inhabit this privileged borderline space of the star, we are always aware that the specialness itself is performed.

Film is a violent medium with its fragmenting shots of the human form, its close-ups, its body-searching attention, the scalpel slice of the camera's look that opens up the face in order to expose character. The aggression with which the camera gaze forces the body to give up the secrets of the soul is participated in by the viewer and also identified with. Moreover, the scandalous exposés of the "real" lives of celebrities entail an aggressive pursuit of another kind of interior.

As I noted in the last chapter, our interest in the sexual secrets/scandals of movie stars has been matched if not surpassed by our fascination with their surgeries. This is part and parcel of the sadistic "anatomizing fascination" Ballard finds at the intersection of science and celebrity culture—a pornographic knowledge achieved through turning the outside in. The repressive structure of sex and sexuality has been supplanted by the "deep" cosmetic secrets of the movie-star body. The routine tabloid exposés of "the plastic surgery secrets of the stars" underscores this nexus I'm describing between aggressivity, movie-star culture, and plastic surgery. The putative expert appraises gleefully what he insists are the various surgeries undergone by these celebrities, although the tabloid's own objective is a hostile one—to "out" more celebrities. The expert is ruthless in his assessment of actresses he claims have thus far avoided the knife—or who "need" more work. About Candice Bergen he laments: "Candice is aging quickly. Only a couple of years ago she looked much better. She's obviously had a chemical peel to resurface her skin and possibly a face-lift, but she really needs more. Her skin is sagging and she has serious wrinkling in her lower eyelids. She could use a complete overhaul." Or about Melanie Griffith: "Melanie is certainly showing her age. Her wrinkles are painfully obvious. She's had her lips enlarged, but to run in the Hollywood big leagues she desperately needs more work, including work on her eyelids and a face-lift" ("Stars' Plastic Surgeries" 24). This attack is especially ironic in light of the noticeable changes Griffith has made to her appearance in the past few years. There is a viciousness in assessing these celebrities from the perspective of how much surgery they have had and/or need. It is as though their beautiful images pressure us to scrutinize them ever more closely, un-

Figure 18.   Goldie Hawn saving her youth.

pack them, discover all their flaws, imaginatively rebuild them. "Poor Goldie!" laments a headline on the cover of *Globe*, "She fights to save her fading beauty" (1). With their telephoto lenses the paparazzi have discovered her sordid secret, her cellulite, her wrinkled skin. What will happen, they wonder, to her relationship with the younger and still desirable Kurt Russell? Yet just a few months later, we find Goldie on the cover of the *National Examiner* cast as one of the beauties who resorts to injections to maintain her apparently eternal good looks ("Anti-Aging Drug Craze!" 1) (see fig. 18).

Routinely, tabloids show the stars without makeup to expose their basic "ordinariness." "Gotcha! Stars with No Makeup" reads one recent *Globe* headline, promising even more unvarnished faces inside. In addition to the aggression unleashed by the idea of catching stars unaware, in revealing potentially less than beautiful images, is the notion that being without makeup is indeed the opposite of being a celebrity. This headline works because we assume the inevitable relationship between image-improving makeup and star culture. Their faces are "made-up" *for* the camera apparatus—and this is the very apparatus with which we in part identify, as a looking-machine that expects to find on the other end a certain kind of face. When you turn to the inside story, you find an array of camera-unfriendly faces. "Those Pretty Hollywood Faces Aren't Always What They Seem . . ." we learn from a headline that emphasizes both the trickery of makeup as well as other forms of technological artifice and our own proximity to these otherwise impossible beauties. In order to make the stars seem even more like ordinary women, their pictures are captioned with "advice" reminiscent of magazine makeover accounts of regular women. Pamela Anderson needs "an eyebrow pencil, lipstick, foundation and puffy eye concealer" (24). Alicia Silverstone simply requires eye shadow and mascara, while "Roseanne needs her signature red lipstick and glossy back eyeliner to look her best" (25). Not only have star faces been "unmasked" for their intrinsic everyday-ness, we also get to feel as though we know what it takes (eyeliner and red lipstick) to look like them. *Globe* simultaneously indicates glee over finding them undisguised and chides them for revealing a chink in the mandatory impermeability of Hollywood skin, reflecting the double position of star as rival and role model.

Leo Lowenthal and Richard Dyer have charted extensively the ways in which "stars become models of consumption for everyone in a consumer society" (Dyer, *Stars* 39). We want to know where they live, what they eat, what they wear, their hair color and styles. "Their fashions are to be copied, their fads followed, their sports pursued, their hobbies taken up" (39). In *All about Eve*, Eve's rapid accomplishment of celebrity

involves universal consumption of her life and habits. In a voice-over at
the beginning of the film, we hear: "Eve, the golden girl, the cover girl,
the girl next door, the girl on the moon. Time has been good to Eve, life
goes where she goes. She's been profiled, covered, revealed, reported,
what she eats and what she wears and whom she knows and where she
was and where she's going. Eve. We all know all about Eve. What can
there be to know that you don't know?" Of course the irony is that no
one knows the truth about this star, whose every waking moment is on
display for the multitudes. The craving for knowledge is chastened by
our recognition that the star's life is part of the show, part of the cultivation of celebrity, and that almost everything we learn about one is
carefully produced and orchestrated by her or his array of image managers (Gamson 61). It's not as though the public doesn't know on some
level that the glimpses of authenticity are no more authentic than the
roles stars play. Perhaps this is why surgery seems like something "real"
about the star that is the deep underside of the image-making process.
Paradoxically, one of the mainstays of star making and keeping, cosmetic
surgery ultimately gives up the show. Sometimes, in their effort to maintain their image as inaccessible (they are hyperbeautiful and they never
age), they go too far, and we catch a glimpse of the bloody machinery
that transforms mortals into images. Consider this tantalizing blind item
from the *Movieline* web site:

MOVIELINE JULY 1999 BLIND ITEM #2

The cast and crew of that big, expensive event flick recently tripped
out when a very friendly but strange looking guy walked onto the
set, parked himself in a chair and seemed to wait for instruction.
When the director got word of the weirdo, he sent headset-wearing
lackeys to alert security and have the benevolent psycho escorted
off the premises. Potential embarrassment was averted when the
film's cool leading lady deliberately engaged the guy in up-close-
and-personal conversation and quickly discovered he was actually
her leading man in the movie. Turns out he had undergone so much
plastic surgery in Europe to make himself camera-ready he was un-

recognizable as the clean-cut hunk he was once. That's what the director gets for hiring an actor without having actually seen him in at least five years.

The glee with which Internet fans pounced on this item and speculated widely (Mickey Rourke, because he's a known plastic surgery junkie? Treat Williams, because he was cast opposite Michelle Pfeiffer in an upcoming film? Kevin Kline, for the same reason?) and my own participatory excitement in following the thread to see if they ever decided suggest that there is cultural pleasure to be had in unmasking the idealized figures of our own making.

For a while, there was a running category on "worst plastic surgery" on alt.showbiz.gossip. The invitation to us was: "Please post your nominations for worst celebrity plastic surgery."

1. Michael Jackson's nose—an absolute atrocity
2. LaToya Jackson's nose and breasts—almost nonexistent facial feature and painful looking chest bumps
3. Tori Spelling's collapsing nose and uneven breasts—evidence as to why you should not be able to have major reconstructions done before your body stops growing
4. Debbie Harry's botox-nightmare face—frozen like a nightmare in wax

A leitmotif is the public's annoyance with the stars' bad taste. With all their money and native good looks, shouldn't they be able to achieve superior surgical results? There is a power struggle here. To be able to evaluate the image is to imagine (momentarily) that you have some power over the very celebrity-paradigm who shapes your response to your own face and body. If celebrities offer up their images as a lure, it is inevitable that the public will assess their *management* of these images. Stars—perhaps in order to conceal the labor behind beauty, mystify it, and thereby fiercely cleave to the fiction of their superiority to the vagaries of the flesh—deny rumors of surgery. Elizabeth Taylor remains so wedded to her surgery-free story that even when she was being operated on for a brain tumor, she used her shaven scalp as "proof" that there were "no scars." Yet, as I discuss in chapter 6, we, the audience, are in possession of the archives of the evolution of their images. As one discussion-list participant puts it regarding Demi Moore's breast implants: "The proof is in the pictures." Stars deny the incommensurability of their bodies to their images, because to admit as much would be to dematerialize altogether—to acknowledge the utter *dis*identification of image and body. They would be nothing in themselves. For the actor, who is no more than the labor power behind the image, this false identity of body and image is necessary to the preservation of a notion of their individual talent and value.

Melanie Griffith's surgical changes seem to invite the most acrimony. Consider the following, from an Internet-based discussion list:

> This old Bitch needs more plastic surgery, Antonio will be moving on to some young stuff soon.

> Did anyone catch Melanie on Access Hollywood last night? Looks like she just stepped out of the plastic surgeon's office. If her face were any tighter, her eyes would be where her ears are. . . . she looked horrible. Guess she's trying to stay young for hubby.

It is the picture of her desperation that turns her audience into ravening beasts; this is how we instantly uplift our own miserable self-images into vampire criticism. The famous beauty becomes the repository for all our frustrations and self-loathing.

BORDERLINES/BORDERLANDS

Hollywood, writes Lary May, became the "modern utopia" for the unfolding of happily ever after (169). "Stars had to make the happy ending an extension of their own lives, for fans had to see that their idols could make it a reality" (169). "Hollywood" is the metonym for the film industry, the word we use to refer to the entirety of the production-making machinery. Hollywood is also a place where people live, you can drive down its streets, have a zip code there, and do the marketing. "Hollywood" stands for the place that generates images of fictional visual worlds—lures to identification. What's Hollywood showing these days? Who should I be tomorrow? Hollywood is the place where screen images become models for the three-dimensional world. Hollywood, in this sense, occupies what I will call a borderline place in the culture— both materially real and the site of illusions, created expressly to house the emergent film industry yet also the imaginary place to which many aspire ("I'm going to Hollywood!" exclaims the radiant young girl, starlet-fever igniting her eyes).

If "Hollywood" is a metonym for the film industry, it likewise has its own assorted metonyms: Grauman's Chinese Theatre, Universal Studios tour—the tour itself is the ultimate expression of borderline space in which house-lined streets are revealed to be no more than a series of facades. I recall as a small child being taken on that tour through streets on the Universal lot set aside for television programs like *Leave It to Beaver* that required undifferentiated suburban settings. The drive down the "street" conveyed me into the calm world of middle-American suburbia until we turned the corner and encountered the emptiness behind, just planks supporting the scenery; we crossed the borderline separating the TV life from "real" life.

But when you come to think of TV life as establishing a kind of paradigm for the rest of the country—*Leave It to Beaver*, for example, with its model of and for an American family that few if any viewers recognized as personally available—when you consider how expertly we learned how to carve ourselves in the image of what was no more than an image (two-dimensional in all respects, just turn the corner and see that there's no house behind the facade), you cannot help but ask to what degree our very experience of reality is modeled on two dimensions. The 1998 film *Pleasantville*, for example, reveals in all its profound despair the confusion between screen and three-dimensional worlds. A present-day brother and sister get stuck in the black-and-white world of the brother's favorite 1950s TV show, *Pleasantville*. This TV show has been for the brother an idealized calm and happy world where he shut out the noise of his broken 1990s family. Yet, heroically, the siblings rescue the black-and-white world of Pleasantville with color (which now stands for passion and vitality). The wonder of this film, its grand feat, is to recast the nostalgic and imperturbably pleasant black-and-white landscape of Pleasantville as in need of a strong dose of our violent, endangered, live-and-in-color, three-dimensional world. The film identifies as repressive (and ultimately dangerous) the "false front" of Pleasantville as it contrasts with the emotional untidiness of "real life." By the end, instead of continuing to hope his actual family becomes like the one on *Pleasantville*, the brother models the no longer idealized Pleasantville on "real life."

No longer, says Baudrillard, do we find the essence of the cinema on Hollywood Boulevard or in Universal Studios. Instead, it is "all around you outside, all of the city," and even more,

> even outside the movie theatres the whole country is cinematic. The desert you pass through is like the set of a Western, the city a screen of signs and formulas. . . . That is why the cult of stars is not a secondary phenomenon, but the supreme form of cinema, its mythical transfiguration, the last great myth of our modernity. Precisely because the idol is merely a pure, contagious image, a violently realized ideal. They say that stars give you something to dream about, but there is a difference between dreaming and fascination by images . . . they are a system of luxury prefabrication, brilliant syntheses of the stereotypes of life and love. *They embody one single passion only: the passion for images*, and the immanence of desire in the image. They are not something to dream about; they are the dream. (*America* 56)

As the three-dimensional landscape takes orders from screen images, movie stars and their cinematic lives can seem more primordially authentic than one's own life and one's own body. Hollywood was created as a place for movie stars to work and live, a place invented as a borderland between real and screen worlds. Those who perform within its charmed circle, Hollywood's representative product, movie stars, perform on the edge of the borderline space articulated by the emergence of Hollywood as such.

The idea of a body turned idealized image, then, is the founding concept for Hollywood—the borderland space designed especially for bodies to live and thrive in character—butlers serving intoxicatingly beautiful drinks to the gorgeous few by the side of their heart-shaped swimming pools. Their gorgeousness is part of the spatial decor. Their surgeries are calling cards into this realm—the inscription on their bodies of the separation of spheres, crossing the line from the three-dimensional into the screen world. Their flesh has become good enough to transcend the flesh and become image. Picture perfect for you and me.

Our extreme susceptibility to cinematic reality is perhaps both cause and effect of our loss of a clearly defined trajectory of representation; no longer can we assume that the celluloid world is based on a material one. Richard de Cordova tells of what he considers a transitional moment in the history of cinema, when in 1907 an uninitiated and unwitting street audience mistook a filmed bank robbery for the real thing:

> "In the most realistic way, the 'robbers' broke into the bank, held up the cashier, shot a guard 'dead' who attempted to come to the rescue, grabbed up a large bundle of money, and made their escape. Thus far all went well. The thieves were running down the street with the police in pursuit, just as the picture had been planned, when an undertaker, aroused by the racket, looked out of his shop. One glance sufficed to tell him that the time had come at last when he might become a hero. The 'robbers' were heading toward him, and, leaping into the middle of the sidewalk, he aimed a revolver at the foremost fugitive with the threat: 'Stop, thief, or I'll blow your brains out.'" (*New York Times* 3 June 1920, qtd. in de Cordova 32)

As an example of what he insists are simulated and no longer actual repressive social apparatuses, Baudrillard invites us to "organize a fake holdup," because we will discover that there's no way of keeping separate fake and real; it will become "real."

> You won't be able to do it: the network of artificial signs will become inextricably mixed up with real elements (a policeman will really fire on sight; a client of the bank will faint and die of a heart attack; one will actually pay you the phony ransom), in short, you will immediately find yourself once again, without wishing it, in the real, one of whose functions is precisely to devour any attempt at simulation, to reduce everything to the real. (*Simulacra* 20)

If we set Baudrillard's version of the impossibility of playacting in the realm of the hyperreal alongside de Cordova's anecdote, we can see the degree to which the playacting of film and television is embedded in and produces a crucial realignment of pretend and "real" events. In contrast to de Cordova's story, now the sight of bank robbers rushing down the street might incite us to look for cameras. Life's thrilling action moments, chase sequences, robberies, shootings are the stuff of the intoxicating two-dimensional screen world, which the real world only dully reflects.

TELEVISION AND THE SYMBOLIC VIOLENCE AGAINST THE FAMILY

Television is perhaps the most pivotal invention in our relationship with screen images. The "small screen" situated within the home casts the screen actors as integral to our lives. Lynn Spigel describes the advent of television in the American home as simultaneously cure and poison in relation to the "dangerous" outside world. "Numerous commentators extolled the virtues of television's antiseptic spaces, showing how the medium would allow people to travel from their homes while remaining untouched by the actual social contexts to which they imaginatively ventured" (191). But there was a "dystopian underside." "Here, television's antiseptic spaces were themselves subject to pollution as new social diseases spread through the wires and into the citizen's home" (194). Spigel distinguishes between real and electrical spaces, and the dangers she points to are the typical ones excoriated by social commentators—violence, sex, and so forth. What I would add to her account is the experienced spatial disruption of the domestic space by the screen that masquerades as three dimensions. This poison that is a cure is in fact itself an aggressive eruption in the increasingly defensive familial space. At the same time that we watch a potentially chaotic and dangerous world from the safety of our couches, also thrust upon us is the representation of a better world than our own, a better living room, a superior family, a two-dimensional model. The advent of television is deeply associated with the imposition of these idealized families on the American consciousness.

That the (Ozzie and Harriet) Nelson family was "real" is critical to the didactic imposition of a certain style and shape of "family" on the American public.[12] The obligatory family life purveyed by a *Leave It to Beaver* can do more symbolic violence to the American family than glimpses of a far-off war. *Leave It to Beaver* and *The Brady Bunch* impress their two-dimensional vision within and onto the family that is trapped before the morally superior vision of the world presented in these programs. Danger may lurk in images imported from the extrasuburban landscape, but true violence (in the sense of a direct assault on one's identity) is experienced at the hands of the two-dimensional televised family.

In "The Precession of Simulacra," Baudrillard stresses the dissolution of the distinction between an active and a passive relationship to one's culture, a distinction that perfectly captures the relationship between screen images and the three-dimensional world. As an example of what he means by the confusion between screen and real life, he considers the 1971 television experiment with the Loud family, in which this so-called average family was filmed nonstop for seven months.[13] He recalls the controversy following the breakup of the Louds' marriage, when many wondered if their divorce resulted from the intrusion of the

248 / *Being and Having*

television cameras into their real lives. "What would have happened," Baudrillard asks, "*if TV hadn't been there?*" (*Simulacra* 28). The ordinary person is a TV star now—look at the Loud family—people just like you and me, their everyday thoughts and experiences transformed into subjects of extreme public fascination. If TV didn't ruin their family, we may consider that it's what the TV stands for that ruined their family. For the Louds, it was as though they traded places with any of the idealized television families of their time. Suddenly, you wake up in television space, where, as a family, you cannot help but see yourself in relation to other television families. You realize you don't belong there, in television space, held up to the television family-values of the late 1960s and early 1970s; your family doesn't know its lines. You will fall apart. Divorce.

The word "model" contains the etymological unfolding of the reversal Baudrillard observes between the order of the real and representation. According to the *Oxford English Dictionary*, "model" originally meant a "representation of structure" or "a description of structure." Subsequently (in 1625) it came into use for "a representation in three dimensions of some projected or existing structure, or of some material object artificial or natural, showing the proportions and arrangement of its component parts" and (in 1639) for "an object of imitation." Not until 1788 was "model" used in the sense of "a person or thing eminently worthy of imitation; a perfect exemplar of excellence." In other words, no longer just an object of imitation, "model" has come to mean "a superior excellence." The very temporal order between model and "real" structure is unclear. A model structure can imitate a preexisting structure or, through functioning as projection, it can precede what thus will necessarily be a form of imitation on a larger scale. Even in its seventeenth-century usage, the word "model" as an object of imitation suggests an inherent confusion in the very idea of imitation, projection—and, ultimately, perfection itself. Not only is the distinction between material reality and representation complicated, but additionally unsettled is the question of where perfection is located, in the past or the future. It is specifically within this ambiguity that *simulation* will be dissevered from representation.

"Model" defined as "an artist's model" was first recorded in 1691; not until 1904 was this use transferred to the notion of a clothing model: "A woman who is employed in a draper's or milliner's shop to exhibit to customers the effect of articles of costume by attiring herself in them." Originally meant to illustrate what the clothes would look like on the person who would come to own them, the model nevertheless implicitly offered a "perfect" version to the consumer's eye. It is through insufficiency patterns of consumption and the ascendance of a retail-based economy that the model's body (in the sense of a projection of what the consumer will come to *have*) becomes imaginatively part of the whole package. In order to sell the product, the model's body must be the perfect form to reveal the clothing to its best advantage. As many have noted, bodies are thus necessarily subordinated to the clothing, for which the "best" body is the body best suited to the design of the clothing. That the model wearing the merchandise is a representation of how the consumer might appear in the same outfit seems self-evident until we consider whether the consumer's desire is to become the model/clothing package itself. The World War I shift from displaying women's clothing on headless dressmaker dummies to more lifelike wax models indicates a significant shift in the perceived relationship between the "model" body and the "real" consumer body. Gail Reekie shows that the implications of the changeover were consciously understood by the window dressers. She quotes one window dresser's expressed preference for the headless dummies:

> [It] leaves something to the imagination, so that the customer can easily visualise her own figure in the frock. . . . the simple suggestion of a drape [leaves] the rest to the customer's imagination. She gets a real pleasure in fancying how she will look in this or that material etc. Don't deprive her of that pleasure. She can't imagine herself as the theatrical young lady with the pearly complexion and ruby lips of the wax model. (143)

The "theatrical young lady" of course alludes to actresses as the official type of glamorous beauty. As wax models became ubiquitous, "the customer had no choice but to attempt to match her bodily appearance with that of the full model in the window" (143). Increasingly, the buyer's pleasure would be to imagine herself *looking like the model when she donned the dress.* The "original" is no longer the consumer but rather the model, whom the consumer aims to emulate. But even the model's status as original is derailed, inasmuch as the model is both ideal body and projection of the consumer body. Hence the simulacral effect. It is not just that the simulation *precedes* the real ("the precession of simulacra"); rather it is the *undoing* of precedence that undoes the reliable structure of representation as well.

Television performs all three kinds of "models"—the model as perfect exemplar, the model as projection of a future material reality, and the model based on a (prior) material reality. That, from its inception, television has offered "model" families suggests its collusion with the processes of reversing the order of the real. Far more accessible and more familiar-looking than films, where the stories have typically focused on larger-than-life characters and experiences that seem far removed from daily life, television has focused on the minor mishaps that might preoccupy any of us. Lynn Spigel writes that "in quite contradictory ways, the ideal sitcom was expected to highlight both the experience of theatricality and the naturalism of domestic life. At the same time that family comedies encouraged audiences to feel as if they were in a theater watching a play, they also asked viewers to believe in the reality of the families presented on the screen" (157). It is in the apparent familiarity that television can do damage; entreating us to watch people just like us, television induces a slow reversal and the replica models become exemplary models.

Focusing on the Loud family, Baudrillard inquires into the very concept of "TV verité." "A term admirable in its ambiguity, does it refer to the truth of this family or to the truth of TV? In fact, it is TV that is the truth of the Louds, it is TV that is true, it is TV that renders true" (*Sim-*

ulacra 29). The Louds arrive on the edge of the reversal of the real and the imitation, as though to reassure the audience that TV characters can and should be like us. But, as Baudrillard claims, this family "was already hyperreal by the very nature of its selection: a typical ideal American family, California home, three garages, five children, assured social and professional status, decorative housewife, upper-middle-class standing" (28). All this statistical perfection, this apparently inviolable image, could not arm them against a more extreme perfection, the very imitative social space upon which they built their actual lives. Lost in the televisual world, the Loud family was shattered by the violence done to their image. It was in being transplanted from audience to the very place where model families are fashioned and deployed that the Louds came to terms with their insufficiency.

COLONIZING THE AMERICAN BODY

Television is a favorite and easy target for media critics. In the 1960s, Daniel Boorstin pointed to television as the main forum for what he called the "pseudo-event." Pseudo-events supplant what Boorstin calls "spontaneous events." They are staged for us by the visual media and, because of their theatrical drama, have much more power over us than the uncontained and fragmentary nature of "real" spontaneous events. Celebrities, for Boorstin, are "human pseudo-events." Most worrisome, "what happens on television will overshadow what happens off television" (39). This is because television seductively frames and makes compelling what otherwise is just life. Television for Boorstin reverses the order of and preference for the original and the make-believe. "The Grand Canyon itself became a disappointing reproduction of the Kodachrome original" (14). Neil Postman has accused television of being the most pernicious form of mind-numbing "amusement" that has supplanted an engaged print culture. Richard Schickel claims that because it is positioned in our very own homes, television most nearly invites the false sense of intimacy with celebrities. What all these critics have in common is the worry that television puts us to sleep intellectually, leads us to conform mindlessly, anesthetizes any impulse for social criticism or resistance—not to mention causes the more general anxieties around television as the origin of everything from violence to drug culture in its influence on the nation's young.

While the vilification of both technology and popular culture has significant historical antecedents, what is specific to a televisual culture is the spatial relocation (and resizing) of celebrities. Not only does television have the effect of containing and normalizing the previously larger-than-life "film star," but also both stars and their practices seem within reach by virtue of sheer proximity and possession (they are caught within our household space). If, as Schickel argues, it's true that we feel increasingly "intimate" with those who appear within the confines of our own homes, then we also feel as though their bodies are more achievable role models. This shift from the outside of our homes to the inside, however, has always been met with a kind of slow panic. For, if we feel that we can appropriate or own *their* bodies, we are at the same time worried that they might colonize *ours*. Although the spate of 1950s films about alien invasions are commonly read as the cultural residue of "red scare" anxiety, what if they were recording anxiety over a different kind of invasion—one closer to home? [14] Rod Sterling's *Twilight Zone* series, which ran from 1959 to 1964, often self-reflexively points to its own medium as a central player in the dystopic transformations of the culture.

Both Susan Bordo and Elizabeth Haiken, in their commentaries on cosmetic surgery, have pointed to a famous *Twilight Zone* episode, "The Eye of the Beholder," as the paradigmatic story of the normalization of society through appearance. The protagonist, Janet Tyler, is being treated for apparently hideous ugliness—so extreme that others treat her as an object of terror. When we first see her, her face is concealed under layers of bandages. This is her eleventh treatment in the hospital, where doctors struggle to make her appear "normal." When Miss Tyler's bandages are removed, she and the doctors lament her unchanged condition. She will, they tell her, need to be transported to "the colony," where she can live out her life with others of her own unfortunate kind. The dramatic irony of the episode lies in the fact that, when the bandages are unwrapped, we see a woman whom we would call conventionally beautiful, played by Donna Douglas in fact; most important, she has the ideal female appearance for the time period, softly blonde and curvy. The doctors and nurses, conversely, are grotesquely pig-faced. Certainly the intention of the episode is a condemnation of a society in which people all have to be alike—hence the power of the ironic contrast between the beautiful Tyler and the monstrous doctors. Yet this very episode is ironically (and interminably) complicit with the normalizing practices it condemns. It is only *because* of a culturally shared code of beauty that this episode works. So dependent is the episode on exactly the kind of shared convention of physical beauty it claims to repudiate, that two actresses were hired to play the character of Janet Tyler, one with and one without bandages. As the director of the episode, Douglas Heyes, explained:

> The important surprise is that the girl who emerges from the bandages is incredibly beautiful by our standards. . . . So it doesn't really matter, I said, if that girl is a great actress or not so long as she's a great beauty. It *does* matter that the girl under the bandages is a great actress, but we're not going to be able to see her. Now, it's very difficult to find a great beauty who is that great an actress, so my original concept was that it would be easier to find a great actress who could do the voice and then find a great beauty who could look like that. (Zicree 147)

Television and film best achieve this combination (one actress to speak and the other to appear), which Heyes takes for granted as an artistic necessity. That Tyler's physical appearance plays a central "role" in the narrative is an element to which we have become accustomed in film and television. Ultimately, Maxine Stuart was cast as the voice of the bandaged Tyler. She noted the degree to which the casting wound up confirming the very conformity the episode attacks: "'It's absolutely right for Hollywood to do a script about conformity and then demand that your leading lady conform to a standard of beauty'" (147). But how else can a beauty-centered culture be defined without appealing to these powerful, already shared conventions? The fact that there was no other way to express the point suggests that the televisual apparatus could not help but be complicit with the social order it was challenging — that every challenge to the beauty industry would involve yet another submission.

Rod Serling introduces each episode by beckoning us into "another dimension, a dimension not only of sight and sound, but of mind, a journey into a wondrous land whose boundaries are that of imagination. Your next stop — the twilight zone." Isn't this dimension promised by Serling no more and no less than the medium through which he tells his stories — television? And then you don't have to travel very far — only as far as the boundaries of your closest television screen. Some episodes seem remarkably like allegories of television. "I Sing the Body Electric," in which a family purchases a robot in the form of a kindly grandmother to replace the dead mother, is ostensibly about the fantasy of overcoming separation and loss ("I can't die," the robot assures them), but just as clearly seems to be about the new role of television in the modern family. As Serling puts it, the robot is "a woman built with precision with the incredible ability of giving loving supervision to your family." Not only blamed for a host of social ills, the television is also made the cultural representative of absent parents, of mothers who abandon their children to a whole range of substitutes, including electronic ones. What if the television were better than a real mother — not only because it's immortal, but also, and more to the point, because it's always there for you?[15]

Jean Baudrillard sees television as the culture's primary vehicle of the hyperreal — "a miniaturized terminal that, in fact, is immediately located in your head — you are the screen, and the TV watches you — it transistorizes all the neurons and passes through like a magnetic tape — a tape, not an image" (*Simulacra* 51). Critics find television's menace lurking—like the monsters or aliens or whatever happens to be invading our peaceful planet—in the way it simulates *us*, the TV viewer. Typically, *Twilight Zone* episodes chart the panic of being colonized by aliens who "look like" us. In "Will the Real Martian Please Stand Up?" the challenge is to distinguish between the "real humans" and the Martian who is passing as human. What we learn is that there are not one but two aliens, a Martian and a Venusian, both having been sent ahead to begin colonization of earth. Similarly, in "Monsters Are Due on Maple Street," the denizens of the most typical of suburban American communities kill each other in a frenzied search for the aliens among them who they imagine are passing as just another average American family. Worse yet, they lament, we are now the object, the secondary effect even, of the television that somehow looks more real than those who watch it. We are socialized by TV, which is, according to Baudrillard, yet another *result* of the simulacral structure. "Everywhere socialization is measured by the exposure to media messages. Whoever is underexposed to the media is desocialized or virtually asocial" (*Simulacra* 80).

Television is associated with a kind of cultural and social death. When television isn't universally lowering our standard of taste along with our IQ, it is prodding us into unspeakable acts of violence, debasing our morals, supplanting the family, and, most insidious, luring us into a world of simulacra from which there is no escape. This is exactly the point of Peter Weir's film *The Truman Show*, in which an "unwanted child" is adopted by a television studio and made to grow up alongside actors on a fictional set that he, Truman, takes for "real life." Almost a parody of the Loud documentary, *The Truman Show* suggests that an entire life can happen within the confines of a television set. The whole nation has been watching Truman for thirty years—we see people who are tuned in twenty-four hours a day, as though Truman's life (which is pure television) has replaced their own life; or rather, the lives of the viewers become as deeply televisual as Truman's. Plotting a TV studio's adoption of an unwanted child takes literally television's baby-sitting function in the contemporary United States—as though to suggest that the child who chronically views television may as well grow up *within* the frame.

The movie opens, however, with Truman's dawning sense of the unreality of his environment. He spends the first half of the film learning where he is and the second half trying to escape. Haunting the film is the question of how he would know the difference between a television set and real life; indeed, the film engages the fantasy that there *is* one. While the series producer, Cristof, is so desperate to keep Truman locked within his world that he almost kills his own character, the audience eagerly identifies with Truman's bid for freedom. When Truman finally escapes, there are great cheers among his viewing audience—and why not? The film's plot, as though to prove there is more to life than the televisual, releases them, too, from this program, which can no longer exist without its central player. Why would we resent so deeply a technology that is so central to American experience, leisure, and pleasure?

Lynn Spigel charts a 1950s panic around television as an instrument of surveillance: "The new TV eye threatens to turn back on itself, to penetrate the private window" (118). In other words, we all risk becoming Louds to one extent or another. This surveillance, Spigel points out, can feel sadistic (118). What is crucial to add here, what "The Eye of the Beholder" makes plain, is that surveillance is actually a form of evaluation. Not just a neutral overseeing gaze, the TV assesses us in relation to the images it puts forth—images uncannily familiar yet superior. It is in their domestic familiarity, in their simulacral power, that these images work on us. If you don't submit to the televisual gaze, you risk being an outcast, an alien to your society, a monster. Your failure to emulate the television would make *you* look like the failed copy.

One of the *Twilight Zone*'s most famous episodes, "Number Twelve Looks Just Like You," parodies the social compulsion to model oneself on "model" bodies. We find ourselves in some future society where, at the age of seventeen, everyone is expected to choose one of two possible bodies (one male model and two female) for surgical transformation. Seventeen-year-old Marilyn is resisting undergoing the "transformation," which is initially represented as optional but turns out to be compulsory. Marilyn's mother, Lana, is played by the United States' first supermodel, Suzy Parker. Parker was cast for just this reason, because she epitomized a general image of "great beauty." Moreover, it is in this final transition into a culture with supermodels that the model altogether exceeds even the clothing and makeup she markets. Whatever she wears, she is in fact selling us her exemplary body.

Lana urges her daughter to choose "number 12," her own model number. To her mother and a friend, Marilyn insists upon free will and the importance of difference, but they can't comprehend why anyone would refuse the proffered "beauty." Marilyn also tries to sway the male doctors (a surgeon and psychiatrist—both played by Richard Long), who recognize her threat to the social order. Ultimately, she is forced to undergo the transformation.[16] In the end, Marilyn rushes from the operating room, exuberant over her new body, which seems to include an entirely new personality as part of the package. With so many visual doubles in the vicinity, it's hardly necessary for Marilyn to turn to the mirror to see what she looks like, but that's what she does. As she admires herself, she squeals to her friend: "And the nicest part of all, Val, I look just like you!" Serling's closing commentary is predictably critical of the culture of narcissism: "Portrait of a young lady in love—with herself. Improbable? Perhaps, but in an age of plastic surgery, body building, and an infinity of cosmetics, let us hesitate to say impossible."

Like "The Eye of the Beholder," the episode suggests that we can only criticize normalizing social practices from *within* their very terms. The show features the very idealized bodies that lead us viewers to want them for ourselves—especially in a show detailing the consumption of bodies through "choice" that isn't really much of one. After all, there are just two models, which implies not just social conformism but the rigidity of beauty standards.[17] Having the effect of a *mise en abyme*, the characters choose from the models, just as viewers are expected to choose models for our own looks from television. If, when we turn to the mirror, we find ourselves instead of "Valerie," what happens? What is the degree or nature of our disappointment? Here's the secret of the show, what confers on it a kind of brilliance apart from its trite social message: many of us might wish we too had the opportunity to choose between the two perfect bodies. Indeed, beneath the surface didacticism of this episode lingers the temptation to experience the very soul-numbing transformation we are instructed to condemn.

This transformation into a model is implicitly violent. Although everyone calmly explains to Marilyn the reasons for submitting as they reassure her that no one has ever been forced against her or his will, a climate of social control is increasingly evident. Moreover, we are led to believe that their "personalities" remain intact. We learn that Marilyn's father committed suicide because he couldn't come to terms with the imposition of the perfect body that stripped him of his individuality. Since this mishap, however, the scientists have corrected the problem of a personality that continues to resist social imperatives despite the body's capitulation. When she is finally transformed, we have the sense that the "real" Marilyn has been killed (in Stepford-wives fashion), so radically is her personality altered.

This episode directly links anxieties around plastic surgery to those surrounding the death of the subject through commodified reproduction. Walter Benjamin worried that "by making many reproductions [the technique of reproduction] substitutes a plurality of copies for a unique existence" (221). What he's really worried about is the death of the individual subject. When one's essence is so widely dispersed, what happens to the original person? Has something been stolen? "Number Twelve" suggests that in the mass reproduction of conventionalized bodies, singular identity dies.

While the order of the simulacral is the consequence of Western styles of power, specifically capitalism's, it also constitutes the fundamental undoing of power, as Baudrillard shows. The unveiling of the simulacral is deeply transgressive; hence, it's safer, as Baudrillard observes, to believe that a person is truly mad than that she or he is able to simulate madness. Power itself is unhinged, because it rests on nothing of substance. Similarly, the plastic surgery of the multitudes could be read not only as the culmination of the incursions of star culture but also as its ultimate undoing. Star culture, its beauty in particular, is dependent on a universal conviction of great beauty as special and privileged. Once their beauty turns out to be surgical, something any of us can have for the purchase, then we are no longer in thrall. By ourselves entering the order of illusion, there is no longer any illusion as such, because there is no difference between them (the illusion of celebrity bodies) and us (real bodies). So, is this an accomplishment of sorts? A repudiation of a certain structure of power that can no longer organize us through a radical separation of the star body from that of the viewer? If I am right about the trajectory of star culture that has culminated in a culture of cosmetic surgery, then wouldn't it stand to reason that with the dissolution of the identificatory power residing in star culture would come the end of the surgical impulse? But what if the identification is double-edged? Just as the television watches *us*, perhaps we are now the models—or rather, models of models, whose thoroughly internalized two-dimensionality functions as the ever-receding basis for "human" performances.

BECOMING-CELEBRITY

I arrived late for the face-lift. The first thing I noticed was that her eyes were open and black. This disgusted me. I felt as though I were looking at dead eyes, at something dead and inert even as the surgeon was working on her to give her the ideal facial contours of the supermodel/actress Paulina Poriskova.

You are a celebrity. You are an image. On television or in film. In a magazine. We all are. These are the images we transform ourselves into. Our "self-made" culture finds its logical extreme in surgical self-fashioning—becoming a star in our own right.

The surgeon slipped a silastic implant under the skin of her jawline, and I
marveled at the difference it made. "She likes the angular bone structure of
models," he noted. It was like watching a photograph develop as her face
progressed through the stages of what was a combination of subperiosteal
face-lift and alloplastic implants to alter her facial shape. Her face was con-
stantly unsettled, reconfigured. The addition of jaw implants made her look
very different, and then the implantation of a septum into her nose to
straighten out the bridge changed her look even further.

You can imagine yourself rising from rags to riches in the wild American highway of upward mobility and class freedom; you can start life in
a poor family in the ghetto and become a corporate executive.

After surgery, you wake up, peer into the mirror, and you are someone else.
The creation of the new image entails a destruction of the old image.

You can't really, or at least the odds are against you, but we feel as though
such achievement is possible, because instead of identifying with a character in a novel onto which we need to project something of ourselves,
we identify with two-dimensional images that give themselves to us entirely at the same time that they swallow us whole.

As the days pass, you watch for the bruised and swollen face in the mirror
to "become" a new face. The surgeon sees the new version on the table—has
a glimpse at least—before swelling and bruising overcome his handiwork.
We all wait anxiously. Sometimes, it takes years.

"Most patients," a plastic surgeon told me, "have very reasonable expectations. They don't expect to look like Sharon Stone." Is he right?
Isn't the process of surgical transformation itself bound up with celebrity
images? Isn't celebrity itself an image you can possess and become?

Suddenly the scalpel was sweeping along the edges of her face, and what
was formerly the pristine intact fabric of her facial skin was rent and lifted.
As the surgery progressed and her muscles were rearranged and tissue was
realigned over the bones in order to recreate the contours of youth, I began

to think of the surgery as the repair and the aging as the force that had shattered her face.

A cosmetic-surgery patient explained to one interviewer that "in her fantasies, she taunted her husband to fits of passion in the body of Vanna White. . . . Vanna had become an icon of feminine beauty, a Barbie doll in the flesh" (Schouten 418). Another commented on the emergence of a perfect face in the surgeon's preoperative drawing: "'Grace Kelly I will never be, but that picture was looking better and better'" (420).

The aging face was supplanted by the scalpel, and the scalpel seemed like the salvation of the face, now returned to its moorings, smoothed out, re-attached, restoring unruffled, smooth lines to a face that, retrospectively, seemed ruined before the scalpel grazed it.

A culture of cosmetic surgery is also a culture of celebrity and vice versa. And so, you will hate yourself or hate them—perhaps both.

This woman will wake up and see her swollen face and be shocked for five minutes before resigning herself to the wait for her new face to emerge. By the time she meets her new face, however, it will be her old face. It will belong to her as much as any old face she wears for the day.

By the end of the surgery, I didn't recall what she had looked like to begin with. Neither, for that matter, will she. She will rely on photographs.

EIGHT

Addicted to Surgery

When you look in the mirror and begin to imagine the imperfect part traded in for the improved version, you cannot help but see your body as in need of or lacking the pretty jawline or upper eyelid. The economic aspect only underscores the flows of exchange, deficit, possession. You buy a nose.

What did it cost you?

Did you get what you paid for?

Did you find love through the new body part? A partner? Does your mother love you now? Your creator?

Your surgeon?

So what are the consequences of becoming surgical? The lifetime effects? These are questions I have asked myself throughout this study. Some people have a few carefully spaced surgeries—say, a teenage rhinoplasty, a thirty-something eyelid lift, a fifty-something full facelift. Others may start much later but then pursue it with intensity—like a patient I interviewed who began with her eyes in her late fifties and took it from there. What are the combined circumstances that might lead to a "plastic surgery junkie"? Or is there any difference, really, between the person who undergoes repeated procedures and the one who simply has incorporated a moderate surgical schedule into her or his life?

IN THE BEGINNING

I observed the rhinoplasty of an eighteen-year-old girl whose preoperative nose appeared, well, uneventful. It was small, regular in shape, no humps, no bulges. I felt surprised. As it turned out, another surgeon had refused to operate. I can't imagine *anyone* twenty years ago performing surgery on this girl's nose. No, she didn't have Candice Bergen's nose, or Christy Turlington's, or anyone with that very narrow hyper-Anglo-Saxonized nose that registers perfect on the American aesthetic meter. She had a regular nose. But its failure to be paradigmatic, a "model" nose, somehow disturbed her enough to have it operated on.

This is normal. Twenty years ago the attempted refinement of normal features into perfect ones would have been the province of actors— not ordinary people, who would never expect to be evaluated so closely. Now that we've started to appraise our own faces and bodies with the carefulness formerly reserved for screen actors, however, all of us seem to have flaws. Should we be correcting them? Each and every one of them? We only need turn to the host of magazine articles discussing what once would have been dismissed as "minimal defects" to know how far we have come. Moreover, how does it make us feel to see ourselves blown up on the big screen of our anxieties? Can any single surgery solve what drives us? Two or three perhaps?

This is a far cry from the "Jewish nose" that stood out as different from the "American nose" and sought assimilative invisibility. Elizabeth Haiken has documented that many midcentury recipients of nose jobs weren't Jewish but were mistaken for Jews once they immigrated here— as though the "Jew" was difference itself, a difference emblematized in any nose weighing in as too big. Similarly, as Haiken shows, features linked to blackness, such as large lips and wide noses, were potentially racializable traits that white people would correct because of their aesthetic guilt by association.

This is a different landscape. Although white, Anglo-Saxon, Protestant aesthetic standards still reign over Western society's sense of proportion and contour, racially variegated traits are in style as long as there's just a smattering—large lips, say, or exotically slanted eyes— adding a sensual but controlled irregularity to otherwise strictly Anglo features and skin tone. Large noses can "work," and there are far fewer ethnic noses being bobbed. Features that used to be considered worrisome because of their *racial* valence have been supplanted by a whole new category of the slightly imperfect.[1]

After a century's worth of immersion in the close-up camera torture of star culture, we have come out on the other side with the ferocious perspective of a cinematographer. Every day, the list unfurls against the mirror, trails us through a day of fixing makeup, catching a glimpse in the rearview mirror, adjusting belts, fixing pantyhose, pushing hair to cover an awkward hairline—all those exhausting encounters with our bodies. Is your brow too low or too high? Is there an extra teaspoon of fat threatening to distort the line of your bathing suit? What about your knees? Are they too prominent or too pudgy? Does your upper arm flesh pucker against your short-sleeved top?

So here was this nose that no one, I mean *no one*, would ever have noticed one way or the other; moreover, because of its innocuousness, it wouldn't have had any effect on her overall facial appearance—yet she wanted it fine-tuned. Toward that end, she had been pressing her parents for the past year to agree to her nose job. I asked her if she expected it to look different, for people to notice. She didn't—it was for her. For her own eyes, for that private unveiling everyday in the mirror, however, she wanted it to seem significantly different. This is one of the paradoxes associated with surgery. You imagine a change that will make you look so much better to yourself—better enough to justify surgery—at the same time that you don't want the surgery to be visible to others. Oh, sure, you want people to ask you if you've changed your hairstyle or been on holiday, but you don't want them to glimpse the radical nature of your addiction to the ebb and flow of your body image.

It's not that you don't want them to see you as vain. Who cares, really? There are worse character flaws. This eighteen-year-old discussed why she didn't want people to know. "I don't want them to think of me as insecure." I might put it even more strongly: it's that we don't want people to know this secret (but overwhelming) necessity about us. It's as though the whole world assumes the position of the analyst, the one who glimpses the most hidden recesses of our identity. For people to realize that you are someone who would go "that far" is to know too much about you. In a sense, to be seen as insecure enough to have cosmetic surgery is to become inadequately defended from the gaze of the world. Curiously, in order to heal one's insecurity, the nose job now stands for (and in place of) the emotional deficit.

Who goes far enough to have surgery, and who doesn't ever consider surgery as an option? Subculture has much to do with these decisions. Those with friends and family members who are surgical typically picture surgery on our horizon. Of course, magazine articles and television programming has made it seem like part of all our lives, but there is still a big difference between those of us for whom surgery is no problem and those who cannot imagine going to such lengths.

As one surgeon told me: "It's certainly not desperation that drives someone to a plastic surgeon, but to actually make an appointment and walk into an office with the purpose of getting one of the most important parts of your body altered with no guarantee that this will come out the way you want it to is usually only done by people who've really tried mostly everything else. They're not desperate, but there isn't any other way to get what they want. So they come in." One patient tried every under-eye concealer imaginable before she had her lower lids cropped. Another wore shaping undergarments before she gave in to a tummy tuck. There is always the Wonderbra. You can use makeup to make your nose appear narrower. Try it. But those of us who have surgery want the change to feel permanent—not provisional.

Having had surgery on my nose when I was eighteen, I could not help but identify with this young woman. At the same time, it was in the differences between her situation and mine that I located my reaction to the surgery. She had to talk her parents into it; I, conversely, had been the reticent one in the face of my mother's insistence. This woman's nose was being operated on by a skilled surgeon, who made a minimal but attractive change to refine and narrow the tip, a surgeon who said he wouldn't break the bone and indeed did not break it. But her parents had reason to be concerned. She was pretty and her nose was unobtrusive. It was really a fine-tuning operation—and what if it went wrong? Rhinoplasty remains among the most difficult operations because of the size and limited visibility of the field of surgery. Even in the most experienced hands, there can be unwanted results. Surgeons repeatedly expressed to me their enjoyment of the procedure because of its technical challenges along with their awareness of the high risk of error: "That's the most satisfying operation. It's hard to learn it because of the long delay to see the follow-up. You have to look right five years later—because you see a lot of fake-looking noses, and they didn't look that bad right after surgery. In general, you don't always see your follow-ups five years later. And that's the problem. That's why it takes so long to learn it, because when you do see them, they come back for something else later on and you say, Hey, I thought that was a good rhinoplasty, and now it looks awful—there's this big hill here and a little ding or dent there." Here was this young woman who already looked very good. What if the surgeon inadvertently left a dent in her nose while refining it, from misjudging the difference between surgical swelling and cartilage by just a millimeter; it would be several years before anyone knew.

Her father pulled me aside before the surgery to express his serious misgivings. He was himself a surgeon, and he had little understanding, he said, of going under the knife for such a patently "unnecessary" procedure. Interestingly enough, many plastic surgeons who specialize in cosmetic surgery are attracted to just this low-risk, high-satisfaction combination. They didn't want to work in the dismal field of poor prognoses and death, like neurosurgery, for example. The father's condemnation of the unnecessary aspect of cosmetic surgery was so very familiar to me that I steeled myself for a vigorous account of the differences between life-threatening problems and what was merely superficial. So,

I was more than surprised by what followed: "For example, a few weeks ago my wife had an abdominoplasty. That was *necessary*. She had tried everything, running, working out for hours. Nothing worked, there was absolutely nothing she could do about it but surgery. *That* I understand, but this . . ." Prepared as I was for the conventional excoriation of plastic surgery as a "vanity" operation, I was taken aback that he considered his wife's major surgery (tummy tucks have a long down time, a significant scar, and a higher rate of complication) more reasonable than the very minor operation his daughter was undergoing; indeed, they weren't even breaking the bone. But, then, his wife is his sexual partner, so her interventions in her physical attractiveness might seem much more necessary.

During my postoperative interview with the rhinoplasty patient, she said she liked cosmetic surgery and had no doubt that some day in the future she would have additional procedures, such as rejuvenating surgeries. She contrasted the simplicity of surgery with the protracted experience of braces. "You wear braces for two or three years. With surgery, you go in, and two hours later you wake up different."

Joan Kron describes her own first experience with plastic surgery (a face-lift) as so gratifying that she went for more surgery five years later—another face-lift, endoscopic brow-lift, rhinoplasty. If "it turns out well," she notes, "you will very likely want more" (*Lift* 5). What I am saying is a little different; you could very well want more regardless. Indeed, if it turns out badly you are stuck wanting/needing more. Kron's own account of her two face-lifts five years apart seems naggingly less than straightforward. Why so soon, I might ask? She offers excuses. She was over sixty, and her doctor said that face-lifts after sixty average only five years of stopping the clock. She was having additional procedures (the brow, the nose, her sinuses), so why not go in and "tug" the lift (86)? Her genial doctor threw in the redone lift for free, referring expansively to warranties and expiration dates. The fact is, she's misleading the reader. In reality, five years is a bit past warranty. Since Kron frequently publishes on plastic surgery in mainstream magazines and is well known by these surgeons, her second surgery should more accurately be called complimentary. I wonder just how successful that first surgery was. Reading between the lines, hers is a typical surgery story; she was escorted halfway to her dream face, where she had that rapturous glimpse; but then when the swelling subsided, skin and muscle reverted. It would be much harder to lose what you had momentarily possessed. In a mournful panic, you watch as the spell dissipates.

FARRAH'S FACE

"Look at Farrah Now" urges the headline of the 4 July 2000 issue of the *National Enquirer.* I look at Farrah's face and don't recognize her. In her place I see a generic post-op woman, plumped up lips, cheek implants, one eyelid hiked a bit too high, profile with a particular surgical lilt to the tip of the nose. Nothing like Farrah. The article explains that eight years ago Farrah "had work to smooth wrinkles and sun damage" (29). Later, after the breakup of a relationship, claims the *Enquirer,* she had a brow-lift. Subsequent to her performance as Robert Duvall's wife in the film *The Apostle,* she received many "offers of work." "And she was convinced plastic surgery was responsible." So why not even more? "When Farrah landed the role in 'Dr. T and the Women,' as Richard Gere's wife, 'the last thing she wanted was to look old and tired in her close-ups. So, she had a major overhaul,' added the insider" (29). True or not, this is the story of surgical addiction—and why, once you believe that surgery "works," you will keep doing it.

Farrah supposedly needed more surgery to play Gere's wife. It's not just actresses playing the role of the wife who have surgery to keep their faces in check for the hellish close-up. It's also wives who desperately take arms against their faces and bodies to keep their husbands "interested." It's not just actresses who struggle to hold the camera's affection. It's also ordinary women (so many of us) who think that what makes us worthwhile, worth anything, is a pleasing physical appearance.

Joyce D. Nash, a psychologist, recounts what she terms a case of surgery addiction:

> Often the surgery addict feels she is fighting a war of attrition with her looks. This was the case for "Barbara." Although Barbara claimed her age was 48, she was actually 54. Despite her blonde hair, endless array of skin creams, and frequent shopping trips for new clothes, Barbara was having difficulty holding her marriage together. Her husband (age 55) was a wealthy businessman who traveled around the world and had casual affairs whenever he could. . . . Barbara had had her face lifted twice in attempts to remain youthful, and while these interventions were technically successful, they never altered her worried and guilty manner. She was very attached to her plastic surgeon, always bringing flowers for his secretary and returning regularly to have the state of her face checked by him. (90)

Nash, who herself had a face-lift, is here trying to distinguish between a normal concern with keeping up one's appearance and the desperate plight of poor Barbara, who blames her aging body for her bad marriage. But Barbara has imbibed thoroughly the cultural lesson about the necessity for women to look good. If her life isn't better, then that must mean she needs another face-lift. Comparing Barbara's story with Farrah's, we have here two different but related plastic surgery addiction narratives: Farrah's is the race against time. In one less than vigilant moment, all might be lost. Barbara, on the other hand, thinks she might have a happy life if she could just get it right this time. If this straying husband was faithful early on in the marriage, then it must be that she is no longer the same. She will go to her plastic surgeon and place her face in his competent hands. He will take care of her—even if her husband won't. Why is Barbara doing this? we might ask. Doesn't she realize that no amount of surgery will transform a chronically unfaithful husband into the picture of fidelity? But she has found another man now, her surgeon, who will restore to her these lost treasures. Losing the love of the camera might feel no different from losing the love of the husband. This is where the surgeon comes in—to rescue the fair princess, unlock the crone body in which she's trapped, release her to her real and happy life. She takes her bow. She is loved once again. Waves of love wash over her, just as Eve Harrington imagines.

It would be hard not to become addicted. It would be hard to stop once you found out it worked. It would be equally hard to stop if you believe it should work and you just haven't yet found the right formula, surgeon, procedure. Whether it's for reconstructive or purely aesthetic reasons, the ongoing sense of imperfection pushes us forward.

BETTER

It is important to understand and come to terms with the psychology of these practices, because then we are in a better position to know what drives us. Moreover, we need to think about the relationship between our personal practices and culturewide trends and transformations. It is true that as more and more of us begin to change ourselves surgically, our distinctions, our variations will be less obvious. Consider, for example, a world in which, by fifty, every single one of us has had rejuvenating surgery. When surgery becomes the standard of what fifty looks like, what might it mean to refuse surgery? In a culture where younger people have a better time in all respects, why wouldn't you want to look young—given the chance? Perhaps such possibilities strike us as frightening *because* they are so very tantalizing. One surgeon put it all very crisply: "We live in a very competitive culture, and you start looking old and saggy, everybody stops talking to you. I did a very large liposuction two days ago on a seventy-year-old woman. She had just gotten back from a motorcycle trip. She's seventy years old going on thirty, and there are a lot of them out there. You know, they're healthy and they're young and she's going to live to be 110. When you're seventy and you think you've got another thirty, forty years, you don't want to sit on the porch and rot. You want to stay in the game." Somehow, when he puts it this way—that in order to "stay in the game," more in the world, you need to have surgery—it all begins to sound rather coercive. The practice I or my friends or my family engage in for our personal gratification and sense of urgency seems simply like a choice of one sort or another, albeit a choice made in the context of powerful social forces. But what happens when those social forces become so very powerful that no one dare resist them without risking total exclusion? You will be fired from your job and replaced by someone "tidier"; you will be replaced by the youthful-looking at dinner tables; your partner will leave you for someone better maintained; your children will be embarrassed to bring their friends home to see their out-of-control parent; you will for all intents and purposes be socially dead. The rest of the crowd, who are with the program, as it were, will act as though they are among the living.

These social forces are all the more powerful because, as I discussed in chapter 7, we have no tolerance for stories of decline. We need movement, travel, stories about going someplace. The trajectory must be from bad or okay to wonderful. Aging isn't something to look forward to, clearly. It slows you down. Youthful possibilities dry up around you, and you leave a desert trail in your wake. To travel, to move, from Old Europe to New America, where one can thrive unrestricted, change social status, be "self-made"—or to venture far from your imperial and powerful world to find some "undiscovered" land, burgeoning with raw materials and land and free labor, you could make your fortune here.

Stories of travel enfold and shape us. We always head into opportunity. Cosmetic surgery stories are inherently future-oriented, are by their very nature about overcoming obstacles through making a change. In the case of the aging and/or defective body, an operation on the horizon becomes a hope toward which one moves with optimism. It is forward moving, expectation generating. For someone with a defect, plastic surgery can become an ongoing story of preoperative expectations followed by postoperative depression. A prominent surgeon talked to me about his early experience with cleft palate patients: "There was a mythology that was passed from patient to patient, and my group knew each other, because they would come in the summertime when school was out to have revisional surgery. There was a mythology that had developed that, when you were sixteen or seventeen and fully sized, then there would be the operation that would make everything look normal. I can't tell you how many times I've had to sit with weeping teenagers and tell them that there isn't anything further that can be done—which is tough." How did such a mythology arise if not through the very cultural association of plastic surgery as the story of "happily ever after"? Whatever the problem—deformity, ugliness, old age—you will be made anew. The end will be better than the beginning.

The fantasy that surgery can transform one is enormously wrenching for people who are disfigured—either congenitally or as the result of an accident. One accident victim fantasized about getting "the finest cosmetic surgery, which would make her defects disappear, and that she would buy the finest artificial arm, a true 'bionic' appendage" (Bernstein 145). Lucy Grealy describes the story of her own obsessive pursuit of a normal face. She had numerous operations involving a range of implant methods and materials, all of which eventually resorbed. She considered abandoning further treatment: "But, again but, how could I pass up the possibility that it might work, that at long last I might finally fix my face, fix my life, my soul" (215). Ultimately, a series of operations in Scotland proved reasonably effective. Grealy describes the difficulty of beginning to live without another surgery on the horizon, without "the framework of *when my face gets fixed, then I'll start living*" (221, emphasis in original).

The surgeon who discussed the cleft palate mythology more recently encountered a patient who would not be satisfied with the result of her scar surgery, nor was she willing to give up. "She was assaulted in a carjack and shot through the face and jaw and has this deformity of her lip. And she's had beautiful plastic surgery. She came to me because she had heard of my face-lift operation. She had had a face-lift, but she didn't feel that it looked as good, and I redid it. She's very happy, but she wants to have more. And I can't think of anything further that's going to make her appear entirely normal. Surely, you're well aware that even people who have no deformity and never had any kind of injury . . . But still, in the deal of the cards, we can't all be Sharon Stone."

We know that—and we don't.

From the wistful expectation that the next surgery will finally correct the disfiguring damage to the wishful thought that it might give you the movie-star level of looks denied you by nature, it's difficult to resign yourself to the mortal limitations the very practice of plastic surgery seems to transcend—at least in our cultural imaginary.

THE SLIPPERY SLOPE

A friend who has had several rejuvenating surgeries sat across the table from me and asked which surgeon I would recommend for further surgery and what she should have done this time. I was surprised, because, frankly, she looked wonderful—better than she had looked for quite some time. In part, what was nice about her appearance was that her last face-lift had relaxed somewhat, loosening the early post-op stiffness. I didn't know what to say, but I wanted to help. What would do it—her brow? she wondered. No, her brow looked fine. Everything was perfect. Any more and she would look too pulled. But it was clear as she pointed to each sector of her face that there was no satisfying her now.

One woman told me that even now, after two face-lifts, every time she looks in the mirror she thinks about her chin—a little tuck, some kind of intervention. But then she turns away—no, not now, not yet. As a consolation, she will have the laser zap her spider veins.

And the young woman with the rhinoplasty, whose tip will be just as slender as she ordered, will have future surgeries on that nose for several reasons. One reason is that she didn't ask for what she really wanted, which was an entirely new nose. So concerned was she to appear absolutely reasonable, a person who knew what she wanted—yet moderated by a sense of limits—that she would never have divulged the whole truth of her deepest desire for something like what swoops down from the midface of Michelle Pfeiffer or Jody Foster. These thin, straight, slightly uptilted noses were what she had in mind, but she wasn't going to expose (no, not for anything) the length and breadth of her yearning. Next time she visits a surgeon, however, she will ask for a little more—which won't seem quite as far from the surgical nose she now possesses.

She will also have more surgery because she's surgical. I've made this point all along, and I'm going to reiterate it, because becoming surgical is the cornerstone of the contemporary experience of cosmetic surgery. You will not necessarily have a lot of surgery, perhaps just a touch-up here and there; it doesn't mean you become a polysurgical addict. It's just that surgery has now entered your world as a remedy for the body's flaws.

There is nothing on her face and body that will slip past an inspection informed by a surgically attuned eye. The body that has been operated on becomes the most critically vulnerable of all bodies. I could say that we internalize the surgeon's gaze. But then again we had surgery to begin with because we were already identifying with him . . . in advance—as well as transferring onto him the priestly function of distinguishing normal from aberrant, reasonable expectations from immoderate craving. One patient told me that what she liked best about her surgeon was his confirmation of her own obsessive but guilty concern with her face: "He acknowledged that it wasn't in my head."

The surgeon can function as the limit-term of what might feel like our excessive desire for transformation. We know, instinctively, that if in our requests for surgery we don't act the part of the "normal patient," we might be turned away: "We call them junkies. You have to be very careful. When a patient comes in for surgery, one of the things I try to do in my interview consultation is determine what is it that they want changed. If the patient comes in and says, well, I'm getting a divorce and I want to start a new life and so forth and is unable to really tell me exactly what they want changed, what is it that really bothers them about their appearance, I'm very leery of that patient." This surgeon's account of the protocol for assessment is fairly standard. Yet, culturally speaking, we wind up here with what seems like a paradox. The surgeon is in many ways the legitimator of our otherwise embarrassing preoccupation with physical appearance. In the plastic surgeon's office, you are in the place of unsuppressed narcissism—the place where your otherwise absurd concern with the angle of your chin will feel entirely "normal." It will feel scientific even, as the surgeon measures and evaluates the arrangement of your features. He will make you feel that all your trivial little obsessions are absolutely justifiable—like any therapist, he's there to support you. "You know what happens is that, as soon as people start talking about appearance, we immediately equate that with being shallow and superficial," a surgeon remarked. Then he paused, looked at me, and pronounced the core truth of his professional life: "We can make that comment all we want. But the fact of the matter is, we live in a very visually oriented society. You can talk about all the inner beauty you want, but the fact of the matter is that appearance makes a tremendous difference insofar as sexual appeal or for jobs."

You would be crazy not to be operated on when doing so will change your life—you will be loved, you will be successful. You would be crazy to refuse all that. Yet this very same surgeon, in another mode, explained quite emphatically the difference between the normal patient and the pathological: "I spend at least an hour talking to people before surgery. And while on the surface I'm just getting information about the operation they want, I'm also doing a psychological evaluation. How stable is this person? What is their true motivation for doing this? Why surgery now? I have one fellow who returns to me every year. He comes back to see me because I'm the only one who won't operate on him. I think that his concern needs to be dealt with not through plastic surgery but through therapy—that's what I've told him. And he comes back after he's had another two surgeries."

"There *are* people who are overly narcissistic. There are people who are overly concerned with their appearance. . . . I turn away thirty percent of cosmetic patients," boasted one surgeon, while another surgeon claimed a turn-down rate of "one out of three." But no one I know and no one I've interviewed has been turned away—ever—by any surgeon.

Anthony Napoleon did an extensive study comparing preoperative personality profiles of patients and their postoperative reactions. Although largely focused on the variables of patient pathology, Napoleon does pause to note the following:

> With regard to the relationship between patient satisfaction and expectation, a conflict can arise between promoting plastic surgery results and promoting realistic postoperative expectations. Most surgeons, at the very least, compile a flattering portfolio of excellent results for prospective patients to review. Some surgeons advertise, oftentimes presenting before and after photographs that are extremely positive and show dramatic improvement. Overstated "marketing" is not conducive to patients maintaining realistic postoperative expectations. (200)

Recall the surgeon who cajoled me into surgery through his photographs of the makeup model. He would certainly be a prime example of the hard sell—as well as someone apt to create dissatisfied customers by fueling hopes he couldn't possibly fulfill. Over the course of my interviews many surgeons spoke grandiosely about results of their "miracle" surgical approaches, which I know are somewhat overstated (especially when it comes to rejuvenating surgeries), because I've seen with my own eyes the published photographs. Perhaps Napoleon is speaking to just this problem of surgeon grandiosity when he writes: "With reference to increasing medical malpractice suits, a pernicious synergy between physician personality and patient personality, both similar along the dimension of Narcissism, was found in more than one-half of the malpractice suits reviewed in this study" (206).

And what of the surgeons recommending procedures? In my interviews I often related the story about a friend of mine who went to a highly respected surgeon for a rhinoplasty and was advised by the surgeon that he would remove her under-eye bags as well. She didn't object and claims that she was delighted with the results of the eyelid surgery.

When I queried her about the ethics of recommending additional surgery, she countered that she didn't know about this procedure and was grateful for the advice—especially since the eyelid surgery pleased her more than the rhinoplasty. As it turns out, this surgeon has a reputation for doing wonderful eyelid surgery. Unsurprisingly, then, he focuses on the eyes of all prospective patients. This "flaw" is somehow magnified for him. He can't control his impulse. He must operate to cure the unsightly and wayward bags.

The surgeons I interviewed condemned unsolicited intervention but at the same time pointed out that it was important to let patients know what combinations of surgery ultimately would make them happy. A surgeon gave me an example illustrating how cautious the surgeon needs to be around the patient's self-image:

SURGEON: This young lady came to my office. Her nose looked like it had been busted a few times—it was twisted, it was dented, and she sat where you're sitting.

And I said to myself, I know why she's here—there's no question in my mind: it's for this nose. And I leaned over and looked at her right in the face, and I said, "How can I help you?" never taking my eyes off her nose, because I was already thinking about what I would do. She said, "I have this mole that bothers me." I actually had to pause, because I just couldn't believe it. She had a mole, no question about it. All I could think of was that ugly nose she had, yet never once in the course of the conversation did she ever allude to that nose, never—never, never, never. As you can see, the problem is, you and I see things on a person and say, My god—this woman here, if she were at a plastic surgery convention, she probably wouldn't make it out the back door without someone doing her, but that was not what she wanted. And I have this all the time. I'll see someone with baggy, baggy eyelids, and they say—that doesn't bother me

at all, Doctor, it's this I can't stand. Now the fact is,
however, that sometimes you have to expand the
menu.

AUTHOR: Do you ever tell people that they need more done?

SURGEON: More done? Yes, let's take a face-lift—I see a woman
who comes in and says this is what bothers me. I say, I
can't do that without doing this, OK? This is what you
might get—you still have to make an incision here. If
that disturbs you, I can't do it, because geographically,
anatomically, these two are intertwined—I can't do one
without the other. I can't paint the door without painting both sides.

It's a fine line, this question of pleasing the patient. Surgeons told me
that they know the patient won't always be happy with what the patient
imagines is the right operation. This makes perfect sense in terms of the
harmony of facial change. You have your nose resized, and suddenly you
become aware that your chin isn't quite what it should be. Many surgeons assured me that patients with "weak chins" won't like the results
of the rhinoplasty if it isn't accompanied by a chin implant or advance-
ment. Or they won't like their face-lifts if their eyes stay baggy and
droopy. Or they won't like the under-eye surgery if they don't have the
upper eyelid hoisted to go along with their freshened new look. One patient reported that her surgeon suggested her upper eye might bother
her a bit after her lower lid blepharoplasty, but there was nothing she
could do about it, because she couldn't afford the additional surgery.
When I later interviewed her about her surgery experience, she had for-
gotten altogether that it was his recommendation and presented it as her
own (albeit minor) concern: "My upper eyes are kind of droopy. If I had
no job and all the money in the world, maybe I'd want to get it fixed."
This is how cycles of surgical necessity can begin.

Plastic surgery and body-image tinkering are filtered through the
practices of consumer capitalism. You can begin to feel as though you
want the whole package. It's how the surgeons present it. Consider this

passage from the interview I quoted at length above: "I can't paint the door without painting both sides." Another surgeon made plain to me the relationship between finances and surgery: "One surgeon has repeatedly said that he feels that everybody should have everything done at the same time so there's harmony in the aging process. And that's fine. If people have unlimited money, they can do that. But a lot of folks walk in, and they say, 'You know, my eyes are bothering me.' 'What about your jaw?' 'Well, what about it? Just get my eyes looking better, and I'd be real happy. How much, Doc?' They say, 'I can afford my eyes, great,' and I explain, 'Well, your jaw's going to be this much more.' So, they respond, 'I can't afford that, Doc. I need a new car.' I think you should choose."

The surgeon presents you with a menu of possible options that you might appreciate, and you can choose on the basis of prioritizing exigency. What tortures you right now, this minute? What can you postpone, save for? A new car? A sleek new jawline? Although cosmetic surgery can seem like fun, like another consumer plaything (as the patient said, if one had all the time and money in the world, I might like that particular surgery), it can also feel like the solution to a sense of desperation. For example, although the patient could dismiss the brow-lift as something she could ill afford, the bags under her eyes seemed like a necessity: "When I was in my early thirties, I rather suddenly developed terrible bags under my eyes, and I became pretty fixated on them. I looked in my mirror, and all I saw were these bags, and I felt like they distorted my whole face, like they pinched my whole face in toward my nose. I felt like the rest of my face was aging just fine, and this was just so dramatically worse than everything else. Also I felt they made me look really ugly when I otherwise would have looked fine. It's uneven, it's unfair, it's distorted, in terms of aging; it was way ahead of the rest of my face."

Like everyone who begins to feel uncomfortable with a certain element of her or his body, she became fixated on these things. "It was all I saw. It really distorted what I felt was my otherwise perfectly acceptable face." Katharine Phillips would call this body dysmorphic disorder, this heavily distorted view of the offending feature, in which it becomes both magnified and isolated from the other features, but she is what plastic surgeons recognize as the perfect surgical candidate. These patients know what they want. There is a match between surgeon and patient insofar as they both recognize the need for a surgical remedy.

THE FIX

I said to my friend, face it, you will never be entirely happy with what you look like. Surgery will make it better for a short time; then it will seem all the worse. She replied that I was right, that for a time it does its work and you feel great even though you already scrutinize the defects—eyes that aren't quite even or a bulge you thought would flatten entirely—and then later it doesn't look good at all, and you need another fix.

Surgery temporarily gratifies the hole in your narcissism that requires attention *some place*, and why not start on the surface if you can't locate the "interior" unconscious origin of the demand for repair. By the way, let me be clear that when you decide you want surgery to correct what you perceive to be a defect on your face and body, the defect feels quite real. It's not as though a little dose of self-esteem could ever be expected to vanquish those crow's feet or, more important, caring about those crow's feet.

Once you have surgery you will either have it again or want it again. I know two people who have assured me, after a face-lift, that they would never have one again. One has gone on to have several other surgical procedures. The other is very recently post-op. Studies are insufficient; they don't track people. Patients go to different doctors for their multiple surgeries, and so no one knows or traces the surgical circuit. Even people who claim to adore their surgeons often visit other surgeons, because when the nature of the subject is a certain experience of perfection, it's hard to believe you've found it in either the result or the surgeon. It is a circuit that takes you from one doctor to the next, from one procedure to the next; for a while you are exhilarated, as you wait for the beautified part to emerge from the swelling, and then you are back to the mirror, the drawing board of your desire.

MOVIE-STAR DREAMS

As I argued in my reading of Frankenheimer's film *Seconds*, the deepest wish associated with cosmetic surgery is that it might make one movie-star gorgeous. This is not grandiosity. Nor is it especially literal. Rather, it's a wish derived from the cultural position of movie stars as paradigm. Note what happens to women, regular-looking women, when they come under the severe look of the camera. Like the Loud family caught in the televisual landscape, they see themselves as inadequate. And so does the audience. Their hairstyles, wardrobes, noses, circumference of their thighs, you name it, are now topics for public discussion. Marcia Clark, the prosecuting attorney of the O. J. Simpson trial, revamped her look entirely during the trial, to the delight of all the commentating journalists. Or consider Linda Tripp, persecuted by the media for her unattractiveness, who lost weight and had extensive plastic surgery: "including liposuction, removal of bags from under her eyes, a facial peel, resculpturing of her nose and removal of the fat from underneath her chin and neck. . . . 'The ugly jokes about Linda finally got to her'" ("Linda Tripp's Plastic Surgery" 8). Being seen in the place reserved for beautiful-looking people, the actually quite normal-looking Tripp appears ugly by comparison. "'What made it worse was the fact she was going back in the public eye. She simply couldn't face going to trial later this year and becoming the butt of an entire new onslaught of jokes'" (9). When she is in the public eye, in the televisual world, the expectations around her appearance change, no matter what *we* look like. Members of *America Online* were invited to vote on whether they preferred the pre- or post-op Linda. At the same time, they were asked to decide whose surgery they liked best, Jennifer Gray's nose job or Linda Tripp's face-lift? It wouldn't be surprising if Linda Tripp were to become "addicted." Courtney Love became famous for being unpretty and profane in the world of the surgically tinkered-with (even rock stars, even punk rock stars, if they're women, are supposed to be beautiful). Disheveled, unsvelte, proud of it. Then one day all that changed. She had her nose done, combed her hair, and showed up in Vera Wang gowns at celebrity events, doing her Monroe turn. What happened? Cintra Wilson thinks it all started with a photograph—big-nosed, chunky Courtney was photographed repeatedly next to "best-friend-of-the-minute Amanda de Cadenet" and saw herself as the ugly one beside de Cadenet's "model type" of glamour-prettiness (85). Although Courtney had resisted for so long succumbing to beauty in the thick of celebrity culture, when she took her measure beside de Cadenet, she folded.[2] But Wilson acts as though Courtney, aggressively unkempt as she was, wasn't perfectly attractive to begin with—pre–nose job.[3] This is because of the "Hollywood effect" of making attractive women seem and feel unlovely next to superhuman beauty. Judy Garland was often cast as the ugly duckling— but how many women would look adequate next to Hedy Lamarr and Lana Turner (in the *Ziegfeld Follies*)? Pretty Janeane Garofalo routinely plays the "plain one." Beautiful actresses like Minnie Driver gain weight (momentarily) to play the "fat homely one" in films like *A Circle of Friends*, because the screen has such a low threshold, as I discussed earlier, for "real" and permanent plainness. Even comedians like Carol Burnett and Phyllis Diller, in part known for their offbeat looks, have become two of the most famous surgical bodies in Hollywood. Time and again the surgeons I interviewed remarked on these two beauty-victims. It was always the same—Diller's work was "wonderful," but "poor Carol Burnett has ruined her career." "How could you laugh at a face like that?" sighed one surgeon. None of them saw the equivalence between the two surgeries, the necessity for the "ugly duckling" to be transformed in the land of astounding metamorphosis.

Cosmetic surgery takes place in the domain of star culture, as I've been arguing all along. When we have surgery, we are also identifying, however remotely, with the transformational practices of celebrities. Hence, rejuvenating surgeries aren't necessarily intended to recover one's *actual* lost youth but rather a fantasmatic lost youth, a youth in which one becomes retrospectively beautiful as well. In contrast to the sinister story told by *Seconds*, *Ash Wednesday* is entirely complicit with this fantasy of surgery restoring the lost original ideal. Elizabeth Taylor simply folds back into Elizabeth Taylor. It is as though any woman in her fifties could walk into the remote and mysterious hospital run by some brilliant Swiss surgeon and come out looking like a screen goddess. This is, of course, what we want (really want) when we go under the knife. A surgeon told me the story of a woman he described as ugly who asked him to make her look more like Elizabeth Taylor during her face-lift surgery. She was apparently convinced that her features already had much in common with Taylor, and a little tweaking would do the trick. As he listened to her, the astonished surgeon thought, "*You?* You think *you* can look like Elizabeth Taylor?" But why not? Isn't this exactly the underlying promise of these body surgeries? That you can "be" someone else—Elizabeth Taylor, for example? And aren't we endlessly encouraged to think about which movie star we most resemble in order to determine our "type"? "Find your inner celebrity," beckoned a recent article on *America Online*.

Barbara, from *Ash Wednesday*, tells her unsuspecting husband on the phone: "This little separation has helped a lot darling. I'm really a different person." She both is and isn't of course, and *Ash Wednesday* is too caught up in conventional fantasies surrounding movie-star beauty and the youth-serum secrets of the rich and famous to pay attention to its overbrimming contradictions. Thus, on one level, she isn't a different person at all. Rather, she's the same person she used to be, more like the woman her husband married. The "different person" is the old woman she's trying to escape. On another level, however, the level of our deepest fantasies associated with rejuvenating surgery, she *is* a different person. She is Elizabeth Taylor, who is just what you and I want to look like (or any of her current screen goddess versions) after we go under the knife. It is in part because of the incommensurability of the outcome to the expectations that people can become addicted to surgery. The addiction is built into the practice.

In the March 1998 issue of *Ladies Home Journal*, the soap opera actor Linda Dano tells us her story in "My Face-Lift." She explains her decision in a way that clearly articulates the conflicts (and anger) involved in making such a choice: "I believe we, as women, must get to a place where seeing other beautiful women doesn't make us feel bad about ourselves. But I was once a model, sought after by men. Now I have this double chin, and I don't feel like me. Still, some part of me thinks I've sold out" (Dano 56). It isn't difficult for me to imagine Dano on the set of a soap opera for many years, aging all the while as a series of beautiful young women (soap operas are their birthright) pass through the show, upstaging her not only in appearance but also in the attention lavished on their romantic plots. Like the tummy-tucked women past their Chevrolet-dating prime referred to by the surgeon, aging actresses must forgo plots based on their delectably youthful bodies. At the same time, the faces and bodies of the young and beautiful are interminable fetishistic points of interest for hovering cameras that land on the postforty female face with great hesitation. Once Linda Dano was the center of the camera's attention; now, she's a lighting challenge.

Being the audience is nightmarish enough as I watch the romantic stories of twenty-year-olds supplant those of actors my age. At the same time I am well aware of the surgical interventions on the faces of soap opera actors I have followed over the years—some of whom would be unrecognizable if compared with their younger versions. This neverending influx of the young and beautiful, who are coded as more gazeworthy, contrasted to the surgical but nevertheless transparently aging faces of actresses is almost too much for me. I am swept away in the performance of the body's anxiety—that daily unfolding of aging beauty witnessed by the soap opera genre. The young women are brought in to attenuate the escalating hysteria sweeping through the show as the central characters are processed through lens filters and scalpels. These visible protests against the aging process seem all the more painful as they flail against the invincibility of young beauty.

Who else but actresses so aptly represent the struggle between waxing and waning beauty? The bodies of actresses are affixed with otherwise more inarticulable and diffuse cultural experiences and representations of femininity. This is why what happens to their bodies (literally, as in surgery) can have such profound effects on the culture. It is because we have projected onto them a certain representational status of the female body—of how we are supposed to look at her, feel about her, contain her, experience her, what angles we are allowed to see, and what angles are interdicted by the camera—by the actress herself.[4]

PROMISES, PROMISES:
THE NEW WORLD OF CONSUMER CHOICE

In the July 2000 issue of *Vogue*, you will find one of this magazine's many predictably high-culture accounts of our fascination with cosmetic surgery. In contrast to something like, say, *Marie Claire*'s middle-class menu of new and fabulous options for the masses, *Vogue*'s articles tend to sustain the upscale associations of the process—Park Avenue surgeons, Soho dermatologists, Aspen socialites, and so on, alongside coy and ironic critique. The author of this piece, Elizabeth Hayt, poses such socially rigorous questions as "So has fake become the new standard?" (200). It's important for the self-reflexive aspects of the upscale articles to offset their true purpose—the menu, the possibilities, the excitement of it all.

Here's how you can tell. When you finish this kind of article you have a mild sensation of intellectual fulfillment (after all, this is supposed to be an intelligent overview of a cultural trend) wedded to a surge of desire (only, of course, if you are already predisposed) for at least one among the many new procedures described. Whether we like it or not, the reader is carried along on the wave of paranoia, competition, and consumer enthusiasm. On the surface, such articles make it sound

like so much fun. The writer and her interview subjects are both practical, indolently tongue-in-cheek ("'Artificial beauty? Is there any other
kind?'") and armed with the most up-to-the-minute information on
preserving their bodies intact forever. Even the addictive components
are presented as amusingly commonplace. Indeed, such articles can participate in addiction, yoking as they do our narcissistic vulnerability to
the rigors of vigilant consumer practice. Almost veiled, but not quite, by
the trendiness of Hayt's presentation, are the feelings of destitution and
loss and panic underlying even the most well-heeled encounters of the
jet set with their Beverly Hills or Park Avenue surgeons: "Another of
Hidalgo's patients, a former model . . . an avid skier who lives in Col-
orado and has a body to rival Gisele Bündchen's—is used to the reactions of disbelief when she confesses her age, 47. Twelve years ago, after
her (beastly) former husband told her he never dated women over 35, she
decided to stop the clock" (200). Since this time, she's had several procedures, and she reports, "'I look to my plastic surgeon to guide me. He
is my VIP, as are my dentist and my trainer'" (201). Why might women
be turning over their bodies to a maintenance crew? We might dismiss
this example because, after all, she's a *model*, whose self-esteem for most
of her life has been located in what can only be a transient beauty.

How can we recognize an addict when we see one? Talk to people
about their surgeries, and you soon find out that they typically compare
their own "minimal" interventions with either "serious" plastic surgery
or "someone who's addicted." A woman who has had her breasts augmented, her nose fixed, and her eyelids trimmed and is now contem-
plating a full face-lift considers herself entirely in the "normal range"
of body maintenance in contrast with people who "overdo" it. Another
woman who had a nose job as a teenager and lower eyelid surgery at
forty compares herself with people who are "real surgery junkies." Actresses who confess to surgery often say something like, "Well, I've only
had my jawline tucked, not a whole face-lift." The jawline "tuck" *is* a
face-lift, in case you're wondering. Even patients suffering from the

effects of silicone breast implants engage in acrimonious comparison. Those whose implants are postmastectomy criticize those whose surgeries were for pure vanity, as though that group deserved their complications.⁵ Why do we need to cast other people as "worse," more "addicted," the true victims of surgery fever? It's never us—we're prudent, careful, reasonable.

THE PERVERSE CYCLE OF ADDICTION

They are called delicate self-cutters, most often adolescent females who cut their skin in moments of intolerable anxiety. They make shallow rifts across the surface of their skin. "The cuts are carefully wrought, sometimes simple parallel lines but also intricate patterns; rectangles, circles, initials, even flowerlike shapes" (Kaplan 373). These cuts can be a work of art, elevating the body from what is felt to be its abject changes (menstruation, for example) and longings; they can reassert the distinction between the inside and the outside. At the same time, the cuts can function as counterphobic responses to a sense of internal mutilation. The delicate self-cutter becomes herself the agent of a mutilation she dreads passively experiencing. Psychoanalyst Louise Kaplan observes that "a perversion, when it is successful, also preserves the social order, its institutions, the structures of family life, the mind itself from despair and fragmentation" (367). Like many who undergo cosmetic surgery, Kaplan's perverts experience a deep-seated shame that needs correcting and feel defiant rather than guilty about their perversion, which they nevertheless take to be a violation of the moral order.

The surgical patient's shame is intolerable, the thing that drives her or him to the doctor—aging or ugliness or just not being quite beautiful enough. Just outside the operating room, a surgeon explained to me that the patient inside was the "ugly duckling" of her voluptuous family. She was now in the middle of divorce and wanted to improve her appearance. Who can imagine her shame? How can I express the shame I

288 / *Addicted to Surgery*

felt for her as her surgeon pronounced the shameful "truth" of her un-loveable body.

The genetically blessed, hypertoned, strategically lit bodies of ac-tresses can induce shame in the woman with an ordinary flesh-and-blood body. But even the "real" actress's incapacity to maintain such a body is humorously treated in Mike Nichols's film *Postcards from the Edge*. Actress Suzanne overhears the head of wardrobe complaining to the director about the difficulties of tailoring clothing for the actress's out-of-shape body. They can't put her in shorts because the top of her thighs are shockingly "bulbous." They can't film her on her back during the love scene because her breasts are "out of shape" and will no doubt "disappear under her armpits." They express regret that they hadn't managed to cast in her place another actress whose body was supposed to be "perfect." Many of the women I know, not actresses, just ordinary women, worry about being seen in public in bikinis or short-sleeved tops or shorts rising much beyond the knee, clothes that would disclose to all a shameful and secret part that we keep hidden from view—our flabby thighs, our postpartum middles, our middle-aged arms. Said one surgeon: "I know of many women whose husbands have never seen them nude. I know of women who never go to doctors because they don't want to be seen by them." So, finally they offer themselves up to the surgeon for aesthetic body work, and they are transformed. They can be seen, held, admired. Little by little, we are all becoming movie stars—inter-nally framed by a camera eye.

"The little mutilations take up her mind and enable her to temporar-ily escape the frightening implications of being transformed physically and emotionally into a woman with the sexual and moral responsibili-ties of adulthood" (368–69). Kaplan is writing as though the transition is just one, from girlhood to womanhood, which, for the delicate self-cutter, proves intolerable. What if we were to rethink this universal transition (puberty to womanhood) through the terms of the twenty-first century, where we find the chronological body supplanted by a two-dimensional prototype that is an impossible combination of fashion-centric transitions and age-defying stasis? This is a body always in flux. It can't land on the other side. It can't become and stay comfortably a woman, because it's so difficult and there are always new challenges to face as well as perils to ward off.

Princess Diana was a self-cutter, or so claims biographer Andrew Morton. "On one occasion she threw herself against a glass cabinet at Kensington Palace, while on another she slashed at her wrists with a razor blade. Another time she cut herself with the serrated edge of a lemon slicer; on yet another occasion during a heated argument with Prince Charles, she picked up a penknife lying on his dressing table and cut her chest and her thighs" (qtd. in Favazza 241). Reminiscent of Elizabeth Taylor, Diana was a celebrity who seemed literally to embody the shift from flesh to image and back again. Her confessed eating disorder made her beautiful image seem more available, closer up, or rather heightened the exciting tension between flesh and image.[6]

And so how different is going under the knife in search of youth and beauty from some ritual and hidden adolescent cutting? Just because the culture has normalized our pathology (of course, it's thoroughly normal to want to look rested and vigorous enough to compete in the youth-centered workplace), it doesn't mean that cosmetic surgery isn't like any other practice that has us offering up our bodies to the psychical intensities that angrily grip us. Ballerina Gelsey Kirkland describes the experience of her initial round of cosmetic surgeries: "The operations found me laid out on a table, yielding to the touch of their probing fingers. I watched my life through the eyes of their needle, penetrating my heart as well as the outer layers of my skin. I would become hooked on the pain, addicted to the voluptuous misery that bound my sexual identity to ballet, to an ever-increasing threshold of anguish" (58). On the operating table, face up, waiting for hands to crawl inside and tug out the ugliness that is like entrails that eventually regenerate and need to be taken out yet again. We struggle up from intolerable bodies vanquished in the exquisite moment of surgical battle in the theater of operations. I recall the scene of a face-lift. One minute she was lying in the swamp of her aging and flaccid skin, and then slowly her face rose from the chaos, sleek, tautened—as though taking shape out of some primal sea—the shards of her outgrown and useless flesh left behind, spirited away by the surgeon's magic.

You will look in the mirror, smile back at the image reclaimed, and relish the grace period between this operation and the next one. The beast-flesh will grow back.

NOTES

1. THE PATIENT'S BODY

1. This question of chin size seems to be a vexing one among surgeons. Some surgeons routinely do chin implants with their face-lifts, for example, because they believe that the chin has atrophied. Other surgeons think this is a medical fantasy. I know one woman whose surgeon augmented her chin during her face-lift with very unsatisfactory results. It is clear that this, like so much of plastic surgery, comes down to each surgeon's personal aesthetic.

2. See Phillips; Cash and Pruzinsky; Thompson et al.; Vargel and Ulusahin; Sarwer; Pertschuk et al.; Bower; Kalick; Castelló et al.; Ozgür et al.; Sarwer et al.; and Monteath and McCabe. Worse yet, there is evidence that even the presurgical assessment of the mental stability of people whom the surgeon considers unattractive is influenced by appearance. As Michael Kalick implies, some "recessive" insecure types are rejected by surgeons who imagine they could have a psychiatric problem on their hands (251). Sarwer et al. recommend that surgeons screen out patients with body dysmorphic disorder prior to surgery. First, they maintain that such patients typically do not respond well to cosmetic surgery. Second, "there is some concern that cosmetic surgery patients with body dysmorphic disorder may become violent toward themselves or the surgeon and his or her staff" (368).

3. See Clifford and Walster; Cusack; Dipboye et al.; Dion; Efran; Mc-Grouther; Dahlbäck; Gitomer.

4. For discussions of body dysmorphic disorder in men, see Pertschuk et al.; Nakamura et al.; and Edgerton et al.

5. Surgeons who operate on non-European patients have extensively discussed the difficulty of using the surgical techniques developed in operations on white European skin and features. On surgery for nonwhite patients, see Matory; and Hoefflin. One difference is the relative thickness of nonwhite skin, which doesn't tend to redrape over the post-op feature in the way that white skin does. See also Farkas et al.

6. It is well known among surgeons that men make the worst cosmetic surgery patients. See Nakamura et al.; Guyuron and Bokhari; and Goin and Goin.

7. Many other surgeons discourage silastic implants. They often cause infection, or they move or leave a visible implant line demarcating the augmentation area.

8. It is the fastest-growing surgical specialty for women, mainly, as I've been told, because they are operating predominantly on women's bodies. Women coming in for breast implants or other bodywork often prefer women surgeons. Indeed, one woman surgeon compared it to gynecology, the other surgical specialty open to women.

9. See Goin and Goin.

10. While one could make the same claim for the detachability of the penis in relation to assessment and penile-augmentation surgeries, male bodies aren't fragmented into quite so many fetishized "part-objects."

11. As James Kincaid reminded me, the penis is equally detachable. Any psychoanalyst would agree with him, and it's not surprising that the most talked-about male surgery (even though it's certainly not common) is penile augmentation. Curiously enough, most penile augmentation patients claim to be doing it for display in the locker room rather than for female sexual partners, suggesting that we all (both men and women) see ourselves as being looked at and assessed by men! See Brooks; Rosenthal; John Taylor; Haiken; and Fraser.

12. As my argument about the effects of star culture makes clear, when it comes to a culture in the process of becoming surgical, more than gender difference is at stake.

2. UNTOUCHABLE BODIES

1. See Zimmermann for an excellent account of the reported effects of silicone.

2. See Dull and West on the ideal surgical candidate.

3. Dull and West note this pattern as well in their own interviews of plastic surgeons.

4. An earlier study of *Körperschema* (schema of the body) was published in 1923 under the title *Seele und Leben* before Schilder's major contribution on the topic, *The Image and Appearance of the Human Body*.

5. Of course, there are many psychologists who concede to the powerful psychological cure offered by cosmetic surgery. See Cash and Pruzinsky; the work of Goin and Goin; and Gilman's *Creating Beauty to Cure the Soul*, which charts the relationship between becoming "happier" through external transformation. Specialists in body-image studies divide roughly into two quite different and at times contradictory camps: one evaluates and treats poor body image while the other focuses on the consequences of personal appearance. Attractiveness studies typically prove that life is better in all respects for the good-looking; body dysmorphic disorder studies tend to pathologize individuals for their excessive concern with appearance.

6. Natural selection materials on beauty tend to differ with this perspective, generally arguing that similar canons of beauty have obtained always. See, for example, Nancy Etcoff's *Survival of the Prettiest*. In *The Evolution of Allure*, art historian George Hersey argues that not only are physical types of beauty more or less consistent through time and space but our idealized works of art participate in raising the stakes on real bodies, thus motivating us to "breed . . . for beauty" (2).

7. Vivian Sobchack, Conference on Women and Aging, Center for Cultural Studies, University of Wisconsin–Milwaukee, Apr. 1996.

8. The average-income statistics tell as much. See Kalb 32; Kruger 56; and Kirkland and Tong 153. When I asked Leida Snow, director of media relations for the American Society of Plastic and Reconstructive Surgeons, she responded, "There are over five thousand board-certified plastic surgeons in this country, not to mention all the ear, nose, and throat doctors and opthamologists and gynecologists doing cosmetic operations. It stands to reason that they can't just be operating on rich people."

9. I interviewed only board-certified plastic surgeons. This means that they did their residency in plastic surgery and had to qualify to become members of the American Society of Plastic and Reconstructive Surgeons. There is considerable controversy over nonspecialists practicing plastic surgery. Many board-certified plastic surgeons are angry about the public ignorance—the fact that people don't know the difference between, say, the Society of Cosmetic Surgeons or the Society of Facial Plastic Surgeons and the two so-called legitimate plastic surgery societies, which are the American Society of Plastic and Reconstructive Surgery and the American Society for Aesthetic Plastic Surgery. See Deborah A. Sullivan's excellent account (chapters 4 and 5) of the ethically tumultuous turf wars taking place between board-certified plastic surgeons and physicians from other specialties.

10. By putting an advertisement in the newspaper, I was at risk of finding mainly disgruntled patients who wanted an opportunity to complain. For the most part, people who live in my region of the country, the Southeast, keep their surgeries to themselves if they are satisfied. I also looked at cosmetic surgery discussion lists for a broader sense of patient experiences. An especially helpful web site is www.faceforum.com.

11. See Viner.

12. In reaction to ubiquitous representations of idealized female bodies along with the marginalization of postforty women, feminists have perhaps gone overboard in berating a concern with appearance; we risk overlooking the potential pleasures achieved through attention to the body. Moreover, why must the "real" female body (especially the "real" middle-aged body) be depicted as overweight or unsculpted, as art historian and bodybuilder Joanna Frueh asks in *Monster/Beauty*. Frueh attempts to distinguish between culturally mandated and hence passive forms of beauty ("photogenic") and the "erotogenic" forms involving the active pursuit of aesthetic and sensual pleasures on our own terms. "I posit the erotogenic as an antidote to the photogenic and as a feminist model of beauty, rooted in aphrodisiac capacity and not simplistically reliant on appearance. The older aphrodisiac body does not strain for glamour that is only artifice, and it is not rabid with longing for youth" (67). What Frueh so importantly recuperates for feminists is the critical distinction between what we do for pleasure and what we do out of shame. Given the degree to which the erotogenic has become reducible to the photogenic, however, I wonder if Frueh's distinction fades.

13. See Bordo; K. Davis; Balsamo; Dery; Haiken, *Venus Envy* and "Virtual Virility"; and Morgan.

14. For accounts of men's increasing interest in surgery, see Haiken, "Virtual Virility"; and Penn. Sometimes the figures are misleading, however. Jean Penn, for example, tells us (in 1996) that "25 percent of all cosmetic surgery is now performed on men," but the lion's share of these "surgeries" are hair transplants.

15. In her enormously influential book *Purity and Danger*, feminist anthropologist Mary Douglas discusses the body as a "clean and proper place" that needs to be maintained through elaborate food rituals and eating taboos. In our current culture, however, various health fads have led to an entirely new relationship between the inside of the body and external threats. We now need to take vitamins to *supplement* what we otherwise lack. In contrast with the former use of purgatives to detoxify the body (although we certainly continue to use various detoxifying agents), vitamin and mineral supplements suggest a body that can find its health only through supplementary practices.

16. Nonsurgical procedures include botox and collagen injections and so forth. According to the American Society for Aesthetic Plastic Surgery (ASAPS), "There was a 25% increase in the total number of procedures performed between 1999 and 2000. There was a 173% increase between 1997 and 2000." These statistics are now available on their web site: www.surgery.org.

17. His expressed preference is atypical, by the way; for the most part, women are the preferred patient.

18. Chancer is after a "democracy of beauty" entailing a wide-scale cultural transformation that would allow women "*to still be viewed as attractive when aging without such surgery*" (96, emphasis in original), which is an appealing proposition but perhaps overlooks the historical point. The current forms of beauty culture are deeply interconnected with how and why women want to be viewed as attractive into old age. The degree to which beauty is now part and parcel of consumer culture certainly has profound effects on the ways in which we all want to still feel marketable/consumable at any age.

19. In *The Most Beautiful Girl in the World*, Banet-Weiser shows the perils experienced by black women when "white" beauty contests opened up to them. This apparent opening up simultaneously seals black bodies in the demands of white beauty culture. Similarly, Ann Ducille comments on the cultural double bind of "black Barbie" in *Skin Trade*.

20. It is important to note, the body isn't simply situated in the political realm of race and class; it also, as Tim Dean points out, needs to be articulated "in terms of [what Lacan calls] real, symbolic, and imaginary" orders (200). To limit accounts of beauty and morphology strictly to hegemonic cultural constructions of race and class is to miss the complicated way in which the symbolic order creates beauty as a locus of desire.

21. See Tseëlon; and Goffman.

22. See, for example, Bordo, *The Male Body*, 222.

23. For this perspective see Bartky; Bordo, *Unbearable Weight*; and Stearns.

24. Abigail Bray and Claire Colebrook have questioned corporeal feminism's conviction of this "false body" somehow supplanting an authentic body that would finally spring into unsuppressed life if only all those oppressive representations of beauty and slenderness would fade away. See Bartky for an account of how to liberate the female body from these oppressive beauty regimes.

25. Indeed, as Gilman notes, cosmetic surgery comes to be considered a "form of psychotherapy" (*Creating Beauty to Cure the Soul* 11).

26. See, for example, de Cordova, whose argument I cite in chapter 6.

27. Mark Dery, Anne Balsamo, and Naomi Wolf assume this position as well.

28. Theorists of the beauty imperative and cosmetic surgery include Susan Bordo, Joanne Finkelstein, Kathryn Pauly Morgan, Kathy Davis, Sandra Lee Bartky, Naomi Wolf, Alice Adams, Lynn Chancer, Anne Balsamo, and Rosemary Gillespie.

29. Leida Snow, news release, American Society for Aesthetic Plastic Surgery, 3 May 2001.

30. There were 5.7 million procedures total, but approximately only 2 million involved surgery.

31. Deborah A. Sullivan as well writes: "Individuals who turn to cosmetic surgery to carve a more attractive appearance, like the Padaung women who elongate their necks with rings and the Africans who decorate their bodies with elaborate patterns of scars, are making a rational response to prevailing cultural values that reward those considered more attractive and penalize those considered less attractive. Cosmetic surgery can be a means of achieving upward social mobility in such a culture" (28).

32. Susan Bordo makes just this point in *Unbearable Weight*. Criticizing the ahistoricism of postmodern celebrations of the mutable body, Bordo writes: "What Foucault himself recognized and his more postmodern followers some-

times forget is that resistance and transformation *are* historical processes" (295; emphasis in original).

33. See especially Heinz Kohut's *The Restoration of the Self* and *How Does Analysis Cure?* for accounts of how the particular family dramas that precipitated Oedipal-level crises of Freud's neurotics no longer obtain in families that both avoid emotional attachment and expect children to fulfill adult idealizations.

34. Consider magazines like *Mode* for "plus-size" women and *More* for women age forty and over. The plus sizes aren't very plus at all, and the over forty is barely over—as though we cannot help but get stuck on the edge of beauty, whatever its outermost limit is. Recently, the publisher of a new men's adult magazine, *Perfect 10*, said that he would "refuse to use models who have had breast implants or other obvious plastic surgery." As the reporter wryly notes, however, "As for . . . taking a stand for real women, it's easy to figure out that shunning plastic surgery is hardly a political decision for the 15 mostly European and American models featured in each issue. They're already beautiful" (Tharp).

3. THE PLASTIC SURGEON AND THE PATIENT

1. This remains an ongoing point of disagreement among surgeons. Some surgeons argue that once the brow has started to drop in, say, the late thirties, the best intervention is the full coronal incision. Others claim they can get a better result with the minimal incision of the endoscopic procedure. Certainly, younger patients are encouraged to choose the endoscopic approach because of the reduced scarring, which leads me to observe that, like so many other innovations in cosmetic procedures, endoscopic brow-lifts are targeting a younger market in order to broaden the patient population.

2. Elizabeth Grosz writes that the "depth, or rather the effects of depth, are thus generated purely through the manipulation, rotation, and inscription of the flat place—an apposite metaphor for the undoing of the dualism" (117).

3. Journalist John L. Camp says of breast augmentation surgery: "Of all the operations done by plastic surgeons, the breast enhancement, technically called an augmentation mammoplasty, is the most like magic. The change in the body is immediate and dramatic and generally unobscured by the bruising and unsightly sutures left by most surgery" (78). It's true that it has a more "magical"

effect than a face-lift, because the change is so swift and doesn't appear visually wedded to the surgical process in the way bruised and swollen body parts do.

4. See Emily Martin's *The Woman in the Body: A Cultural Analysis of Reproduction* for one of the most extensive and influential accounts of the multiple ways in which women are fragmented, including the separation of mind and body, and the medicalization of our "natural" functions like menstruation, childbirth, and menopause.

5. See Marchac et al. and Tonnard et al. for recent examples of surgeries designed around minimal incisions with lower risk of complications.

6. See Malcolm D. Paul on changes regarding approaches to brow-lift.

7. Annie Reich suggests in response to Freud: "It seems as though he were largely thinking of a fixation at early levels of object relationship. At these early levels, passive attitudes are more frequently found than an active reaching out for an object" (298). Reich is here referring to the infant's originally passive relation to its mother. While I disagree with Reich and read Freud as emphasizing regression more than fixation, a regression precipitated by the castration trauma, her emphasis on the binary of active-passive is crucial to the way in which I will develop my theory about the surgeon/patient identification.

8. Both Sarah Kofman (50–65) and Leo Bersani (644) logically point out that this roundabout route of identifying with the very narcissism they claim to have forfeited suggests a narcissistic style of loving for men as well.

9. Freud, "On Narcissism" 67–102.

10. The recent interest in penile augmentation surgeries suggests that the narcissistic investment in the penis is no longer so hidden or displaced.

11. Hoefflin's wedding ceremony received the same kind of journalistic attention given to celebrities. See Lacher.

12. By the end of the book, moreover, we are treated to what amounts to an advertisement of Man's own special skin-care line!

13. Many scholars and journalists have been pursuing the transformations in representations and experiences of "masculinities" over the course of the twentieth century. See especially Bordo; Faludi; Pfeil; Silverman; Theweleit; and Studlar.

14. Anne Balsamo believes that plastic surgery generally preserves the conventional heterosexual order, but I am here arguing that it is in fact always on the edge of collapsing what it so desperately tries to sustain—in terms of both gender difference and subjectivity.

15. See Ludmilla Jordanova's excellent account of the history of the Enlightenment and post-Enlightenment feminization of nature in relation to masculine science, especially the tension between nature's benign and dangerous forms.

16. A similar interest in the relationship between inner character and outer appearance informs the 1989 film *Johnny Handsome*, where the extremely deformed convict is reconstructed as part of an experiment to rehabilitate criminals through cosmetic surgery. The psychologist in charge of Johnny's (Mickey Rourke's) transformation insists that if given a new face to compensate him for a life as a social outcast, Johnny will leave behind his criminal ways. Instead, the new face gives Johnny the opportunity to seek revenge on the criminals who previously double-crossed him. Such rehabilitative surgeries are actually being undertaken at various prisons around the country. See Kevin M. Thompson.

17. See Radsken.

18. It is important to note that he divorces his wife, who is the one with a beautiful face but no heart—in contrast with his "perfect" Galatea, the plastic surgery patient.

19. Hoefflin originally fell into opportunity, as it were, in 1984 when he was the on-call plastic surgeon who treated Michael Jackson's burn injuries after his hair caught fire during a shooting for a Pepsi commercial.

20. See Joan Kron's article on Hoefflin, "Knife Fight," where she touches on the ethics of being a Hollywood surgeon.

21. See Kettle.

22. In 1938, the notorious "quack" surgeon Henry J. Schireson compared the face to a house: "He looks at the face as the architect looks at a house. When the architecture is bad, it stands out to affront the eye. When it is good, one does not see the details; he sees only a harmonious dwelling blended into and pointing up a beautiful landscape" (76). In a recent "Image" note in *Harper's Bazaar*, the following appeared: "There's a growing number of plastic surgeons exploring . . . creative pursuits [in their marketing strategies]. 'If you see something they've painted, it will inspire confidence in their aesthetic sense,' explains plastic-surgery consultant Wendy Lewis." See also Tolleth; and C. A. Stone; as well as works by Romm underscoring the artistic aspects of aesthetic surgery.

23. In *Beneath the American Renaissance*, David Reynolds discusses the influence of contemporary patterns of erotic voyeurism. Hawthorne was very inter-

ested in the new science of photography (Daguerre fixed his first impression in 1839). His novel *The House of the Seven Gables* features the daguerreotypist Holgrave among its protagonists. See Alan Trachtenberg's reading.

24. Barbara Johnson notes the "profound complicity between aesthetics and medicine" (256).

25. This image of the hand is also linked to the general assumption that photography was the perfect evidence and to confidence in the camera's technological neutrality; only the facts were presented. That the birthmark is what the camera captures of Georgiana is thus linked to the camera's nineteenth-century function as an instrument of criminal surveillance.

26. Johnson has compared Hawthorne's story with Charlotte Perkins Gilman's "The Yellow Wallpaper" and Freud's case history of the patient Dora to demonstrate her theory that psychoanalysis depicts femininity as the ground (blank, neutral) against which masculinity emerges as a clearly defined figure.

4. FRANKENSTEIN GETS A FACE-LIFT

1. Even menopause has been listed as a contraindication. See Goin and Goin, *Changing the Body* 81.

2. For an extensive consideration of this subject, see Sander Gilman's *Creating Beauty to Cure the Soul* and *Making the Body Beautiful*.

3. See Elizabeth Haiken's *Venus Envy* on our culture of inferiority complexes and self-improvement.

4. See, for example, Meninger; Kalick; Gifford; Groenman and Sauër; Edgerton and Knorr; Knorr et al.; Vargel and Ulusahin; Thomas, Sclafani, et al.; Thomson et al.; Newell; Greer; Mohl; Goin and Goin, "Psychological Understanding and Management"; Slator and Harris. See, for example, Updegraff and Menninger; MacGregor and Schaffner; and Stekel.

5. The "significantly psychologically disturbed patients" documented in this article were all treated with psychotherapy in combination with their surgeries. Nevertheless, it seems apparent from all the accounts that it was the surgery that gave them relief, even though they had agreed to the therapy in order to be approved for surgery. Much of the literature on this combined approach seems to cling to the psychiatric model for transformation despite evidence that these people feel better because of the surgery.

6. Freud avers that what amounts to a regression to narcissistic identification could happen only because the object choice was of the narcissistic variety to begin with ("Mourning and Melancholia" 249).

7. Winnicott specifies the mother in his account, and he has written at length on why the mother is best suited to be the infant's primary caregiver. See especially "Primary Maternal Preoccupation."

8. Goin and Goin write: "Early anxiety about and vulnerability to the possibility of abandonment remain dormant somewhere in the immense circuitry of the brain. Changes in a body part decades later can often evoke anxiety that is unconsciously related to fears of separation and abandonment" (*Changing the Body* 64).

9. I am using this term here in the sense employed by Freud in his 1915 essay, "Mourning and Melancholia," and elsewhere. Later in the chapter I will discuss the distinction Torok and Abraham make between introjection and incorporation.

10. Sandor Ferenczi, another member of Freud's psychoanalytic circle, contended that masturbation and other forms of bodily self-stimulation are "imaginary substitutes on [one's] own body for the lost object" (23–24).

11. See Woodward, *Aging and Its Discontents*, chapter on Barthes's *Camera Lucida*.

12. The day after Lucy's first lover broke up with her, she noticed that her bone graft was beginning to resorb, thereby cementing the relationship between the mirror image and feelings of being unlovable (208).

13. Otto Fenichel describes "primary identification," the early ego formation that happens through forging oneself through identifications with caregivers, as a psychic defense against the original and universal experience of loss. He writes that "it can be conceived of as a reaction to the disappointing loss of the unity which embraced ego and external world" (101).

14. As Lacan says, "in a symmetry that inverts it" ("Mirror Stage" 2).

15. Nancy Friday writes about the reverse mirror in plastic surgeons' offices: "The flip side of the mirror shows the face that others see when they look at us" (18). She associates this view with the look of unloving parents.

16. There is much discussion about the impact of a child's disfigurement on parental caregivers. See Bernstein; and Rogers-Salyer et al. Rogers-Salyer and her colleagues write: "Behaviorally, mothers of craniofacially deformed infants spent much less time demonstrating toys and smiling at their infants, and

were rated as being significantly less sensitive to their infants" (483). MacGregor et al. describe the guilt most mothers experience (114–15).

17. MacGregor et al. also suggest that parental response to the deformity gets permanently internalized as "lack of parental love," for which no amount of later corrective surgery can compensate (51).

18. Stories of racial passing typically focus on the possibility of the child's betraying the material racial history that the parents hid so well. African American women who are passing as white in Nella Larsen's *Passing* discuss this worry. A passing family in the 1949 film *Lost Boundaries* urges their daughter to give birth at home instead of the hospital, just in case.

19. Worse yet, non-Jewish people with large noses were mistaken in this anti-Semitic country for Jews. "Jane Hatch arrived from England in 1941 to find that her nose—which in England was acceptably British—was, in the United States, assumed to be Jewish" (191).

20. Of course, this question of assimilation plagues other countries with immigrant populations who experience themselves as physically marginalized. See Niechajev and Haraldsson.

21. See Mead on just this question of how parental surgery might affect the child's body image.

22. For example, Marin Cureau de la Chambre's *L'Art de connoistre les hommes* and *Les Charactères des passions*, both mid-seventeenth-century works.

23. See Walker, *Beauty in Women*.

24. This surgeon's perspective is confirmed routinely by studies on body image. Thomas F. Cash writes: "For both males and females, physical attractiveness was predictive of greater intimacy and satisfaction in one's heterosexual interactions" ("The Psychology of Physical Appearance," 55). He also observes that what he terms "beautyism" "may be more detrimental to homely persons than it is beneficial to comely individuals" (56).

25. MacGregor et al. give a case history of a patient from the upper classes whose beautiful face was ruined in an automobile accident. Although she was extremely disfigured, she managed to marry (more than once) and have a highly successful business career.

26. Here Judith Butler's theory of performative identities is useful. The only reason identity feels continuous is that every moment one is reiterating the discourse that keeps it in place. If this is true, the creation of new identities through

transformations of the surface appearance will be experienced as continuous with former identities, because the *process* remains the same.

27. See Ariès; Lawrence Stone; and Shorter.

28. Somehow, the story of Mary Shelley's birth and marriage, along with her subsequent losses (husband, children), has created a powerful frame of mourning through which many of us have read this novel. See Moers; Rickels; and Mellor, for example. We seem to be incapable of disengaging Mary Shelley's famous birth from the events of the novel.

29. Most notable of these actions is the creature's slaughter of the very woman Victor has for so long delayed marrying.

30. Not just buried, but likely unmourned—bodies furnished by the "dissecting room" and the "slaughter-house."

31. Jay Clayton has argued that it is the monster's looking back at Victor that distresses Victor more than what the monster "looks like" (61). This would signify the demand for the object relation that Victor avoids at all costs.

32. See Moers.

33. Tim Marshall, who reads the novel through contemporary debates on the use of cadavers for dissection, points out that with the new laws of 1832, it was "unclaimed" corpses that could be turned over to the anatomist. He discusses the implications for the monster: "'The monstrosity' of Frankenstein's nameless Creature—despite his constitution as a mass of reanimated corpses—arises from the fact that he has no relatives" (139). Thus his body is the very image of his lack of human ties—what simultaneously reflects and leads to his monstrousness.

34. Curiously enough, although the novel centers on the creation of a male body, cosmetic surgery (typically performed on women) has generally been imagined as a version of the *Frankenstein* story. That the story of building a man is culturally reversed into cosmetically altering women illustrates just how much we continue to deny the fragility of masculine identity.

5. AS IF BEAUTY

1. Jamie and his girlfriend joke about Baudrillard's simulacral.

2. The as if personality can be considered an extreme version of what D. W. Winnicott called "the false self." Winnicott's description of the inadequate

mother-child relation leading to the false self is suggestive for the as if person-ality as well. The attuned "good-enough mother," as Winnicott calls her, re-sponds to her baby's need instead of her own timetable, in contrast with the un-attuned mother. Stephen Mitchell describes it thus: "The baby's own impulses and needs are not met by the mother, and the baby learns to want what the mother gives, to become the mother's idea of who the baby is" (10).

3. Although I am primarily discussing the effects of star culture in particular (meaning actors and even singers, who are also adored for the way they dress, physical appearance, etc.), I will often refer to "celebrity culture" as well, because stars and celebrities share many cultural features. Consider Princess Diana, for example.

4. Benjamin McArthur writes: "Actors became both exemplars and meta-phors of modern life: exemplars in that the public followed their cues for per-sonal development . . ." (188).

5. Regarding the "look of youth and purity," the preference for younger ac-tors in the newly formed cinema also echoes what has become a culturewide eroticization of the child. See James Kincaid's *Child-Loving* and *Erotic Innocence* for brilliant readings of this trend.

6. Insisting on the smooth visage of the screen-sized face, Griffith invented "'hazy photography . . . the camera is a great beauty doctor'" (May 76).

7. Pickford offered weekly beauty advice to the masses, to let them in on her beauty secrets as though this is all it takes to emulate the image they see on the big screen.

8. For excellent accounts of the culture of celebrity see Schickel, *Intimate Strangers;* David Marshall; and Gamson.

9. As Benjamin McArthur asks in his analysis and history of the actor in American culture, "What kind of person wishes to devote himself to living the life of another? What prompts the urge for continued display?" (36–37). Mc-Arthur goes on to cite various studies on the personality of the actor that pathol-ogize it. My point would be that if actors suffer from narcissistic pathologies, so does the culture that identifies with/imitates them.

10. To-be-seenness. Being known for being well known, this is the formula captured by Daniel Boorstin in 1962. Sociologist Joshua Gamson remarks about the necessary myth of celebrity that there is "no formula" (70). Rather, it's a spe-cial something, a certain indefinable set of ingredients that no one can name or package, but it marks the otherwise regular person as "special." As Gamson

makes clear, however, it is ultimately "being seen" that makes someone a full-fledged celebrity. Ron Howard's film *EDTV* suggests that simply being seen by large numbers of people can make someone (anyone) special. The most innocuous among us can instantly be catapulted to celebrity status. Just consider the most recent spate of reality shows, such as *Survivor*, which seem to document the very process of becoming celebrity. See "Agent Provocateur" by Tim Williams on an agent who specializes in turning these reality-program "survivors" into celebrities.

11. Interestingly, in *A Woman's Face*, Anna describes herself as feeling "reborn" after surgery.

12. I read California as a code for Hollywood.

13. Indeed star culture itself, with its transformational ideology, dictates the very terms of authenticity. In a film centering on questions of identity and performance, Pedro Almodóvar's *All about My Mother*, a transvestite explains the nature of authenticity to a theater audience. After itemizing the cost of each one of her cosmetic surgeries, she claims: "I'm very authentic. Look at this body. All made to measure. . . . It costs a lot to be authentic . . . because you are more authentic the more you resemble what you dreamed of being." Dreams are now what one must be instead of what one follows, just as "the body" or "the self" is simply a vehicle through which one fulfills the potential of either—or both.

14. The very place of narcissism in psychoanalytic theory reflects a cultural shift from denouncing narcissistic traits to applauding them. Heinz Kohut and Otto Kernberg, two of the foremost theorists of narcissistic personality disturbance, diverge on just this point. While Kernberg treats narcissism as always pathological, Kohut elaborates a separate developmental path for what he terms "healthy narcissism."

15. In contrast with Butler's account of the performativity of gender, I'm focusing here on the experienced gap between feeling "authentically" oneself and feeling "false."

16. Gerald Pratley regarded the casting of Rock Hudson as the film's weakness, not only because he was too different looking from John Randolph (who plays Arthur Hamilton), but also because he was such a well-known star (135–36). Frankenheimer as well thought the casting was flawed, but only because of the height difference. He actually believed that the facial surgery was possible. ("'In reality it's very possible to do that with plastic surgery.'" [Pratley 143]). Originally, Frankenheimer wanted Laurence Olivier for the part, but Para-

mount, as he reports, didn't consider Olivier a "'big enough name'" (Champlin 91). By contrast, "Rock Hudson was the biggest male star in the country at that point" (91).

17. That it is increasingly common for stars to play themselves in their own biopics suggests a complete collapse of real and reel, in which to play a part is to "be yourself."

18. Another way to interpret this film is as an allegory of the closeted life of homosexual men. There is an irony in casting Rock Hudson, who played the "false" part of a straight man in both his real life and on screen. Richard Meyer discusses the doubleness of Rock Hudson's star identity, overt in the late 1980s when he was diagnosed with AIDS, covert as early as the 1950s when fan magazines were threatening to expose his homosexuality (272).

19. See Sennett on this trope.

20. Judith Mitrani considers Klein's version of projective identification similar to Esther Bick's concept of "narcissistic identification" (Mitrani 66).

21. This enhanced body is also frequently a body of technology. Although I don't believe that plastic surgery bodies are cyborg, because the patients don't experience themselves as merging with technology, I certainly think that cyborg shares this pattern of projective identification. For accounts of cyborg subjectivities, see Bukatamen; Dery; Haraway; Gray; Penley and Ross; and Balsamo.

22. Debord is highly critical of celebrity culture, which epitomizes the culture's "identification with mere appearance" (38).

23. Freud's split between wanting to be (identification) and wanting to have (desire) has been challenged by Teresa de Lauretis (in *The Practice of Love*), Judith Butler, Diana Fuss, and Jackie Stacey.

24. Minghella expressed concern that his account of a psychopath who is also homosexual would be misread as a homophobic pathologization of homosexuality (see Rich).

25. In a 1922 essay, Freud traced certain instances of homosexual object-choice to repressed rivalry. According to this model, the shift into homosexuality takes place both because of the repressed aggression *and* because of an attempt to become (once again) the primary object of the mother's interest and love. Homosexuality is a way of reconciling the simultaneous identifications with the mother's desire and the desirability of the hated rival ("Some Neurotic Mechanisms" 231).

26. After he has murdered Dickie, Tom lies beside him and places Dickie's

arms around him as though to emblematize the bloody skin he has wrested as his rightful portion of both love and identity. By the end of the film, Tom has taken on the skin of his second love object–victim, Peter; he is seated on the bed wearing the coat of his slain partner.

27. Judith Mitrani believes that the mirror image can have the containing effect of the skin ("Unintegration" 71–72). Clearly Tom's problem is that his own image doesn't serve this containing function.

28. Hollywood skin does indeed seem to be the most invulnerable of containers—because its an image instead of flesh.

29. Yet another ironic layer involves Max Factor makeup's connection to the film industry. Writes Kathy Peiss: "All [Factor's] advertisements prominently featured screen stars, their testimonials secured in an arrangement with the major studios that required them to endorse Max Factor" (126).

30. See, for example, John Ellis's *Visible Fictions* (35).

31. We could further speculate that while he is effacing his blackness, as so many observe, many whites are busily effacing their whiteness—through lip augmentation and other alterations of traditionally white-aesthetic features. In an article on the effect of television images on black women, Karen R. Perkins points out that it's not simply that there will be an instant recognition of the difference between the idealized image and the viewer; rather, initially the viewer will identify with the ideal and only later be let down by her own "real" mirror image. Thus, identification is the problem—more than just difference itself. See Haiken, "The Michael Jackson Factor," in *Venus Envy*.

32. See Balsamo, who considers video imaging part of a general trend of using technology in the service of sustaining highly conservative versions of the gendered body. For literature on computer imaging, see Bronz; VanderKam and Achauer; Papel and Park; Larrabee et al.; Maves et al.; Kohn et al.; Vannier et al.

33. Thomas et al.'s study shows "28% felt that the process led them to consider additional changes not considered previously" (Thomas, Freeman, et al. 794).

34. Plastic surgeon Robert Goldwyn quotes one of his patients, euphoric over the marvels of computer imaging: "'He has this computer, and I could really see what kind of a nose I could be getting (as if she is ordering a dress from a catalog)'" (*The Operative Note* 89).

35. Meanwhile, there are unscrupulous surgeons out there who profit from patient fantasies about the infinite transformability of flesh and blood. Pamela

Kruger quotes a woman who was promised Elizabeth Taylor looks by one surgeon: "'I don't want to look like Elizabeth Taylor. This is *my* face'" (58).

36. It is important to note that the plastic surgeon simply services the media; indeed, he's being exploited as much as the models.

37. Presumably so the company can avoid paying the models, although this is never fully explained.

38. In *The Four Fundamental Concepts of Psycho-Analysis*, Lacan describes the way in which the scopic drive involves both voyeurism and narcissistic components. It's in the reconciliation of the two that we find pleasure, he argues. See Henry Krips's brilliant account of this pairing of needs in the drive in *Fetish: An Erotics of Culture*.

6. THE MONSTER AND THE MOVIE STAR

1. Many reviewers have commented on the unbelievable contradictions in this film arising from Streisand's struggle between the plain-Jane story and needing to represent herself as a glamour-puss. See, for example, the following reviews of the film: Ansen; Rozen; Schickel; Simon; and Brian Johnson.

2. See Jane Gaines's *Contested Cultures* for an important history and theory of the legal ownership of celebrity images.

3. Some silent films specifically addressed changing one's life through surgery. Callé and Evans describe the films *Musty's Vacation* and *The Mishaps of Musty Suffer*: Musty "wants to resemble a man in a photograph. After surgery, he is several inches taller, has a large nose, wider feet, and high forehead" (422). Another silent film, *Minnie*, "features an ugly girl who falls in love with a man who sees her inner beauty. She is transformed by surgery, and they become a handsome couple" (422). Note the identification with a photograph in the *Musty* films and the externalization of "inner beauty" in *Minnie*.

4. Tellingly, after her husband leaves her, the wife throws out a copy of *Motion Picture Classic*, as though to underscore the effect the motion picture industry has had on her personal life. For extensive accounts of these films, see Sumiko Higashi's *Cecil B. De Mille and American Culture: The Silent Era*. De Mille's 1936 film, *Madame Satan*, is similarly focused on such metamorphosis. In this case, an uptight upper-class wife becomes more alluring in order to win her husband back from his chorus-girl mistress, achieving thereby the increasingly requisite amalgamation of class types.

5. Many nonspecialists (meaning doctors who are not board certified in plastic surgery) practice in outpatient facilities. While hospitals typically require doctors performing plastic surgery to hold these formal credentials, there are no state regulations requiring that plastic surgery be performed by specialists. This is a subject of much consternation among board-certified surgeons, needless to say. The United Kingdom has its own version of the popular clinics where non-specialists perform bulk surgeries.

6. Especially a problem when sitters had to stay still for protracted periods of time, waiting for the image to expose.

7. Early on, actors had their portraits taken and mass produced. See Jane Gaines on portrait photography and celebrity (42–83); and Benjamin McArthur, who writes on how theatrical portraits as well as the use of actresses for advertising intensified beauty culture (41–42). McArthur also documents the degree to which such portraits of actors quickly overlapped commercially with "girlie magazines" (148). See Linda Williams for her analysis of why visual technologies, like the camera, would be inextricably linked to pornography; because developers of visual technologies capitalized on the discoveries being made around the workings of the eye, these technologies were interdependent with the body. See also John Tagg, who argues that there was "a whole class of middling people eager to measure themselves against the image of their social superiors" (49).

8. At the same time, "the news that the camera could lie made getting photographed much more popular" (Sontag 86). The camera not only revealed one's appearance, it could improve upon it—hence the convergence of beauty with the after picture.

9. Sarah Kember writes: "[Photojournalists] want their external world to stay where they imagined it was, to be there for them (to represent). However, photography was considered to be the means of representing this reassuring world in which everything appeared to stay in its time, space and place" (21).

10. Photography played a double role in the history of the body's identifiability. Tom Gunning writes that "attempts to reestablish the traces of individual identity beneath the obscurity of a new mobility were central to both the actual processes of police detection and the genesis of detective fiction" ("Tracing the Individual Body" 20). This concern with evidence is historically recent. Mark Taylor connects our obsession with surface and depth to the detective story: "The drama of investigation is set in motion by tensions between surface/

depth, outer/inner, appearance/reality, pretext/text, and so forth" (17). The nineteenth century is the century of the detective story, from Edgar Allan Poe to Nathaniel Hawthorne and Wilkie Collins. The story of detection captivated a society invested in the enormous discrepancy between what was seen and what was hidden from view. Ultimately, Sigmund Freud becomes the master detective in his search for unconscious motivations in the fabric of surface events: slips of the tongue, errors, jokes. *Frankenstein*, too, is a story of detection. Not only is Victor concerned with "tracing Nature to her hiding places"; much of the story involves police hunting down suspects for the various crimes. It can be manipulated, but at the same time it seems to be the best record of historical truth. Sarah Kember has contrasted photography to the "new imaging technologies [and] their ability to generate a realistic image out of nothing—to simulate it from scratch using only numerical codes as the object or referent (21).

11. In part, as Benjamin suggests, because through photography, for example, we can see "those aspects of the original that are unattainable to the naked eye yet accessible to the lens . . ." (220).

12. John Tagg charts the simultaneous use of the photograph as a record of criminality and class ascension (through portraiture).

13. This is the moral associated with the novel *The Portrait of Dorian Gray*— that you cannot hide your history (in a closet); eventually it will catch up with you. Of course, there are critics who argue that this is not in the least the moral value promulgated by the novel. See Halberstam; Gaines; and Bowlby.

14. As Ronald R. Thomas writes: "The immediate appropriation of photography for the bureaucratic procedures of personal documentation and identification by policing agencies seemed as natural as its instantaneous popularity among the middle classes as a form of self-promotion" (87). That plastic surgery became a way of changing one's criminal identity is a direct by-product of the mug shot. *Dark Voyage*, starring Humphrey Bogart and Lauren Bacall, treats this very theme, as a convicted felon undergoes dramatic surgical revision in order to find the man who framed him. See Elizabeth Haiken's account of this trend in *Venus Envy*.

15. Gunning, "Tracing the Individual Body" 36.

16. Victoria Duckett points out that central to the performance artist Orlan's staged surgeries is her making public what is so typically concealed.

17. As Freud makes clear, often the scene is a fantasy and was never actually experienced.

18. The question of identification with the camera apparatus and/or the screen images is one that has a long history among psychoanalytic film theorists. See especially Metz; Mulvey; Rose; and Kaja Silverman. Jackie Stacey has criticized what amounts to a preoccupation with the intrapsychic without any concern for the society in which such identifications take place.

19. John Ellis has described moviegoing as "a very precise urban experience, that of the crowd with its sense of belonging and of loneliness" (26). Spatially, the theater brings together total strangers who nevertheless are proximally linked through the shared viewing experience. This physical proximity, in which audience members remain entirely indifferent to if not unaware of each other, is reversed in our relationship to the screen stars, who seem so much closer at the same time that their bodies are in an altogether different register. Such a predicament, built in to the cinematic experience, suggests how we can begin to feel closer to images than we do to material bodies. Moreover, the disjuncture between feeling close and being far away can function as a lure—to touch the stars or, failing that, to know everything there is to know about them.

20. Sarah Bernhardt had already had her first face-lift in 1912. See Kron, *Lift* 42.

21. Crum often performed surgery publicly. Haiken refers to his "theatrical approach" (*Venus Envy* 80). Crum himself, in his book, *The Making of a Beautiful Face*, underscored his work on actresses: "We have frequently operated in the morning on actresses who appeared on the stage the same night, and, in fact, did not miss a single performance on account of their visit to the plastic surgeon. If we were at liberty to do so, we could mention some of the most prominent actresses who have done this very thing. But, of course, all reputable plastic surgeons hold the names of their patients in confidence" (45). Note that as early as 1928 we see this particular combination of associating surgery with actors at the same time that it has to be kept secret by surgeons, who nevertheless cannot help but reveal that they operate on celebrities.

22. One journalist remarks on the difference between model Esther Canadas's lips in "2-D" versus "in the flesh, [where] her face looks weirdly proportioned." See Blanchard for the *Observer*.

23. See Callé and Evans, who note: "Most doctors in movie plots have extraordinary operative talents and surgical prowess. Their results are often dramatic and unrealistic" (432).

24. This story of plastic surgery's making one love-worthy is reiterated in a

recent tabloid outing of Jane Fonda's putative overhaul. "'The effort to regain her youthful looks is part of her plan to reunite with the love of her life—Ted Turner,' disclosed an insider" (Nelson et al. 34).

7. BEING AND HAVING

1. "Estimates from the early 1990s indicate ordinary citizens account for fifty-one percent of stalking targets but celebrities comprise only seventeen percent of all stalking victims; the remaining thirty-two percent of stalking victims are lesser-known entertainment figures" (Radosevich).

2. "'When I think about her I feel that I want to become famous and impress her,'" Bardo wrote in his diary (Tharp). See Ros Davidson's article "Hollywood Lives Made Hell by the Celebrity Stalkers." Also see Pitts for an account of how celebrities seem like "public property."

3. Again, consider Richard Sennett's account of the changing force of the trope *theatrum mundi*.

4. Explaining why she eventually had her implants removed, Anderson claimed she wanted to look "more natural" (B. Thomas, "Image"). This whole process of becoming a parody of the movie star and subsequently winding back one's body (very publicly) suggests endless possibilities for transformation and emulation.

5. From the earliest days of the screen actor, the actor's body was broken down into a series of body parts and traits. Hortense Powdermaker, an anthropologist who in the 1940s took Hollywood as her cultural field, distinguishes between two types of screen actors, the "look what I can do" type and the "look at me" type. "Hollywood stresses and gives importance to the 'Look at me,' 'Look at my body' type. All the camera tricks, the close-ups, give intimate details of the actor's physical being This exhibitionism is carried still further by emphasizing certain parts of the actor's body. An actress becomes known for her comely legs, and these are accented in every picture. Another one is known for her bust; still another for her husky, sensuous voice" (207). The fetishistic pattern here goes without saying; what is most interesting is the way the spectator goes on to identify with the disassembled bodily parts.

6. Facial peeling for rejuvenating was originally called skinning; ironically, all the young women victims in this film literally have their faces "skinned,"

implying that the restoration of the perfect surface is always understood as aggressive.

7. As Deleuze and Guattari discuss in *A Thousand Plateaus*, the face is the privileged locus of representation of the subject. It is through the face that we experience each other as differentiated subjects.

8. Parveen Adams describes her experience upon observing Orlan's facial surgery. Under the skin there is nothing, she claims. The face is the place where we are represented as human to one another; so much rests on the relationship between one face and another. So much of what we take to be human lives on the surface of the face. So, when you raise the skin, Adams argues, you realize the deception of the face—that underneath there is nothing at all (141–59).

9. Hortense Powdermaker describes the "peep show" relationship of the fan to our film icons: "Fan magazines give details of the star's domestic and so-called private life, with pictures of his home, his garden, his swimming pool, his family, his dogs and his cats. The columnists in the daily paper expand this with what type of underwear he wears, whether he prefers noodle soup to tomato" (249).

10. Among our most aggressive responses to celebrity was the public hysteria surrounding the death of Princess Diana.

11. See Gamson; McArthur; and May.

12. Moreover, the Nelson family loudly proclaimed the closeness between their real and their televised lives. See Spigel.

13. This is the original reality programming.

14. Wheeler Winston Dixon links post–World War II paranoia to the "disruptive specter of television" (53). He suggests that, because it's free, television threatens both the film industry and, implicitly, capitalist styles of profit.

15. At the same time, the series participates in the very antimedia rhetoric that would mean its own elimination. In "The Obsolete Man," Romney Wordsworth is being "eliminated" because his espoused function as librarian is entirely redundant in a society with no books. As in Ray Bradbury's *Fahrenheit 451*, television has become the society's sole educational vehicle. Indeed, Mr. Wordsworth's execution will be "televised [because] . . . it has an educative effect on the public." Once again, there is a marked link between the machinations of a normalizing "state" and television itself. As the prosecutor says, "It's not unusual that we televise executions, Mr. Wordsworth. Last year, in the mass executions, we televised around the clock."

16. Consider this in light of transformational identifications I discussed in chapter 6.

17. As Lois Banner points out, since the nineteenth century, there have been two basic models of female beauty: the voluptuous woman and the steel engraving lady.

8. ADDICTED TO SURGERY

1. See Kornreich for an elaborate account of how tolerant the culture apparently has become about imperfection in its celebrities, naming actresses such as Claire Danes and Julianna Margulies as "imperfect."

2. It seems common enough that women who seem very attractive in "real life" are made to appear "plain" in the televisual world.

3. Rather, Wilson says Courtney wasn't "ugly" (91).

4. When women identify with soap opera actresses and their relationship to youth and beauty, what are the effects on us? Especially when women our own age, whom we've been following for many years, nevertheless look and behave as though they are much younger. As a student of mine pointed out regarding her mother's favorite soap character (fiftyish in real life), "They have face-lifts, and then they come back to the show and have babies." Having a baby on the show, she decided, is the best way to turn back the clock.

5. See Zimmermann.

6. Apparently on the way to becoming an actress just before she died, Diana has been called "Princess-Grace-in-reverse" (Dixon 33). "Shortly before the opening of his 1997 film *The Postman*, director-star Kevin Costner announced that he and Diana had been involved in a project which would have been a sequel to *The Bodyguard* (1992, dir. Mick Jackson)" (33). As Dixon argues, "Diana in her last months sought to create a space where she could unerringly control her own image, even if it was within the confines of a rigidly structured, generic fiction narrative. Being a film star would allow Diana to seek both a new career and perhaps a new image.... For her entire public life, Diana's image and voice had been mediated by the exigencies of a press that both hounded and flattered her" (34–35). Of course, being an actress wouldn't have given her any more actual control. In fact, Dixon, and perhaps Diana as well, is responding to the culturally *imagined* control of actors as instructors of our body images—as I've been arguing all along. Diana's restless struggle with the surface of her body became her desire to ascend into pure image.

WORKS CITED

Abraham, Nicholas, and Maria Torok. *The Shell and the Kernel: Renewals of Psychoanalysis.* Vol. 1. Trans. and ed. Nicholas T. Rand. Chicago: U of Chicago P, 1994.

Accinelli, Laura. "Eye of the Beholder." *Los Angeles Times* 23 Jan. 1996: E1+.

Adams, Alice E. "Molding Women's Bodies: The Surgeon as Sculptor." *Bodily Discursions: Genders, Representations, Technologies.* Ed. Deborah S. Wilson and Christine Moneera Laennec. Albany: State U of New York P, 1997. 59–80.

Adams, Parveen. *The Emptiness of the Image: Psychoanalysis and Sexual Differences.* New York: Routledge, 1995.

All about Eve. Dir. Joseph L. Mankiewicz. Perf. Bette Davis, Celeste Holm, Ann Baxter, Thelma Ritter, and George Sanders. Warner Bros., 1950.

All about My Mother. Dir. Pedro Almodóvar. Perf. Penélope Cruz, Marisa Paredes, and Cecilia Roth. Columbia/TriStar, 1999.

Allen, Jane E. "Surgeon-to-the-Stars Raises Concern." Associated Press, Los Angeles, 27 Oct. 1997.

"Altered States." *People Weekly* 2 Nov. 1998: 110.

Ansen, David. "Streisand's 'Mirror.'" Rev. of *The Mirror Has Two Faces. Newsweek* 25 Nov. 1996: 78.

"Anti-Aging Drug Craze!" *National Examiner* 20 Oct. 1998: 1+.

Anzieu, Didier, ed. *Psychic Envelopes.* Trans. Daphne Briggs. London: Karnac, 1990.

———. *The Skin Ego.* Trans. Chris Turner. New Haven: Yale UP, 1989.

———. *A Skin for Thought: Interviews with Gilbert Tarrab on Psychology and Psychoanalysis.* Trans. Daphne Nash Briggs. London: Karnac, 1990.

Ariès, Phillipe. *Centuries of Childhood: A Social History of Family Life.* Trans. Robert Baldick. New York: Vintage, 1962.

Ash Wednesday. Dir. Larry Peerce. Perf. Elizabeth Taylor, Henry Fonda, and Helmut Berger. Paramount, 1973.

Ballard, J. G. *The Atrocity Exhibition.* San Francisco: V/Search Pub., 1990.

———. *Crash.* New York: Farrar, 1973.

Balsamo, Anne. *Technologies of the Gendered Body: Reading Cyborg Women.* Durham: Duke UP, 1996.

Banet-Weiser, Lois. *The Most Beautiful Girl in the World: Beauty Pageants and National Identity.* Berkeley: U of California P, 1999.

Banner, Lois W. *American Beauty.* Chicago: U of Chicago P, 1983.

Barthes, Roland. *Camera Lucida: Reflections on Photography.* Trans. Richard Howard. New York: Hill and Wang, 1981.

Bartky, Sandra Lee. *Femininity and Domination: Studies in the Phenomenology of Oppression.* New York: Routledge, 1990.

Baudrillard, Jean. *America.* Trans. Chris Turner. London: Verso, 1988.

———. *Simulacra and Simulation.* Trans. Sheila Faria Glaser. Ann Arbor: U of Michigan P, 1994.

Being John Malkovich. Dir. Spike Jonze. Perf. John Cusack, Cameron Diaz, and John Malkovich. Gramercy Pictures, 1999.

Benjamin, Walter. "The Work of Art in the Age of Mechanical Reproduction." *Illuminations.* Trans. Harry Zohn. Ed. Hannah Arendt. New York: Schocken, 1969. 217–51.

Berger, John. *Ways of Seeing.* 1972. New York: Penguin, 1977.

Bernstein, Norman R. "Objective Bodily Damage: Disfigurement and Dignity." *Body Images: Development, Deviance, and Change.* Ed. Thomas F. Cash and Thomas Pruzinsky. New York: Guilford Press, 1990. 131–48.

Bersani, Leo. "Sociality and Sexuality." *Critical Inquiry* 26 (2000): 641–56.

Bick, Esther. "The Experience of the Skin in Early Object Relation." *International Journal of Psycho-Analysis* 49 (1968): 484–86.

Blanchard, Tasmin. Column. *Observer* 6 Aug. 2000: 26.

Boorstin, Daniel. *The Image: A Guide to Pseudo-Events in America.* 1961. New York: Vintage, 1992.

Bordo, Susan. *The Male Body: A New Look at Men in Public and Private.* New York: Farrar, Straus, and Giroux, 1999.

———. "Reading the Male Body." *The Male Body: Features, Destinies, Exposures.* Ed. Laurence Goldstein. Ann Arbor: U of Michigan P, 1994. 265–306.

———. *Twilight Zones: The Hidden Life of Cultural Images from Plato to O. J.* Berkeley: U of California P, 1997.

———. *Unbearable Weight: Feminism, Western Culture, and the Body.* Berkeley: U of California P, 1993.

Bowlby, Rachel. *Shopping with Freud.* London: Routledge, 1993.

Braidotti, Rosi. *Nomadic Subjects: Embodiment and Sexual Difference in Contemporary Feminist Theory.* New York: Columbia UP, 1994.

Bransford, Helen. *Welcome to Your Facelift: What to Expect Before, During and After Cosmetic Surgery.* New York: Doubleday, 1997.

Braudy, Leo. *The Frenzy of Renown: Fame and Its History.* 1986. New York: Vintage, 1997.

———. *The World in a Frame: What We See in Films.* Chicago: U of Chicago P, 1976.

Bray, Abigail, and Claire Colebrook. "The Haunted Flesh: Corporeal Feminism and the Politics of (Dis)Embodiment." *Signs: Journal of Women in Culture and Society* 24 (1998): 35–67.

Brazil. Dir. Terry Gilliam. Perf. Jonathan Pryce, Robert DeNiro, Katherine Helmond, and Ian Holm. Universal Studios, 1985.

Bromberg, Philip M. "The Mirror and the Mask: On Narcissism and Psychoanalytic Growth." *Essential Papers on Narcissism.* Ed. Andrew P. Morrison. New York: New York UP, 1986. 438–66.

Bronz, Giorgio. "The Role of the Computer Imaging System in Modern Aesthetic Plastic Surgery." *Aesthetic Plastic Surgery* 23 (1999): 159–63.

Brooks, Lida. "Bigger Is Better." *Cosmopolitan* Sept. 1996: 250–53.

Bryant, Marsha, ed. *Photo-Textualities: Reading Photographs and Literature.* Newark: U of Delaware P, 1996.

Bukatamen, Scott. *Terminal Identity: The Virtual Subject in Postmodern Science Fiction.* Durham: Duke UP, 1993.

Burana, Lily. "Bend Me, Shape Me." *New York Magazine* 15 July 1996: 30+.

Butler, Judith. *Gender Trouble: Feminism and the Subversion of Identity.* New York: Routledge, 1990.

Callé, Stuart C., and James T. Evans. "Plastic Surgery in the Cinema, 1917–1993." *Plastic and Reconstructive Surgery* 93.2 (1994): 422–33.

Camp, John. *Plastic Surgery: The Kindest Cut.* New York: Henry Holt, 1989.

Campbell, Laurie. "Roseanne: Plastic Surgery Saved My Life." *Examiner* 13 Aug. 1996: 7.

Carey, Gary, and Jospeh L. Mankiewicz. *More about All about Eve.* New York: Random, 1972.

Carvey, Nick. "The Bigger the Better." *Men's Perspectives,* "The Sex Issue," June 1996: 79–81.

"A Case for Undergoing Facelift at a Younger Age." Advertisement. *Lexington Herald-Leader* 10 Sept. 1995: 11.

Cash, Thomas F. "The Psychology of Physical Appearance: Aesthetics, Attributes, and Images." *Body Images: Development, Deviance, and Change.* Ed. Thomas F. Cash and Thomas Pruzinsky. New York: Guilford, 1990. 51–79.

Cash, Thomas F., and Thomas Pruzinsky, eds. *Body Images: Development, Deviance, and Change.* New York: Guilford P, 1990.

Castelló, José R., Jesús Barros, and Alfonso Chinchilla. "Body Dysmorphic Disorder and Aesthetic Surgery: Case Report." *Aesthetic Plastic Surgery* 22 (1998): 329–31.

Cato, Leigh. *The Other Woman: True Stories of Love, Betrayal, and the Men Women Have Shared as Husbands and Lovers.* Atlanta, GA: Longstreet, 1996.

Champlin, Charles. *John Frankenheimer: A Conversation with Charles Champlin.* Riverwood Press: Burbank, CA, 1995.

Chancer, Lynn S. *Reconcilable Differences: Confronting Beauty, Pornography, and the Future of Feminism.* Berkeley: U of California P, 1998.

Chapkis, Wendy. *Beauty Secrets: Women and the Politics of Appearance.* Boston: South End Press, 1986.

Clayton, Jay. "Concealed Circuits: Frankenstein's Monster, the Medusa, and the Cyborg." *Raritan* 15.4 (1996): 53–69.

Clifford, Margaret M., and Elaine Walster. "The Effect of Physical Attractiveness on Teacher Expectations." *Sociology of Education* 46 (1973): 248–58.

Copjec, Joan. *Read My Desire: Lacan against the Historicists.* Cambridge, MA: MIT P, 1994.

Crary, Jonathan. *Techniques of the Observer: On Vision and Modernity in the Nineteenth Century.* Cambridge, MA: MIT P, 1993.

Crosscope-Happel, Cindy, David E. Hutchins, Hildy G. Getz, and Gerald L. Hayes. "Male Anorexia Nervosa: A New Focus." *Journal of Mental Health Counseling* 22 (Oct.): 365–370.

Crum, J. Howard. *The Making of a Beautiful Face; or, Face Lifting Unveiled*. New York: Walton Book Co., 1928.

Cureau de la Chambre, Marin. *L'Art de connoistre les hommes*. 2 vols. Paris: Chez Jacques d'Allin, 1667.

————. *Les Charactères des passions*. Paris: Chez P. Ricolet, 1653.

Cusack, Lisa. "Perceptions of Body Image: Implications for the Workplace." *Employee Assistance Quarterly* 15 (2000): 2339.

D'Amato, Brian. *Beauty*. New York: Island Books, 1992.

Daniel, Rollin K., and Beatrix Tirkanits. "Endoscopic Forehead Lift: Aesthetics and Analysis." *Clinics in Plastic Surgery* 22 (1995): 605–18.

Dano, Linda. "My Face-Lift." *Ladies Home Journal* Mar. 1998: 56.

Dark Voyage. Dir. Delmer Daves. Perf. Humphrey Bogart and Lauren Bacall. Warner Bros., 1947.

Davidson, Ros. "Hollywood Lives Made Hell by the Celebrity Stalkers." *Scotland on Sunday*, 8 Mar. 1998: 17.

Davis, Kathy. *Reshaping the Female Body: The Dilemma of Cosmetic Surgery*. New York: Routledge, 1995.

Davis, Sally Ogle, and Ivor Davis. "The Good, the Bad, and the Ugly of Celebrity Plastic Surgery." Three parts. *E! Online*. 15 Nov. 2002 <http://www.eonline.com/Features/Specials/Surgery3/>.

Dean, Tim. *Beyond Sexuality*. Chicago: U of Chicago P, 2000.

de Beauvoir, Simone. *The Second Sex*. Trans. and ed. H. M. Parshley. Intro. Deirdre Bair. New York: Vintage, 1952.

Debord, Guy. *Society of the Spectacle*. Trans. Donald Nicholson-Smith. New York: Zone Books, 1995.

de Cordova, Richard. *Picture Personalities: The Emergence of the Star System in America*. Urbana: U of Illinois P, 1990.

de Lauretis, Teresa. *The Practice of Love: Lesbian Sexuality and Perverse Desire*. Bloomington: Indiana UP, 1994.

————. *Technologies of Gender: Essays on Theory, Film, and Fiction*. Bloomington: Indiana UP, 1987.

Deleuze, Gilles, and Félix Guattari. *A Thousand Plateaus: Capitalism and Schizophrenia*. Trans. Brian Massumi. Minneapolis: U of Minnesota P, 1987.

Demarest, Jack, and Rita Allen. "Body Image: Gender, Ethnic, and Age Differences." *Journal of Social Psychology* 140 (2000): 465–72.

Dery, Mark. *Escape Velocity: Cyberculture at the End of the Century.* New York: Grove, 1996.

Deutsch, Helene. "Some Forms of Emotional Disturbance and Their Relationship to Schizophrenia." *Essential Papers on Borderline Disorders: One Hundred Years at the Border.* Ed. Michael H. Stone. New York: New York UP, 1986. 74–91.

Dixon, Wheeler Winston. *Disaster and Memory: Celebrity Culture and the Crisis of Hollywood Cinema.* New York: Columbia UP, 1999.

Dolgoff, Stephanie. "4th Annual Nip and Tuck Awards: Job Security Hollywood Style." *Longevity* (Feb. 1995): 42–43, 106.

Douglas, Mary. *Purity and Danger: An Analysis of the Concepts of Purity and Taboo.* London: Routledge and Kegan Paul, 1966.

Ducille, Ann. *Skin Trade.* Cambridge, MA: Harvard UP, 1996.

Dull, Diana, and Candace West. "Accounting for Cosmetic Surgery: The Accomplishment of Gender." *Social Problems* 38.1 (1991): 54–70.

Durgnat, Raymond. *Franju.* Berkeley: U of California P, 1968.

Dyer, Richard. *Heavenly Bodies: Film Stars and Society.* New York: St. Martin's, 1986.

———. *Stars.* 1979. London: BFI Institute, 1998.

———. *White.* London: Routledge, 1997.

Edgerton, M. T., and N. J. Knorr. "Motivational Patterns of Patients Seeking Cosmetic (Esthetic) Surgery." *Plastic and Reconstructive Surgery* 55 (1971): 551–57.

Edgerton, Milton T., Margaretha W. Langman, and Thomas Pruzinsky. "Plastic Surgery and Psychotherapy in the Treatment of 100 Psychologically Disturbed Patients." *Plastic and Reconstructive Surgery* 88 (1991): 594–608.

EDTV. Dir. Ron Howard. Perf. Matthew McConaughey, Ellen DeGeneres, and Jenna Elfman. Universal, 1999.

Ellis, John. *Visible Fictions: Cinema Television Video.* Rev. ed. 1982. London: Routledge, 1989.

Etcoff, Nancy. *Survival of the Prettiest: The Science of Beauty.* New York: Doubleday, 1999.

Ewen, Stuart. *All-Consuming Images: The Politics of Style in Contemporary Culture.* New York: Basic, 1988.

Ewen, Stuart, and Elizabeth Ewen. *Channels of Desire: Mass Images and the Shaping of American Consciousness.* 1982. Minneapolis: U of Minnesota P, 1992.

"The Eye of the Beholder." *The Twilight Zone.* Dir. Douglas Heyes. Perf. Maxine Stuart and Donna Douglas. CBS. 11 Nov. 1960.

A Face to Die For. Dir. Jack Bender. Perf. Yasmin Bleeth and Richard Beymer. NBC television movie, 1996.

Faludi, Susan. *Backlash: The Undeclared War against American Women.* New York: Crown, 1991.

Farkas, L. G., C. R. Forrest, and L. Litsas. "Revision of Neoclassical Facial Canons in Young Adult Afro-Americans." *Aesthetic Plastic Surgery* 24 (2000): 179–84.

Favazza, Armando R. *Bodies under Siege: Self-Mutilation and Body Modification in Culture and Psychiatry.* Baltimore: Johns Hopkins UP, 1996.

Featherstone, Mike. "The Body in Consumer Culture." *The Body: Social Process and Cultural Theory.* Ed. Mike Featherstone, Mike Hepworth, and Bryan S. Turner. London: Sage, 1991. 170–96.

Fenichel, Otto. "Identification." *The Collected Papers of Otto Fenichel.* Ser. 1. Ed. Hanna Fenichel and David Rapaport. New York: Norton, 1953. 97–112.

Ferenczi, Sandor. *Thalassa: A Theory of Genitality.* Trans. Henry Alden Bunker. New York: Psychoanalytic Quarterly, 1938.

Finkelstein, Joanne. *The Fashioned Self.* Philadelphia: Temple UP, 1991.

Fomon, Samuel. *Cosmetic Surgery: Principles and Practice.* Philadelphia: J. B. Lippincott, 1960.

Frankenstein: The True Story. Dir. Jack Smight. Perf. James Mason, Leonard Whiting, David McCallum, Jane Seymour, and Michael Sarrazin. 1973. Videocassette, GoodTimes Home Video, 1995.

Franklyn, Robert Alan. *Beauty Surgeon.* Longbeach, CA: Whitehorn Pub., 1960.

Fraser, Laura. "The Hard Body Sell." *Mother Jones* Mar. 1999: 31+.

Freud, Sigmund. *The Standard Edition of the Complete Psychological Works of Sigmund Freud.* 24 vols. Trans. James Strachey et al. Ed. James Strachey. London: Hogarth, 1957–99. Referred to below as *Standard Edition.*

———. *The Ego and the Id.* 1923. *Standard Edition* 19: 3–66.

———. "Group Psychology and the Analysis of the Ego." 1921. *Standard Edition* 18: 67–143.

———. *Interpretation of Dreams.* 1900–01. *Standard Edition* 4–5.

———. "Mourning and Melancholia." 1915. *Standard Edition* 14: 237–60.

———. "On Narcissism: An Introduction." 1914. *Standard Edition* 14: 67–102.

———. "Some Neurotic Mechanisms in Jealousy, Paranoia and Homosexuality." 1922. *Standard Edition* 18: 223–32.

Friday, Nancy. *The Power of Beauty.* New York: Harper, 1996.

Friedberg, Anne. "A Denial of Difference: Theories of Cinematic Identification." *Psychoanalysis and Cinema.* Ed. E. Ann Kaplan. New York: Routledge, 1990. 36–45.

Frizot, Michel. "Another Kind of Photography: New Points of View." *A New History of Photography.* Ed. Michel Frizot. Trans. Susan Bennett et al. Milan: Könemann, 1998. 387–97.

———. "Body of Evidence: The Ethnophotography of Difference." *A New History of Photography.* Ed. Michel Frizot. Trans. Susan Bennett et al. Milan: Könemann, 1998. 259–71.

Frueh, Joanna. *Monster/Beauty: Building the Body of Love.* Berkeley: U of California P, 2001.

Fuente-Del-Campo, A. "Superiosteal Facelift: Open and Endoscopic Approach." *Aesthetic Plastic Surgery* 19.2 (1995): 149–60.

Furman, Frida Kerner. *Facing the Mirror: Older Women and Beauty Shop Culture.* New York: Routledge, 1997.

Fuss, Diana. *Identification Papers.* New York: Routledge, 1995.

Gaddini, Eugenio. "On Imitation." *International Journal of Psycho-Analysis* 50.4 (1969): 475–84.

Gaines, Jane. *Contested Culture: The Image, the Voice, and the Law.* Chapel Hill: U of North Carolina P, 1991.

Gamson, Joshua. *Claims to Fame: Celebrity in Contemporary America.* Berkeley: U of California P, 1994.

Gergen, Kenneth J. *The Saturated Self: Dilemmas of Identity in Contemporary Life.* New York: Basic, 1991.

Giddens, Anthony. *The Constitution of Society: Outline of the Theory of Structuratio.* Berkeley: U of California P, 1984.

Gifford, Sanford. "Cosmetic Surgery and Personality Change: A Review and Some Clinical Observations." *The Unfavorable Result in Plastic Surgery: Avoidance and Treatment.* Ed. Robert Goldwyn. 2nd ed. Boston: Little, 1984. 21–43.

Gillespie, Rosemary. "Women, the Body and Brand Extension in Medicine:

Cosmetic Surgery and the Paradox of Choice." *Women and Health* 24 (1996): 69–85.

Gilman, Sander L. *Creating Beauty to Cure the Soul: Race and Psychology in the Shaping of Aesthetic Surgery.* Durham: Duke UP, 1998.

———. *Making the Body Beautiful: A Cultural History of Aesthetic Surgery.* Princeton: Princeton UP, 1999.

Gimlin, Debra L. *Body Work: Beauty and Self-Image in American Culture.* Berkeley: U of California P, 2002.

Gitomer, Jeffrey. "Critical Match—Looking Good and Making Sales." *Providence Business News* 25–31 Oct. 1999: 32.

Gledhill, Christine, ed. 1991. *Stardom: Industry of Desire.* London: Routledge, 1998.

Goffman, Erving. *The Presentation of Self in Everyday Life.* New York: Doubleday, 1972.

Goin, John M., and Marcia Kraft Goin. *Changing the Body: Psychological Effects of Plastic Surgery.* Baltimore: Williams and Wilkins, 1981.

———. "Psychological Understanding and Management of the Plastic Surgery Patient." *Essentials of Plastic, Maxillofacial, and Reconstructive Surgery.* Ed. Nicholas G. Georgiade et al. Baltimore: Williams and Wilkins: 1987. 1127–43.

Goldwyn, Robert M., *The Operative Note: Collected Editorials.* New York: Thieme Medical Pub., 1992.

———, ed. *The Unfavorable Result in Plastic Surgery: Avoidance and Treatment.* 2nd ed. Boston: Little, 1984.

Goodman, Marcene. "Culture, Cohort, and Cosmetic Surgery." *Journal of Women and Aging* 8.2 (1996): 55–73.

———. "Social, Psychological, and Developmental Factors in Women's Receptivity to Cosmetic Surgery." *Journal of Aging Studies* 8 (1994): 375–96.

Gorney, Mark. "Preoperative Computerized Video Imaging." *Plastic and Reconstructive Surgery* 78 (1986): 268.

"Gotcha! Stars with No Makeup." *Globe* 25 Jan. 2000: 1+.

Gray, Chris Hables, ed. *The Cyborg Handbook.* New York: Routledge, 1995.

Grealy, Lucy. *The Autobiography of a Face.* New York: Houghton Mifflin, 1994.

Greer, Donald M. "Psychiatric Consultation in Plastic Surgery: The Surgeon's Perspective." *Psychosomatics* 25.6 (1984): 470–75.

Groenman, N. H., and H. C. Sauër. "Personality Characteristics of the Cosmetic Surgical Insatiable Patient." *Pschosomatic Problems in Surgery* 90 (1983): 241–45.

Grossman, Barbara W. *Funny Girl: The Life and Times of Fanny Brice.* Bloomington: Indiana UP, 1991.

Grosz, Elizabeth. *Volatile Bodies: Toward a Corporeal Feminism.* Bloomington: Indiana UP, 1994.

Grotstein, James S. *Splitting and Projective Identification.* Northvale, NJ: Jason Aronson, 1985.

Guerrissi, Jorge Orlando, and Luis Izquierdo Sanchez. "An Approach to the Senile Upper Lip." *Plastic and Reconstructive Surgery* (Nov. 1993): 1187–91.

Gullette, Margaret Morganroth. "The Other End of the Fashion Cycle: Practicing Loss, Learning Decline." *Figuring Age: Women, Bodies, Generations.* Ed. Kathleen Woodward. Bloomington: Indiana UP, 1999. 34–55.

Gunning, Tom. "Phantom Images and Modern Manifestations: Spirit Photography, Magic Theater, Trick Films, and Photography's Uncanny." *Fugitive Images: From Photography to Video.* Ed. Patrice Petro. Bloomington: Indiana UP, 1995. 42–71.

———. "Tracing the Individual Body: Photography, Detectives, and Early Cinema." *Cinema and the Invention of Modern Life.* Ed. Leo Charney and Vanessa R. Schwartz. Berkeley: U of California P, 1995. 15–45.

Guyuron, Bahman. "The Armamentarium to Battle the Recalcitrant Nasolabial Fold." *Clinics in Plastic Surgery* 22.2 (Apr. 1995): 253–64.

Hadley, Katharine. "'My Facelift Is Great.'" *Mail on Sunday* 3 Sept. 1995: 37.

Haiken, Elizabeth. *Venus Envy: A History of Cosmetic Surgery.* Baltimore: Johns Hopkins UP, 1997.

———. "Virtual Virility, or, Does Medicine Make the Man?" *Men and Masculinities* 2 (2000): 388–409.

Haithman, Diane. "Just Perfect for the Part." *Los Angeles Times* 6 July 1996: F1.

Halberstam, Judith. *Skin Shows: Gothic Horror and the Technology of Monsters.* Durham: Duke UP, 1995.

Hamra, Sam T. "Composite Rhytidectomy and the Nasolabial Fold." *Clinics in Plastic Surgery* 22 (1995): 313–24.

———. "The Role of Orbital Fat Preservation in Facial Aesthetic Surgery: A New Concept." *Clinics in Plastic Surgery* 32 (1996): 17–28.

Haraldsson, P.-O. "Psychosocial Impact of Cosmetic Rhinoplasty." *Aesthetic Plastic Surgery* 23 (1999): 170–74.

Haraway, Donna J. *Simians, Cyborgs, and Women: The Reinvention of Nature*. New York: Routledge, 1991.

Hardie, Melissa Jane. "'I Embrace the Difference': Elizabeth Taylor and the Closet." *Sexy Bodies: The Strange Carnalities of Feminism*. Ed. Elizabeth Grosz and Elspeth Probyn. New York: Routledge, 1995. 155–71.

Harris, D. L., and A. T. Carr. "The Derriford Appearance Scale (DAS59): A New Psychometric Scale for the Evaluation of Patients with Disfigurements and Aesthetic Problems of Appearance." *British Journal of Plastic Surgery* 54 (2000): 216–22.

———. "Prevalence of Concern about Physical Appearance in the General Population." *British Journal of Plastic Surgery* 54 (2001): 223–26.

Hawthorne, Nathaniel. "The Birthmark." 1843. *Hawthorne: Selected Tales and Sketches*. Ed. Hyatt H. Waggoner. New York: Holt, Rinehart and Winston, 1970. 264–81.

Hayt, Elizabeth. "Surreality Check." *Vogue* July 2000: 200+.

Hersey, George. *The Evolution of Allure: Sexual Selection from the Medici Venus to the Incredible Hulk*. Cambridge, MA: MIT P, 1996.

Hesse-Biber, Sharlene. *Am I Thin Enough Yet? The Cult of Thinness and the Commercialization of Identity*. New York: Oxford UP, 1996.

Heymann, C. David. *Liz: An Intimate Biography of Elizabeth Taylor*. Secaucus: Carol Publishing Group, 1995.

Higashi, Sumiko. *Cecil B. De Mille and American Culture: The Silent Era*. Berkeley: U of California P, 1994.

Hirschhorn, Michelle. "Orlan: Artist in the Post-Human Age of Mechanical Reincarnation: Body as Ready (to Be Re-)Made." *Generations and Geographies in the Visual Arts: Feminist Readings*. Ed. Griselda Pollock. London: Routledge, 1996. 110–34.

Hoefflin, Stephen M. *Ethnic Rhinoplasty*. New York: Springer-Verlag, 1997.

Hollander, Anne. Editorial. *New York Times Magazine* 24 Nov. 1996: 90.

"Image." *Harper's Bazaar* Apr. 2001: 138.

Imitation of Life. Dir. Douglas Sirk. Perf. Lana Turner, Juanita Moore, John Gavin, Sandra Dee, and Susan Kohner. Universal International, 1959.

"I Sing the Body Electric." *The Twilight Zone*. Perf. Veronica Cartwright. CBS. 18 May 1962.

Jacobson, Edith. "Ways of Female Superego Formation and the Female Castration Conflict." *Essential Papers on the Psychology of Women.* New York: New York UP, 1990.

James, Henry. *Watch and Ward.* 1867. London: Rupert Hart-Davis, 1960.

Jameson, Fredric. *The Culture of Postmodernism; or, the Cultural Logic of Late Capitalism.* Durham: Duke UP, 1991.

Johnny Handsome. Dir. Walter Hill. Perf. Mickey Rourke, Morgan Freeman, Forest Whitaker, and Elizabeth McGovern. Carolco Pictures, 1989.

Johnson, Barbara. "Is Female to Male as Ground Is to Figure?" *Feminism and Psychoanalysis.* Ed. Richard Feldstien and Judith Roof. Ithaca: Cornell UP, 1989. 255–68.

Johnson, Brian D. Rev. of *The Mirror Has Two Faces. Maclean's* 25 Nov. 1996: 131.

Jordanova, Ludmilla. *Sexual Visions: Images of Gender in Science and Medicine between the Eighteenth and Twentieth Centuries.* Madison: U of Wisconsin P, 1989.

Kalick, Michael. "Toward an Interdisciplinary Psychology of Appearances." *Psychiatry* 41 (1978): 243–53.

Kaplan, Louise J. *Female Perversions: The Temptations of Emma Bovary.* 1991. Northvale, NJ: Jason Aronson, 1997.

Kember, Sarah. *Virtual Anxiety: Photography, New Technologies and Subjectivity.* Manchester: Manchester UP, 1998.

Kent, Allegra. *Once a Dancer: An Autobiography.* New York: St. Martin's, 1997.

Kernberg, Otto. *Borderline Conditions and Pathological Narcissism.* 1975. Northvale, NJ: Jason Aronson, 1985.

Kettle, Martin. "Doc Hollywood 'Mocked and Fondled Stars.'" *Guardian* 18 Feb. 1999: 15.

Kincaid, James R. *Child-Loving: The Erotic Child and Victorian Culture.* New York: Routledge, 1992.

———. *Erotic Innocence: The Culture of Child Molesting.* Durham: Duke UP, 1998.

King, Barry. "Articulating Stardom." *Stardom: Industry of Desire.* Ed. Christine Gledhill. London: Routledge, 1991. 167–82.

Kirkland, Anna, and Rosemarie Tong. "Working within Contradiction: The Possibility of Feminist Cosmetic Surgery." *Journal of Clinical Ethics* 7 (1996): 151–59.

Kirkland, Gelsey, with Greg Lawrence. *Dancing on My Grave: An Autobiography.* Garden City, NY: Doubleday, 1986.

Klein, Melanie. "A Contribution to the Psychogenesis of Manic-Depressive States." 1935. *Love, Guilt and Reparation and Other Works, 1921–1945.* Vol. 1. Ed. R. E. Money-Kyrle. New York: Free P, 1975. 262–89.

———. "On Identification." 1955. *Envy and Gratitude and Other Works, 1946–1963.* Vol. 3. Ed. R. E. Money-Kyrle. New York: Free P, 1975. 141–75.

Knorr, N. J., M. T. Edgerton, and J. E. Hoopes. "The 'Insatiable' Cosmetic Surgery Patient." *Plastic and Reconstructive Surgery* 40 (1967): 285–89.

Koestenbaum, Wayne. *Cleavage: Essays on Sex, Stars, and Aesthetics.* New York: Ballantine, 2000.

Kofman, Sarah. *The Enigma of Woman: Woman in Freud's Writings.* Trans. Catherine Porter. Ithaca: Cornell UP, 1985.

Kohn, Luci Ann, et al. "Anthropometric Optical Surface Imaging System Repeatability, Precision, and Validation." *Annals of Plastic Surgery* 34.4 (Apr. 1995): 362–71.

Kohut, Heinz. *How Does Analysis Cure?* Ed. Arnold Goldberg. Chicago: U of Chicago P, 1984.

———. *The Restoration of the Self.* New York: International Universities Press, 1977.

Kornreich, Jennifer. "Beauties, Perfect vs. Imperfect." *Marie Claire* Sept. 1996: 106–17.

Krastinova-Lolov, Darina. "Mask Lift and Facial Aesthetic Sculpturing." *Plastic and Reconstructive Surgery* 95 (1995): 21–36.

Krips, Henry. *Fetish: An Erotics of Culture.* Ithaca: Cornell UP, 1999.

Kron, Joan. "Knife Fight." *Allure* Sept. 1998: 175+.

———. *Lift: Wanting, Fearing, and Having a Face-Lift.* New York: Viking, 1998.

———. "Nipping and Tucking in Tinseltown." *Allure* May 1995: 166+.

Kruger, Pamela. "Face." *Working Woman* 19 (July) 1994: 54+.

Lacan, Jacques. "Aggressivity in Psychoanalysis." *Écrits: A Selection.* Trans. Alan Sheridan. New York: Norton, 1977. 8–29.

———. *The Four Fundamental Concepts of Psycho-Analysis.* Trans. Alan Sheridan. Ed. Jacques-Alain Miller. New York: Norton, 1978.

———. "The Mirror Stage." *Écrits: A Selection.* Trans. Alan Sheridan. New York: Norton, 1977. 1–7.

———. *The Seminar of Jacques Lacan.* Book 1: *Freud's Papers on Technique, 1953–*

1954. Trans. Sylvana Tomaselli. Ed. Jacques-Alain Miller. New York: Norton, 1988.

———. *The Seminar of Jacques Lacan*. Book 2: *The Ego in Freud's Theory and in the Technique of Psychoanalysis, 1954–1955*. Trans. Sylvana Tomaselli. Ed. Jacques-Alain Miller. New York: Norton, 1988.

Lacher, Irene. "Here's to a Match Made in Medical Heaven." *Los Angeles Times*, 27 Aug. 1997: E5.

Lakoff, Robin Tolmach, and Raquel L. Scherr. *Face Value: The Politics of Beauty*. London: Routledge and Kegan Paul, 1984.

Lambert, Ellen Zetzel. *The Face of Love: Feminism and the Beauty Question*. Boston: Beacon Press, 1995.

Laplanche, Jean, and J.-B. Pontalis. *The Language of Psycho-analysis*. Trans. Donald Nicholson-Smith. Introd. Daniel Lagache. New York: Norton, 1973.

Larrabee, Wayne F., John Sidles, and Dwight Sutton. "'How I Do It'—Head and Neck and Plastic Surgery: A Targeted Problem and Its Solution." *Laryngoscope* 98 (1988): 1273–75.

Larsen, Nella. *Passing*. Ed. Thadious Davis. 1929. New York: Penguin, 1997.

Larson, David L. "An Historical Glimpse of the Evolution of Rhytidectomy." *Clinics in Plastic Surgery* 22 (1995): 207–12.

Lasch, Christopher. *The Culture of Narcissism: American Life in An Age of Diminishing Expectations*. New York: Norton, 1979.

Lavater, Johann Caspar. *Essays on Physiognomy: For the Promotion of the Knowledge and the Love of Mankind*. 4 vols. Translated by Mme. E. de la Fite, H. Renfner, and Mme. Caillard. The Hague, 1781–1803.

Lazzeri, Antonella. "Twindy Dolls: Cindy's Plastic Surgery Clone." *Sun* (London) 21 June 1997: 1+.

Le, Thuy T., Leslie G. Farkas, Rexon C.K. Ngim, L. Scott Levin, and Christopher R. Forrest. "Proportionality in Asian and North American Caucasian Faces Using Neoclassical Facial Canons as Criteria." *Aesthetic Plastic Surgery* 26 (2002): 64–69.

Leiby, Richard. "Face Off: Three of Hollywood's Elite Plastic Surgeons Are at War." *Washington Post* 26 Oct. 1997: F01+.

"Linda Tripp's Plastic Surgery." *National Enquirer* 11 Jan. 2000: 8+.

Lingis, Alphonso. *Foreign Bodies*. New York: Routledge, 1994.

"Liz Plastic Surgery Miracle." *National Enquirer* 2 Apr. 1996: 1+.

Lockwood, Ted. "Lower Body Lift with Superficial Fascial System Suspension." *Plastic and Reconstructive Surgery* (1993): 1112–22.

"Look at Farrah Now." *National Enquirer* 4 July 2000: 1+.

Looker. Dir. Michael Crichton. Perf. Albert Finney, Susan Dey, and James Coburn. 1981. Videocassette. Warner Home Video, 1991.

Lord, M. G. *Forever Barbie: The Unauthorized Biography of a Real Doll.* New York: Avon Books, 1995.

Lost Boundaries. Dir. Louis de Rochemont. Perf. Mel Ferrer, Beatrice Pearson, and Richard Hylton. 1949. Videocassette, Warner Bros., 1997.

Lowenstein, Adam. "Films without a Face: Shock Horror in the Cinema of Georges Franju." *Cinema Journal* 37.4 (1998): 37–58.

Lowenthal, Leo. "The Triumph of Mass Idols." *Literature, Popular Culture, and Society.* Englewood Cliffs, NJ: Prentice-Hall, 1961.

Macdonald, Myra. *Representing Women: Myths of Femininity in the Popular Media.* London: Edward Arnold, 1995.

MacGregor, Frances Cooke, and Bertram Schaffner. "Screening Patients for Nasal Plastic Operations: Some Sociologic and Psychiatric Considerations." *Psychosomatic Medicine* 12.5 (1950): 277–91.

MacGregor, Frances Cooke, Theodora M. Abel, Albert Bryt, Edith Lauer, and Serena Weissmann. *Facial Deformities and Plastic Surgery: A Psychosocial Study.* Springfield, IL: Charles C. Thomas Pub., 1953.

Mahler, Margaret S. "Study of the Separation-Individuation Process." *Essential Papers on Borderline Disorders: One Hundred Years at the Border.* Ed. Michael S. Stone. New York: New York UP, 1989. 433–52.

Mahler, Margaret S., Fred Pine, and Anni Bergman. *The Psychological Birth of the Human Infant: Symbiosis and Individuation.* New York: Basic, 1975.

Maltz, Maxwell. *Psycho-Cybernetics: A New Technique for Using Your Subconscious Power.* Foreword Melvin Powers. Hollywood: Melvin Powers Wilshire Book Co., 1960.

Man, Daniel, and L. C. Faye Shelkofsky. *The Art of Man: Faces of Plastic Surgery.* Naples, FL: Beauty Art Press, 1998.

Marchac, Daniel, James A. Brady, and Portia Chiou. "Face Lifts and Hidden Scars: The Vertical U Incision." *Plastic and Reconstructive Surgery* 109.7 (June 2002): 2539–51.

Margrave, Christopher. *Cosmetic Surgery: Facing the Facts.* Middlesex: Penguin, 1985.

Marshall, David. *Celebrity and Power: Fame in Contemporary Culture.* Minneapolis: U of Minnesota P, 1997.

Marshall, Tim. *Murdering to Dissect: Grave-robbing,* Frankenstein *and the Anatomy Literature.* Manchester: Manchester UP, 1995.

Martin, Emily. *The Woman in the Body: A Cultural Analysis of Reproduction.* Boston: Beacon P, 1992.

Masterson, James F. *The Search for the Real Self: Unmasking the Personality Disorders of Our Age.* New York: Free P, 1988.

Matory, W. Earle, Jr. "Addressing the Needs of the Hostile Patient." In *Ethnic Considerations in Facial Aesthetic Surgery.* Ed. W. Earle Matory, Jr. Philadelphia: Lippincott-Raven, 1998.

———, ed. *Ethnic Considerations in Facial Aesthetic Surgery.* Philadelphia: Lippincott-Raven, 1998.

Mattison, R. C. "Facial Video Image Processing: Standard Facial Image Capturing, Software Modification, Development of a Surgical Plan, and Comparison of Presurgical and Postsurgical Results." *Annals of Plastic Surgery* 29 (1992): 385–89.

Maves, Michael D., Margaret H. Cooper, James E. Benecke, Paul H. Young, and Corey S. Maas. "Three-Dimensional Video Imagining in Otolaryngology—Head and Neck Surgery." *Laryngoscope* 103 (1993): 1174–76.

May, Lary. 1980. *Screening Out the Past: The Birth of Mass Culture and the Motion Picture Industry.* Chicago: U of Chicago P, 1983.

McArthur, Benjamin. *Actors and American Culture, 1880–1920.* Iowa City: U of Iowa P, 2000.

McClelland, Susan. "Distorted Images: Western Cultures Are Exporting Their Dangerous Obsession with Thinness." *Maclean's* 14 Aug. 2000: 41–42.

McLuhan, Marshall. 1964. *Understanding Media: Extensions of Man.* Introd. Lewis H. Lapham. Cambridge: MIT P, 1994.

Mead, Rebecca. "Identity Crisis." *Vogue* Mar. 1995: 326.

Mellor, Anne K. *Mary Shelley: Her Life, Her Fiction, Her Monsters.* New York: Routledge, 1988.

Meninger, K. A. "Polysurgery and Polysurgical Addiction." *Psychoanalytic Quarterly* 3 (1934): 173–99.

Metz, Christian. *The Imaginary Signifier: Psychoanalysis and the Cinema.* Trans. Celia Britton et al. Bloomington: Indiana UP, 1982.

Meyer, Richard. "Rock Hudson's Body." *Inside/Out: Lesbian Theories, Gay Theories.* New York: Routledge, 1991. 259–88.

The Mirror Has Two Faces. Dir. Barbra Streisand. Perf. Barbra Streisand, Jeff Bridges, and Lauren Bacall. TriStar Pictures, 1996.

Mitchell, Stephen A. "True Selves, False Selves, and the Ambiguity of Authenticity." *Relational Perspectives in Psychoanalysis.* Ed. Neil J. Skolnick and Susan C. Warshaw. Hillsdale, NJ: Analytic Press, 1992. 1–20.

Mitrani, Judith. "Unintegration, Adhesive Identification, and the Psychic Skin: Variations on Some Themes by Esther Bick." *Melanie Klein and Object Relations* 11.2 (1994): 65–88.

Moers, Ellen. *Literary Women: The Great Writers.* New York: Oxford UP, 1985.

Mohl, Paul C. "Psychiatric Consultation in Plastic Surgery: The Psychiatrist's Perspective." *Psychosomatics* 25 (1984): 471–75.

"Monsters Are Due on Maple Street." *The Twilight Zone.* Perf. Claude Atkins and Jack Weston. CBS. 4 Mar. 1960.

Monteath, Sheryl A., and Marita P. McCabe. "The Influence of Societal Factors on Female Body Image." *Journal of Social Psychology* 137 (1997): 708–27.

Morgan, Kathryn Pauly. "Women and the Knife: Cosmetic Surgery and the Colonization of Women's Bodies." *Hypatia* 6.3 (1991): 25–53.

Mulgannon, Terry. "Stalker! Stalker!" Three-parts. *E! Online.* 15 Nov. 2002. <http://www.eonline.com/Features/Specials/Stalkers/stalk1b.html>.

Mulvey, Laura. "Visual Pleasure and Narrative Cinema." *Feminism and Film Theory.* Ed. Constance Penley. New York: Routledge, 1988. 57–68.

Nakamura, Yuri, John B. Mulliken, and Myron L. Belfer. "Cross-Cultural Understanding of Aesthetic Surgery: The Male Cosmetic Surgery Patient in Japan in the USA." *Aesthetic Plastic Surgery* 24 (2000): 283–88.

Napoleon, Anthony. "The Presentation of Personalities in Plastic Surgery." *Annals of Plastic Surgery* 31.3 (1993): 193–208.

Nash, Joyce D. *What Your Doctor Can't Tell You about Cosmetic Surgery.* Oakland, CA: New Harbinger, 1995.

Nead, Lynda. *The Female Nude: Art, Obscenity and Sexuality.* London: Routledge, 1992.

Neimark, Jill. "The Culture of Celebrity." *Psychology Today* May/June 1995: 52+.

Nelson, Jim, Patricia Shipp, and Robert Blackmon. "Jane Fonda's Tragic Secret." *National Enquirer* 19 Nov. 2002: 34+.

Newell, R. "Psychological Difficulties amongst Plastic Surgery Ex-Patients Following Surgery to the Face: A Survey." *British Journal of Plastic Surgery* 53 (2000): 386–92.

Niechajev, Igor, and Per-Olle Haraldsson. "Ethnic Profile of Patients Undergoing Aesthetic Rhinoplasaty in Stockholm." *Aesthetic Plastic Surgery* 21 (1997): 139–45.

Nolan, James T. *Face to Face: Men and Women Talk Freely about Their Plastic Surgery.* Wilsonville, OR: Book Partners, 1998.

"Number Twelve Looks Just Like You." *The Twilight Zone.* Perf. Suzy Parker and Richard Long. CBS. 24 Jan. 1964.

"The Obsolete Man." *The Twilight Zone.* Perf. Burgess Meredith. CBS. 2 June 1961.

O'Neill, Ann W. "Plastic Surgeon to the Stars in a Nip and Tuck Case." *Los Angeles Times* 8 Nov. 1998. LexisNexis Academic.

Owsley, John Q. "Lifting the Malar Fat Pad for Correction of Prominent Nasolabial Folds." *Plastic and Reconstructive Surgery* 91 (1993): 463–76.

Ozgür, Figen, Dogan Tuncali, and K. Güler Gürsu. "Life Satisfaction, Self-Esteem, and Body Image: A Psychosocial Evaluation of Aesthetic and Reconstructive Surgery Candidates."*Aesthetic Plastic Surgery* 22 (1998): 412–19.

Pacteau, Francette. *The Symptom of Beauty.* Cambridge, Mass.: Harvard UP, 1994.

Papel, Ira D., and Robert J. Park. "Computer Imaging for Instruction in Facial Plastic Surgery in a Residency Program." *Archives of Otolaryngology Head and Neck Surgery* 114 (1988): 1454–60.

Paul, Malcolm D. "The Evolution of the Brow Lift in Aesthetic Plastic Surgery." *Plastic and Reconstructive Surgery* 108.5 (Oct. 2001): 1409–24.

Peiss, Kathy. *Hope in a Jar: The Making of America's Beauty Culture.* New York: Henry Holt, 1998.

Penley, Constance, and Andrew Ross. *Technoculture.* Minneapolis: U of Minnesota P, 1991.

Penn, Jean. "On The Cutting Edge." *Health and Fitness Magazine* Summer 1996: 85+.

Perkins, Karen R. "The Influence of Television Images on Black Females' Self-

Perceptions of Physical Attractiveness." *Journal of Black Sociology* 22 (Nov. 1996): 453–69.

Pertschuk, Michael. "Psychosocial Considerations in Interface Surgery." *Clinics in Plastic Surgery* 18 (Jan. 1991): 11–18.

Pertschuk, Michael J., David B. Sarwer, Thomas A. Wadden, and Linton A. Whitaker. "Body Image Dissatisfaction in Male Cosmetic Surgery Patients." *Aesthetic Plastic Surgery* 22 (1998): 20–24.

Pfeil, Fred. *White Guys: Studies in Postmodern Domination and Difference.* London: Verso, 1995.

Phillips, Katharine A. *The Broken Mirror: Understanding and Treating Body Dysmorphic Disorder.* New York: Oxford UP, 1996.

Pitts, Leonard, Jr. "Obsessed Fans Make the Fame Game Not So Fun to Win." *Houston Chronicle* 16 Oct. 1998: 2+.

Plastic Fantastic. Dir. Douglas Chirnside. 13 episodes. BBC. Convergence Productions, 1997.

Pleasantville. Dir. Gary Ross. Perf. Tobey Maguire, Reese Witherspoon, and Jeff Daniels. New Line Cinema, 1998.

"Poor Goldie!" *Globe* 24 Mar. 1998: 1+.

Postcards from the Edge. Dir. Mike Nichols. Perf. Meryl Streep, Shirley MacLaine, and Dennis Quaid. Columbia, 1990.

Postman, Neil. *Amusing Ourselves to Death: Public Discourse in the Age of Show Business.* New York: Penguin, 1985.

Powdermaker, Hortense. *Hollywood the Dream Factory: An Anthropologist Looks at the Movie-Makers.* Boston: Little, 1950.

Pratley, Gerald. *The Cinema of John Frankenheimer.* London: A. Zwemmer, 1969.

Pruzinsky, Thomas, and Thomas F. Cash. "Integrative Themes in Body-Image Development, Deviance, and Change." *Body Images: Development, Deviance, and Change.* Ed. Thomas F. Cash and Thomas Pruzinsky. New York: Guilford Press, 1990. 337–49.

Pruzinsky, Thomas, and Milton T. Edgerton. "Body-Image Change in Cosmetic Plastic Surgery." *Body Images: Development, Deviance, and Change.* Ed. Thomas F. Cash and Thomas Pruzinsky. New York: Guilford Press, 1990. 217–36.

Pruzinsky, Thomas, Milton Edgerton, and Jeffrey Barth. "Medical Psychother-

apy and Plastic Surgery: Collaboration, Specialization, and Cost Effective-
ness." *The Handbook of Medical Psychotherapy: Cost Effective Strategies in Mental Health.* Ed. Kenneth N. Anchor. Toronto: Hogrefe and Huber, 1990.
101–22.

Rabid. Dir. David Cronenberg. Perf. Marilyn Chambers. 1976. DVD. New
Concorde, 2000.

Radner, Hilary. *Shopping Around: Feminine Culture and the Pursuit of Pleasure.*
New York: Routledge, 1995.

Radosevich, Amy C. "Note: Thwarting the Stalker: Are Anti-Stalking Measures
Keeping Pace with Today's Stalker?" *University of Illinois Law Review* (2000):
1371. LexisNexis Academic.

Radsken, Jill. "Women Who Love Their Doctors." *Boston Herald* 8 June 2000:
47.

Ramirez, Oscar M. "Endoscopic Subperiosteal Browlift and Facelift." *Clinics in
Plastic Surgery* 22 (1995): 639–60.

Rayner, Richard. "Children of Paradise." Rev. of *Fast Forward: Growing Up in the
Shadow of Hollywood*, by Lauren Greenfield. *Los Angeles Times*, "Book Review" 15 June 1997: 3.

Reekie, Gail. *Temptations: Sex, Selling and the Department Store.* NSW, Australia:
Allen and Unwin, 1993.

Reich, Annie. "Pathologic Forms of Self-Esteem Regulation." *Essential Papers on
Narcissism.* Ed. Andrew P. Morrison. New York: New York UP, 1986. 44–60.

Reynolds, David. *Beneath the American Renaissance: The Subversive Imagination in
the Age of Emerson and Melville.* Cambridge, Mass.: Harvard UP, 1989.

Rhodes, Gillian, Alex Sumich, and Graham Byatt. "Are Average Facial Configu-
rations Attractive Only Because of Their Symmetry?" *Psychological Science* 10
(1999): 52–58.

Rich, Frank. "American Pseudo." *New York Times Magazine* 12 Dec. 1999, sec.
6: 80.

Richardson, Laurel. *The New Other Woman: Contemporary Single Women in Affairs with Married Men.* New York: Free P, 1985.

Rickels, Laurence A. "Cryptology." *Hi-Fives: A Trip to Semiotics.* Ed. Roberta
Kevelson. New York: Peter Lang, 1998. 191–204.

Rivers, Christopher. *Face Value: Physiognomical Thought and the Legible Body in
Marivaux, Lavater, Balzac, Gautier, and Zola.* Madison: U of Wisconsin P,
1994.

Roberts, Yvonne. "Is There a Woman Out There Who Likes Her Body?" *New Statesman* 1 May 2000: 32–33.

Rogers-Salyer, Marcy, A. Gayle Jensen, and R. Christopher Barden. "Effects of Facial Deformities and Physical Attractiveness on Mother-Infant Bonding." *Craniofacial Surgery: Proceedings of the First International Congress of the International Society of Cranio-Maxillo-Facial Surgery.* Ed. Daniel Marchac. New York: Springer-Verlag, 1987.

Romm, Sharon. "Art, Love, and Facial Beauty." *Clinics in Plastic Surgery* 14 (1987): 579–83.

———. "On the Beauty of Lips." *Clinics in Plastic Surgery* 11 (1984): 571–81.

Rose, Jacqueline. "Paranoia and the Film System." *Feminism and Film Theory.* Ed. Constance Penley. New York: Routledge, 1988. 141–58.

Rosen, Harvey M. "Aesthetic Guidelines in Genioplasty: The Role of Facial Disproportion." *Plastic and Reconstructive Surgery* (Mar. 1995): 463–69.

Rosenthal, Jim. "The Science of Size: Current Insights into This Controversial Procedure." *Muscle & Fitness* Nov. 1994: 220+.

Rowen, Norma. "The Making of Frankenstein's Monster: Post-Golem, Pre-Robot." *State of the Fantastic: Studies in the Theory and Practice of Fantastic Literature and Film.* Ed. Nicholas Ruddick. Westport, CT: Greenwood P, 1990. 169–77.

Rozen, Leah. Rev. of *The Mirror Has Two Faces. People Weekly* 25 Nov. 1996: 19.

Sarwer, David B. "The 'Obsessive' Cosmetic Surgery Patient: A Consideration of Body Image Dissatisfaction and Body Dysmorphic Disorder." *Plastic Surgical Nursing* 17 (1997): 193–99.

Sarwer, David B., Thomas A. Wadden, and Linton A. Whitaker. "An Investigation in Changes in Body Image Following Cosmetic Surgery." *Plastic and Reconstructive Surgery* 109.1 (2001): 363–69.

Schickel, Richard. *Intimate Strangers: The Culture of Celebrity.* Garden City: Doubleday, 1985.

———. Rev. of *The Mirror Has Two Faces. Time* 25 Nov. 1996: 108.

Schilder, Paul. *The Image and Appearance of the Human Body: Studies in the Constructive Energies of the Psyche.* New York: International Universities Press, 1950.

———. *Seele und Leben.* Berlin, 1923.

Schireson, Henry J. *As Others See You: The Story of Plastic Surgery.* New York: Macaulay, 1938.

Schouten, John W. "Selves in Transition: Symbolic Consumption in Personal Rites of Passage and Identity Reconstruction." *Journal of Consumer Research* 17 (1991): 412–25.

Schweitzer, Isaac. "The Psychiatric Assessment of the Patient Requesting Facial Surgery." *Australian and New Zealand Journal of Psychiatry* 23 (1989): 249–54.

Seconds. Dir. John Frankenheimer. Perf. Rock Hudson, John Randolph, and Salome Jens. Paramount, 1966.

Sennett, Richard. *The Fall of Public Man.* 1974. New York: Norton, 1992.

Serrano, Nancy. "Insert Here." *Elle Magazine* Sept. 2002: 310–12.

Sharkey, Betsy. "Face Values." *Town and Country* Mar. 1996: 130+.

She-Devil. Dir. Susan Seidelman. Perf. Meryl Streep and Roseanne Barr. 1989. Videocassette. Orion, 1989.

Shelley, Mary. *Frankenstein; or, the Modern Prometheus.* Ed. Marilyn Butler. Rpt. 1818. New York: Oxford UP, 1994.

Shorter, Edward. *The Making of the Modern Family.* New York: Basic, 1975.

"Sick Computer Game Lets You 'Kill' Stars." *Star* 22 Sept. 1998: 4.

Siebert, Charles. "The Cuts That Go Deeper." *New York Times Magazine* 7 July 1996: 20–45.

Silverman, Kaja. *Male Subjectivity at the Margins.* New York: Routledge, 1994.

Simon, John. Rev. of *The Mirror Has Two Faces. National Review* 23 Dec. 1996: 57.

Slator, R., and D. L. Harris. "Are Rhinoplasty Patients Potentially Mad?" *British Journal of Plastic Surgery* 45 (1992): 307–10.

Sontag, Susan. 1977. *On Photography.* New York: Anchor, 1989.

Spigel, Lynn. *Make Room for Television: Television and the Family Ideal in Postwar America.* Chicago: U of Chicago P, 1992.

Stacey, Jackie. *Star-Gazing: Hollywood Cinema and Female Spectatorship.* New York: Routledge, 1994.

Stafford, Barbara Maria. *Body Criticism: Imaging the Unseen in Enlightenment Art and Medicine.* Cambridge: MIT Press, 1997.

Stafford, Barbara M., John La Puma, and David L. Schiedermayer. "One Face of Beauty, One Picture of Health: The Hidden Aesthetic of Medical Practice." *Journal of Medicine and Philosophy* 14 (1989): 213–30.

Starl, Timm. "The Use and Spread of the Daguerreotype Process." In *A New History of Photography.* Ed. Michel Frizot. Trans. Susan Bennett et al. Milan: Könemann, 1998.

"Stars' Plastic Surgeries." *Globe* 28 Sept. 1999: 1+.

"Stars' Plastic Surgery Secrets." *National Enquirer* 23 Apr. 1996: 1+.

"Steal This Look." *In Style* Jan. 2000.

Stearns, Peter N. *Fat History: Bodies and Beauty in the Modern West.* New York: New York UP, 1997.

Stekel, Wilhelm. *Compulsion and Doubt.* London: Peter Nevill, 1950.

Stone, C. A. "Can a Picture Really Paint a Thousand Words?" *Aesthetic Plastic Surgery* 24 (2000): 185–91.

Stone, Lawrence. *The Family, Sex, and Marriage: In England, 1500–1800.* New York: Harper, 1977.

Studlar, Gaylyn. *This Mad Masquerade: Stardom and Masculinity in the Jazz Age.* New York: Columbia UP, 1996.

Sullivan, Deborah A. *Cosmetic Surgery: The Cutting Edge of Commercial Medicine in America.* New Brunswick: Rutgers UP, 2002.

Sullivan, Robert. "Surgery before 30." *Vogue* July 1995: 156+.

Sunstein, Emily W. *Mary Shelley: Romance and Reality.* Baltimore: Johns Hopkins UP, 1989.

Tagg, John. *The Burden of Representation: Essays on Photographies and Histories.* Minneapolis: U of Minnesota P, 1993.

Talamus, Irene, and Luis Pando. "Specific Requirements for Preoperative and Postoperative Photos Used in Publication." *Aesthetic Plastic Surgery* 25 (2001): 307–10.

The Talented Mr. Ripley. Dir. Anthony Minghella. Perf. Matt Damon, Jude Law, Gwyneth Paltrow, and Cate Blanchett. Miramax, 1999.

Taylor, John. "The Long, Hard Days of Dr. Dick." *Esquire* Sept. 1995: 120–30.

Taylor, Mark. *Hiding.* Chicago: U of Chicago P, 1997.

Terino, Edward O. "Implants for Male Aesthetic Surgery." *Clinics in Plastic Surgery* 18.4 (Oct. 1991): 731–49.

Tharp, Mike. Untitled article. *U.S. News & World Report* 17 Feb. 1992: 28.

Theroux, Paul. "Liz: Ms. Taylor Will See You Now." *Talk* Oct. 1999: 162+.

Thesander, Marianne. *The Feminine Ideal.* London: Reaktion Books, 1997.

Theweleit, Klaus. *Male Fantasies.* Vol. 1: *Women, Floods, Bodies, History.* Trans. Stephen Conway, Erica Carter, and Chris Turner. Minneapolis: U of Minnesota P, 1987.

———. *Male Fantasies.* Vol. 2: *Male Bodies.* Trans. Erica Carter and Chris Turner. Minneapolis: U of Minnesota P, 1988.

Thomas, Barbara. "Image: Others Are Openly Talking about Breast Augmentation Reversal after Pamela Anderson Lee Goes Public; Implants Made Them Feel Like Unnatural Women." *Los Angeles Times* 30 Apr. 1999: 1+.

Thomas, J. Regan, Sean Freeman, Daniel J. Remmler, and Tamara K. Ehlert. "Analysis of Patient Response to Preoperative Computerized Video Imaging." *Archives of Otolaryngology Head and Neck Surgery* 115 (1989): 793–96.

Thomas, J. Regan, Anthony P. Sclafani, Mark Hamilton, and Erin McDonough. "Preoperative Identification of Psychiatric Illness in Aesthetic Facial Surgery Patients." *Aesthetic Plastic Surgery* 25 (2001): 64–67.

Thomas, Ronald R. "Double Exposures: Arresting Images in *Bleak House* and *The House of the Seven Gables*." *Novel* 31 (fall 1997): 87–113.

Thomson, J. Anderson, Norman J. Knorr, and Milton T. Edgerton. "Cosmetic Surgery: The Psychiatric Perspective." *Psychosomatics* 19.1 (Jan. 1978): 7–15.

Thompson, J. Kevin, Leslie J. Heinberg, Madeline Altabe, and Stacey Tantleff-Dunn. *Exacting Beauty: Theory, Assessment, and Treatment of Body Image Disturbance.* Washington, DC: American Psychological Association, 1999.

Thompson, Kevin M. "Refacing Inmates: A Critical Appraisal of Plastic Surgery Programs in Prison." *Criminal Justice and Behavior* 17 (1990): 448–66.

Tolleth, Hale. "Concepts for the Plastic Surgeon from Art and Sculpture." *Clinics in Plastic Surgery* 14 (1987): 585–98.

Tonnard, Patrick, Alexis Verpaele, Stan Monstrey, Koen Van Landuyt, Philippe Blondeel, Moustapha Hamdi, and Guido Matton. "Minimal Access Cranial Suspension Lift: A Modified S-Lift." *Plastic and Reconstructive Surgery* 109.6 (May 2000): 2074–86.

Trachtenberg, Alan. *Reading American Photographs: Images as History, Matthew Brady to Walker Evans.* New York: Hill and Wang, 1989.

The Truman Show. Dir. Peter Weir. Perf. Jim Carey, Laura Linney, and Ed Harris. Paramont, 1998.

Tseëlon, Efrat. *The Masque of Femininity: The Presentation of Woman in Everyday Life.* London: Sage, 1995.

Twitchell, James B. *Dreadful Pleasures: An Anatomy of Modern Horror.* New York: Oxford UP, 1985.

Underwood, Nora. "Body Envy: Thin Is in—and People Are Messing with Mother Nature as Never Before." *Maclean's* 14 Aug. 2000: 36–38.

Updegraff, Howard L., and Karl A. Menninger. "Some Psychoanalytic Aspects of Plastic Surgery." *American Journal of Surgery* 25 (1934): 554–58.

Vaisse, Pierre. "Portrait of Society: The Anonymous and the Famous." *A New*

History of Photography. Ed. Michel Frizot. Trans. Susan Bennett, Liz Clegg, John Crook, Caroline Higgit, and Helen Atkins. Milan: Könemann, 1998. 494–513.

VanderKam, Victoria M., and Bruce M. Achauer. "Digital Imaging for Plastic and Reconstructive Surgery." *Plastic Surgical Nursing* 17 (1997): 37–38.

Vannier, Michael W., et al. "Quantitative Three-Dimensional Assessment of Face-Lift with an Optical Facial Surface Scanner." *Annals of Plastic Surgery* 30.3 (Mar. 1993): 204–11.

Vargel, Serpil, and Aylin Ulusahin. "Psychopathology and Body Image in Cosmetic Surgery Patients." *Aesthetic Plastic Surgery* 25 (2001): 474–78.

Viner, Katharine. "Women: The New Plastic Feminism?" *Guardian* 21 July 1997: T4.

Walker, Alexander. *Beauty in Women: Analyzed and Classified with a Critical View of the Hypotheses of the Most Eminent Writers, Painters, and Sculptors*. 1852. Glasgow: Thomas D. Morison, 1892.

———. *Stardom: The Hollywood Phenomenon*. New York: Stein and Day, 1970.

Wallace, Anthony. *The Progress of Plastic Surgery: An Introductory History*. Oxford: William A. Meeuws, 1982.

Warner, Marina. "Stolen Shadows, Lost Souls: Body and Soul in Photography." *Raritan* 15.2 (1995): 35–58.

Weldon, Fay. "Beauty and Pain." *Allure* Jan. 1994: 56+.

———. "Is Thin Better?" *Allure* June 1994: 80–82.

———. *The Life and Loves of a She-Devil*. New York: Ballantine, 1983.

Wells, H. G. *The Island of Doctor Moreau*. Ed. Brian Aldiss. 1896. New York: Everyman, 1993.

Whittell, Giles. " 'Doc Hollywood' under Legal Knife." *London Times* 19 Feb. 1999. LexisNexis Academic.

———. "Face-Lift Expert in Battle to Save His Skin." *London Times* 10 Nov. 1998. LexisNexis Academic.

Why Change Your Wife? Dir. Cecil B. De Mille. Perf. Gloria Swanson and Thomas Meighan. 1920. Videocassette. Grapevine Video.

Wienke, Chris. "Negotiating the Male Body: Men, Masculinity and Cultural Ideals." *Journal of Men's Studies* 6 (1998): 255–83.

Wilde, Oscar. *The Portrait of Dorian Gray*. Ed. Isobel Murray. 1891. London: Oxford UP, 1974.

Wilkinson, Alec. "Lift Off." *Allure* Nov. 1996: 118+.

Williams, Linda. "Corporealized Observers: Visual Pornographies and the 'Carnal Density of Vision.'" *Fugitive Images: From Photography to Video.* Ed. Patrice Petro. Bloomington: Indiana UP, 1995. 3–41.

Williams, Tim. "Agent Provocateur." *TV Guide* 17–23 Nov. 1999: 38–41.

"Will the Real Martian Please Stand Up." *The Twilight Zone.* Perf. John Hoyt and Barney Phillips. CBS. 26 May 1961.

Wilson, Cintra. *A Massive Swelling: Celebrity Re-examined as a Grotesque Crippling Disease and Other Cultural Revelations.* New York: Viking, 2000.

Wilson, Sarah, Michel Onfray, Allucquere Rosanne Stone, Serge François, and Parveen Adams. *Orlan: Ceci est mon corps . . . Ceci est mon logiciel . . . This is my body . . . This is my software . . .* London: Black Dog Publishing, 1996.

Winnicott, D. W. "The Location of Cultural Experience." *Playing and Reality.* London: Tavistock, 1971. 95–103.

———. "Primary Maternal Preoccupation." *Collected Papers: Through Paediatrics to Psycho-Analysis.* New York: Basic, 1958. 300–305.

Wolf, Naomi. *The Beauty Myth: How Images of Beauty Are Used against Women.* New York: William Morrow, 1991.

Wolff, Bob. "He's a Cut Above." *Muscle & Fitness* Feb. 1996: 150+.

A Woman's Face. Dir. George Cukor. Perf. Joan Crawford and Melvyn Douglas. MGM, 1941.

Woodward, Kathleen. *Aging and Its Discontents: Freud and Other Fictions.* Bloomington: Indiana UP, 1991.

———. "From Virtual Cyborgs to Biological Time Bombs: Technocriticism and the Material Body." *Culture on the Brink: Ideologies of Technology.* Ed. Gretchen Bender and Timothy Druckrey. Seattle: Bay Press, 1994.

Les Yeux sans visage (Eyes without a face). Dir. Georges Franju. Perf. Pierre Brasseur, Alida Valli, and Edith Scob. 1959. Videocassette, Interama, 1988.

Zicree, Marc Scott. *The Twilight Zone Companion.* 2nd ed. Los Angeles: Silman-James P, 1992.

Zimmermann, Susan M. *Silicone Survivors: Women's Experiences with Breast Implants.* Philadelphia: Temple UP, 1998.

INDEX

Page numbers given in *italics* indicate illustrations or their captions.

and diversity of aesthetic judgment, 31; dominant culture codes of, 10, 252–54, 314n17; identification with image of, 19–20; internal vs. external, 162–64, 308n3; as locus of desire, 296n20; love and, 115–16, 122; media images of, 297n34; photogenic vs. erotogenic, 294n12; and photography, 211; and two-dimensional imagery, 65

beauty culture: and aging, 295n18; and "false body," 296n24; paradox of, 51–52; race and, 295n19; and willingness to undergo surgery, 59–60

Beauty (D'Amato), 145–46, 231

beautyism, 302n24

Beauty Secrets (Chapkis), 18–19

becoming-celebrity, 154–61, 174, 236, 259–61, 304–5n10

before-and-after, 217–19; beauty, 188–93, *191*; photography, 8, 193–97, 199, 203

Being John Malkovich (film), 174

Benchley, Mrs. (surgery patient), 196

Benefit cosmetics, 175

Benjamin, Walter, 202–3, 258

Bergen, Candice, 237

Berger, John, 83

Bernhardt, Sarah, 311n20

Bernstein, Norman R., 121–22, 129

Berry, Halle, *178*

Bersani, Leo, 298n8

Bick, Esther, 306n20

"Birthmark, The" (Hawthorne), 94–99, 102

blepharoplasty, 67

body: as aesthetic landscape, 70–71; as commodity, 66; cultural reality given to, 53–54; "false" vs. authentic, 296n24; fragmentation of, 37–38, 118–19, 236–37, 292n10, 312n5; in *Frankenstein*, 303n33; maintenance of, 295n15; and photography, 203; politics of, 61–63; public vs. private,

42–43; repression of, 135; as site of mourning, 113, 115–16; subordinated to clothing, 249; surface of, and photography, 93–99; and technology, 306n21. *See also* women's bodies

body culture, men as victims of, 48

body dysmorphic disorder (BDD), 15–16, 280, 291n2, 293n5

body ego, 116, 168

body image: body integration and, 32–33; and conviction of disfigurement, 113–14; defined, 39; deformity and, 122–23; effects of "beautyism" on, 302n24; formation of, 2; identity and, 42–43, 108–9; and objective beauty, 39–40; photography and, 200–202; and separation-individuation process, 114–15, 118–19; tri-dimensional, 116; and video-imaging, *184–85*

body image studies, 3, 293n5

body image theory, 116

body-in-pieces, 118–19. *See also* body, fragmentation of

body integration, 32–33

body landscape, and bodily history, 42–44

Boorstin, Daniel, 56, 251, 304–5n10

borderline personality, 150–51, 152–53, 156

Bordo, Susan, 252; on ahistoricism of postmodernism, 296–97n32; on conventionality of postmodern body-liberating strategies, 57; on male construction of female subjectivity, 26; on resistance to surgery, 61–62, 217

Bowlby, Rachel, 50–51, 52, 152

Bradbury, Eileen, 3–4

Brady Bunch, The (TV show), 247

Bransford, Helen, 207

Braudy, Leo, 201, 224–25

Bray, Abigail, 296n24

Brazil (film), 231

breasts: augmentation of, 70–71, 91, 292n8, 297–98n3; and body integra-

Compositor: G&S Typesetters, Inc.
Text: 10/15 Janson
Display: Janson